Overcoming Hypertension

**Bantam Books
by Kenneth H. Cooper, M.D.**

AEROBICS

**AEROBICS FOR WOMEN
(with Mildred Cooper)**

THE AEROBICS WAY

THE NEW AEROBICS

**THE AEROBICS PROGRAM
FOR TOTAL WELL-BEING**

RUNNING WITHOUT FEAR

**THE NEW AEROBICS FOR WOMEN
(with Mildred Cooper)**

**Dr. Kenneth H. Cooper's
Preventive Medicine Program**

**CONTROLLING CHOLESTEROL
PREVENTING OSTEOPOROSIS
OVERCOMING HYPERTENSION**

Dr. Kenneth H. Cooper's
Preventive Medicine Program

Overcoming Hypertension

Kenneth H. Cooper, M.D., M.P.H.

BANTAM BOOKS
New York • Toronto • London •
Sydney • Auckland
A Bantam Large Print Edition

OVERCOMING HYPERTENSION

A Bantam Book
Bantam hardcover edition / March 1990
Bantam large print edition / September 1990

Bantam Books are published by Bantam Books, a division of Bantam
Doubleday Dell Publishing Group, Inc. Its trademark, consisting of
the words "Bantam Books" and the portrayal of a rooster, is
Registered in U.S. Patent and Trademark Office and in other coun-
tries. Marca Registrada. Bantam Books, 666 Fifth Avenue, New York,
New York 10103.

PRINTED IN THE UNITED STATES OF AMERICA
BG   0 9 8 7 6 5 4 3 2 1

This Large Print Book carries the
seal of approval of N.A.V.H.

NOTE

Fitness, diet, and health are matters which necessarily vary from individual to individual. Readers should speak with their own doctor about their individual needs before starting any diet program. Consulting one's physician is especially important if one is on any medication or is already under medical care for any illness.

Grateful acknowledgment is made for permission to reprint the following charts: "Drugs for Hypertensive Emergency" reproduced by special permission of The Medical Letter, *"The Effect of Age on Selected Risk Factors" reproduced by special permission of William B. Kannel, M.D., M.P.H., "Sources of Dietary Sodium" reprinted with permission from* Environmental Nutrition, *2112 Broadway, Suite 200, New York, NY 10023, "Blood Pressure Monitors," copyright © 1987 by Consumers Union of United States, Inc., Mount Vernon, NY 10553, reprinted by permission from* Consumer Reports, *May 1987, and "Descriptive Information on Devices Tested" and "Devices Passing the Investigators' Tests" reprinted from an article by Evans CE, Haynes RB, Goldsmith CH, Hewson SA: Home blood pressure-measuring devices: a comparative study of accuracy:* Journal of Hypertension *1989, 7:133–42.*

To the 3,000 members of the Dallas Aerobics Activity Center and to the almost 40,000 patients who come regularly to the Cooper Clinic.

The publication of this book has been inspired by your adherence to diet and exercise programs, your commitment to periodic medical evaluations, and your desire to achieve maximum well-being in your life. Your enthusiasm in maintaining your health has convinced me that spreading the good word of preventive medicine is indeed worthwhile. Hopefully, millions of people will benefit from *our* efforts.

Acknowledgments

As I have stated previously in this Preventive Medicine series, I am certainly not knowledgeable in all areas of preventive medicine. Consequently, I have sought advice and counsel from some of the world's experts in these areas.

When I considered the field of hypertension, only one name came to mind—Dr. Norman Kaplan, Professor of the Department of Internal Medicine, University of Texas Southwestern Medical School, Dallas, Texas. Dr. Kaplan has been referred to in the scientific literature as the "expert's expert" in the management and treatment of high blood pressure. From the planning stages of this book through the review process,

Dr. Kaplan's contributions have been innumerable and outstanding. I hope you can see not only his wisdom but his enthusiasm in the following pages.

Bill Proctor continues to work with me in the preparation of manuscripts. His knowledgeable contributions have been essential to the publication of this book.

My senior editor at Bantam Books, Coleen O'Shea, reviews and edits all manuscripts, ably assisted by my literary agent and friend of more than twenty years, Herb Katz.

Dr. John Duncan and Dr. Neil Gordon, exercise physiologists at the Institute for Aerobics Research, made helpful contributions to the sections dealing with exercise and hypertension.

The Nutrition Division at the Cooper Clinic again contributed all of the dietary information. Cindy Klecker, R.D., was primarily in charge, but was assisted by the following: Georgia Kostas, M.P.H., R.D.; Patty Kirk, R.D.; Cindy Wachtler, R.D.; Brenda Reeves, Veronica Costello, Kim Rudy, and Genda Potter. Nancy Ward with *The Word Works* typed all the recipes, menus, and charts.

My personal assistant, Wayne Loney, helped collect and analyze most of the data reference material.

Without administrative assistance from Rachel

Kahl-Meals, my executive secretary, this project would never have reached fruition.

Finally, I want to thank again my wonderful family—my wife, Millie, my daughter, Berkley, and my son, Tyler—for their support and understanding in preparing this, another book.

When Tyler recently asked Millie if I were "ever coming home again," I realized how book promotion and other time spent away from home takes a great toll on my family. Yet, all of the contributors should take pride in this book, since without them it would never have been published.

Contents

Overcoming Hypertension

Introduction

The underlying theory in the practice of preventive medicine might be stated this way: "It is always cheaper and more effective to maintain good health than to regain health once it is lost."

There is no area of medicine in which this statement applies more than in the management and treatment of high blood pressure, which is also known as hypertension. Like so many other medical problems, the onset of this disease is insidious and usually has no obvious symptoms. The first sign of trouble may be an incapacitating, or fatal, heart attack or stroke. So it's not surprising that many studies have shown the benefits of early diagnosis and treatment of hypertension.

Twenty years ago, medical reports revealed that only 15 percent of Americans with hypertension had their condition effectively diagnosed and controlled. By 1989, however, that figure was estimated to be above 50 percent.

As a practicing physician, I have in excess of fifty medications that I can prescribe to treat hypertension, but many of them have troublesome side effects. Unfortunately, even practicing physicians are not always knowledgeable about these side effects, nor are they aware of the best drugs with which to treat hypertension. So, in an effort to spread important information on this disease as widely as possible, I have written this book for both the layperson *and* the practicing physician. Medical references and other source citations can be found in the "References" section in the back of the book and also, in a number of cases, in the text. Shortened forms of references in the text are available with longer citations in Dr. Norman Kaplan's *Clinical Hypertension* (Baltimore: Williams & Wilkins, fourth edition, 1986).

It's quite easy simply to prescribe a drug that will control or mask hypertension. Unfortunately, that's the approach taken by many physicians, with the result that almost invariably, the patient builds up tolerance to the medication. When this happens, either the dose must be increased, the medication changed, or a combination of medications prescribed. A vicious, seemingly endless cycle may then arise, shifting the patient from medication, to tolerance, to more medication.

Because of such dangers, I strongly emphasize in this book the *non*pharmacological approach to treating hypertension, and only if that fails do I encourage the use of medications. The ultimate goal is to cure the problem, not to mask it.

During the past twenty years, considerable improvement has been noted in the incidence of cardiovascular disease, including a decline in heart attacks and strokes. That improvement has occurred not so much because of what modern medicine has done for us—nor even because of what the government has provided through Medicare and Medicaid. Rather, it's a consequence of what we, as individuals, have done for ourselves.

This book is an extension of an educational, self-help process that started with *Aerobics* in 1968 and has gone through *Controlling Cholesterol* and *Preventing Osteoporosis*. Now, with this discussion of high blood pressure, we're dealing with a subject that affects nearly 60 million Americans. I hope that *Overcoming Hypertension* will help you help yourself if you are among those 60 million people.

—Kenneth H. Cooper, M.D.

1

The Much Misunderstood Challenge of Hypertension

Hypertension is an illness of civilization.

Personal and professional stress, poor diet, lack of exercise—these and related features of our so-called advanced societies contribute heavily to the problems of the nearly 60 million Americans who have some form of high blood pressure.

There's a danger that as we progress toward the twenty-first century and life in our cities and suburbs becomes more pressure-ridden and unlivable, the number of those at risk for hypertension will rise. But I'm convinced that this danger can be confronted and conquered—*if*, through extensive public education, we can explain the paradoxes and perplexities of hypertension.

Hypertension is, indeed, a disease fraught with misunderstanding and confusion. For example, there's the question of just how to evaluate the danger of high blood pressure. Without doubt, in many respects hypertension poses one of the most serious threats to our health. The disease is *the* major risk factor for all forms of stroke; furthermore, it can lead to kidney failure or other serious disorders.

Paradoxically, as dangerous as this disease is, one or even several high blood pressure readings are nothing to panic about. To be sure, hypertension is a silent killer, and the first major symptom may be death. But with an early diagnosis, you have time on your side because it typically takes ten to twenty years for hypertension to cause real damage to your health.

Furthermore, for most people with hypertension, the initial approach to treatment doesn't have to turn one's life upside down. The first line of attack usually consists of nondrug treatments rather than medication.

If you are among the 60 million Americans who now confront hypertension, here are some facts you should know:

- Your chances of controlling mild hypertension without drugs are *very good.*

- A single high reading in your doctor's office is *not* conclusive evidence of the disease.

- Your blood pressure readings may vary considerably during any given day—and those ups and downs may be quite normal.

- It's common for many people, with hypertension or without, to have two upward "bursts" of blood pressure in the morning—one immediately on awakening, and another on getting out of bed and walking about.

- Vigorous exertion (especially the type that tenses the muscles), the experience of stress or anxiety, the ingestion of caffeine, smoking, a full bladder, or simply eating immediately before a blood pressure reading is taken *may* lead to an invalid measurement.

- Excessive use of alcohol may lead to elevated blood pressure, but; paradoxically, moderate use has been linked to a lower incidence of coronary disease.

- Your *average* blood pressure (i.e., the average of multiple readings taken over one to two months, rather than one isolated reading) is the key to diagnosing hypertension.

- Many cases of hypertension have a genetic factor: In other words, there's an inherited tendency toward high blood pressure in some people. However, your genes need not be decisive! Changes in lifestyle or the administration of appropriate medications can often offset the influence of heredity.

The main focus of this book is on managing hypertension without drugs. But there are many healthy people who exercise regularly and eat correctly, yet who *can't* control their hypertension through a drug-free regimen.

We live in a high-pressure society that requires millions of those with hypertension to rely both on nondrug treatments *and* on medication. Furthermore, as the following story demonstrates, a patient can have a lot of input into the way his illness is treated.

How One Patient Participated in Choosing His Treatments

William, a busy executive in his early fifties, had been coming in for regular annual medical exams for several years, and the first few times his blood pressure had been normal.

His initial measurement, which was performed as part of a checkup for health insurance, was 130/82 (the meaning of these numbers will be explained in upcoming chapters)—well below the generally accepted "mild" or "borderline" hypertension level that begins at 140/90. During this exam I had followed the classic procedure for taking a first blood pressure, which involved the following steps:

I took several separate readings during that first visit to find how William's blood pressure responded under different circumstances. First of all, using the traditional measuring device called the sphygmomanometer, I checked his right arm while he was sitting in a chair.

The sphygmomanometer is a cufflike inflatable bladder, usually measuring 12 by 23 centimeters, which the doctor or technician wraps around the patient's upper arm and then blows up with a small hand-held bulb pump. The presure created by the inflation of the cuff cuts off the circulation momentarily. Then, as the pressure is released, the physician listens through attached earphones for the first and last sounds of blood rushing back through the arm to determine the upper (systolic) and lower (diastolic) blood pressure readings.

Before taking the pressure, I made sure that William had been seated for at least five minutes and was leaning back in a relaxed position. His right arm, on which I had placed the sphygmomanometer, was supported at about heart level by the arm of the chair.

Then I checked his left arm and found the pressure to be the same as on the right. (Sometimes the pressures in the arms are different, and in such situations we go with the arm that has the higher reading.) Next, I took his pressure lying down on his back and also standing up. As with many people, his standing pressure was somewhat higher than in the other positions.

Finally, to get his true pressure, I took two more readings while he was in the sitting position with the cuff on his right arm. By figuring the average of the three sitting measurements of his right arm, I was able to establish his true blood pressure during that office visit.

As is the case with many patients, William had a higher reading on the first of his sitting measurements than on the two later ones. Specifically, his first measurement was 138/88, which placed him near the mild or borderline hypertensive category.

But this was a normal reaction, since many patients are under greater stress during the first phase of a medical exam than later, when the procedures and atmosphere have become more familiar. And remember the final result: His *average* blood pressure, using all three readings, was 135/80. As William's response suggests, it's important for a physician to take several readings and find the average, rather than just to go with one initial measurement, which may be unusually high. (Another option is to take three measurements, discard the first, and average the last two.)

During the next three years, as William came in for annual physicals, his blood pressure began to creep up. The second year I checked him, his average reading was 134/85; the third year, it was up to 137/88.

Clearly, there was an upward trend. Already he had almost reached the "mild" hypertension category, which begins with a diastolic reading of 90. Furthermore, he was almost up to the "borderline" systolic hypertension level, which begins at 140. In light of these developments, I wanted to be sure that William was doing everything in his power, within normal limits, to control his blood pressure.

As I questioned him, he confirmed that he was still following these instructions for preparation before his exam:

- He urinated before the test (a full bladder will increase pressure).

- He refrained from eating or ingesting caffeine for at least sixty minutes before the test.

- He avoided vigorous exercise just before the measurements were taken.

Also, I knew William wasn't on any drugs, such as steroids, which might raise his blood pressure. Nor was he a smoker or overweight. Furthermore, he had gone on a low-fat diet as part of a personal health program, and he regularly ran about ten miles a week. All these are part of the plan recommended for preventing and controlling hypertension.

But William's pressure still was rising, and I was determined to head it off. I recommended that he adjust his diet further by going on a stricter low-salt regimen. He had been watching his salt consumption, but not very closely. I estimated that he was eating fewer than 4 grams of sodium a day, or somewhat below the national average of 4 to 6 grams daily. But a more severe diet averaging about 2 grams of sodium a day (which works out to about 5 grams of salt) seemed in order. Eager to do all he could to prevent the onset of full-blown hypertension, he agreed to try my suggestions.

In addition, because William was under relatively heavy pressure at work, I recommended that he try some relaxation techniques to reduce his stress level. Again, he said he'd try.

But when he returned in three months for a progress evaluation, the situation was worse. His average blood pressure readings had risen to 145/95. These measurements put him well up into the mild hypertension category on his diastolic (lower) blood pressure number, and the borderline classification on his systolic (upper) pressure.

The nondrug treatments we had tried so far hadn't succeeded in controlling the upward march—so what was the next step?

First, it was necessary to establish a firm diagnosis of hypertension so that I'd have a solid basis for prescribing further treatment. To do this, I followed a well-accepted procedure: I took several sets of average readings over the next month and came up with the same result— an average blood pressure of 145/95.

Because William's pressure had only re- cently moved into the mild or borderline range, I knew we had time to work on the problem. Typically, it may take ten to twenty years before hypertension does any serious damage to the body, and William certainly hadn't had his condition that long. So, knowing that stress was most likely a part of his problem, I decided to try another nondrug approach.

"I know your job is a pressure cooker," I said. "Any way you can change that?"

"I can't quit—this is my life!" he said.

"I realize that. But what *can* you do to reduce the stress you're under at work?"

He thought about it and decided to cut back on his work load and spend more time unwinding with his family in the evenings and on weekends.

I also recommended some sources for learning relaxation techniques, including several books on the subject and also a psychologist who specialized in that area. Some people who practice these methods regularly—and at the same time follow sound antihypertensive health practices, such as a low-salt, low-fat diet, moderate alcohol intake, and regular exercise—have lowered *both* their upper and lower blood pressure readings by 20 points or more.

William agreed to this strategy. But I wanted to know how it was working under real-life conditions, to see how particular lifestyle changes and relaxation techniques succeeded or failed *in practice* in lowering his blood pressure.

Obviously, I couldn't follow William around all day and check his blood pressure under different conditions. So I recommended that he buy a home monitoring device—which can be purchased for less than $60—and take his own blood pressure several times a day. These devices look much like the ones in your physician's office, but they're more compact and simpler to use. For example, many have digital displays, rather than a traditional clocklike dial and pointer, to show the blood pressure measurement.

After I had shown William how to take his

own pressure, we identified several points during his day that would provide a complete picture of his condition. Specifically, he took his pressure (1) when he first got up in the morning; (2) just after he arrived at work; (3) in the midafternoon, when his job pressures were at a peak; and (4) in the evening after dinner, when he was feeling relaxed.

Over the course of a couple of weeks, William's self-recorded readings at these four times averaged out this way:

- First thing in the morning: 135/88
- Arrival at work: 140/92
- Midafternoon: 155/96
- Evening at home: 130/85

By doing this self-monitoring, William provided me with information I could not otherwise have obtained. It was evident from these readings that his blood pressure was quite normal when he was at home, away from the stresses of work. That confirmed my belief that the more time he could spend in the company of his family, the better.

Also, I suspected that his measurements were even lower while he was asleep, as most people tend to have their lowest readings at that time. To check this out, I had William take his pressure a few times when he woke up in the middle of the night. The readings were indeed lower on those occasions than they were after he awakened in the morning.

Blood pressure typically jumps up on awakening, sometimes by as much as 20 points for both the upper and lower readings. There's still another surge upward when the person gets out of bed and begins to walk about. William's total increase in pressure at these times was more on the order of about 10 points for both the systolic and diastolic readings. But he still remained in the normal range during the early morning hours.

However, William was apparently in a mild or borderline hypertensive state throughout his workday. I knew that these higher readings over a period of several hours each day could eventually lead to a permanent hypertensive condition. So I encouraged him to continue to work at reducing his stress.

Unfortunately, he couldn't do anything to bring down his blood pressure levels at work; he said that the demands on him were just too great. Furthermore, as disciplined as he was in other areas of his life, he wasn't able to stay with a regular relaxation program. Typically, these programs require participants to do meditative and breathing exercises twice a day for twenty minutes at each session, day in and day out. Some people take to such a program quite naturally, while others, perhaps because they have doubts about whether it will really work, are unable to get started.

"I just can't find the time for that," William said. "My schedule is already too packed to make time for such things. Besides, I'm just not a natural meditator."

After about six months of monitoring and consultation, William's average readings held at about 148/95. As a result, I prescribed an antihypertensive medication—one of the beta-blocker drugs, metoprolol (Lopressor).

Beta blockers are designed to lower the blood pressure by reducing the pumping action and blood output of the heart. This type of drug isn't usually appropriate for young athletes because it limits the intensity of the physical activity in which a person can engage. But the medication was fine for William because his only exercise was moderate jogging.

Fortunately, too, the possible side effects of beta blockers—which may include such reactions as fatigue, insomnia, or impotence—didn't materialize.

The end result in William's case: His blood pressure on the medication decreased to an average of 129/84—well within normal limits both in the doctor's office and in various stressful situations at work.

The Power of Cooperation

William's experience is instructive in a number of ways—especially as it shows us the value and power of cooperation between the physician and patient in dealing with hypertension.

Obviously, the initial examination and recommendation in this situation had to be made by me—the physician. But by learning to monitor his own blood pressure, both at home and at work, William contributed significantly to the process. He provided information that helped in proving the diagnosis of hypertension and in providing the groundwork for its treatment.

Two important principles underlie this need for cooperation between the hypertensive patient and the physician:

1. Your doctor needs to know your average blood pressure in order to make a definite diagnosis of hypertension. Under his guidance, you can help him gather important information as you monitor your pressure at home and at work.

2. Your doctor's ability to make an accurate diagnosis can also be enhanced if he understands how your pressure responds in a variety of daily circumstances, whether at home, at work, or in other activities. If you experience regular, rela-

tively high peaks of high blood pressure at work—or if your blood pressure stays up at hypertensive levels in other circumstances for sustained periods—that characteristic will place you at greater risk for permanent hypertension.

To identify those peaks and rises, *you* must learn to check your own pressure. Your doctor can't be with you to check you at those moments.

What if your doctor doesn't want this sort of help from you? He *should* welcome your willingness to cooperate with him—even if he recommends that in your case self-monitoring isn't really necessary. If he doesn't appreciate your interest, perhaps you should consider finding another physician.

In the following pages, we'll consider in great detail topics that often lend themselves to your collaboration with your physician in preventing, controlling, and curing hypertension. You'll learn:

- Ways to evaluate your risk for hypertension

- An explanation of how other coronary risk factors—such as high cholesterol, cigarette smoking, obesity, or failure to manage stress well—can actually *multiply* your risk level

- Your personal blood pressure classification

- What your blood pressure readings really mean

- The implications of "high," "low," and "normal" readings

- How to take your own blood pressure

- Why many people experience a marked increase in blood pressure when they're tested in the doctor's office—even though they may not be hypertensive

- How exercise can reduce your blood pressure (To show you step by step how this works, I've included a complete antihypertensive aerobics program.)

- Why weight training may be dangerous if you have high blood pressure

- The levels of blood pressure that make any exercise unsafe

- A special formula to enable those on beta-blocker drugs to find their target heart rate during exercise (You'll recall that beta blockers slow down the heart rate; so those on these drugs must expect to exercise at a lower level of intensity than other athletes.)

- Why older people don't have to settle for relatively high blood pressure readings

  There's an old rule of thumb that says, "Your systolic (upper) blood pressure reading should be no higher than 100 plus your age." Using this approach, many doctors still believe that a reading of 170/90 is quite acceptable for those 70 years of age or older. Yet, I've discovered that exercise and a healthy diet and life-style can keep the average person's blood pressure near the levels of youth.

  In one series of studies at the Aerobics Center, for instance, the median blood pressure for those who were 60 years of age and older was 132/82—a level that would make most 30-year-olds quite happy!

- The healthy levels of blood pressure for children of all ages

- How "salt-sensitive" people can control hypertension through their diets

  There is evidence that some people, but not all, are salt-sensitive. This means that their blood pressure tends to rise when they increase the amount of salt in their diets. By experimenting with your diet and watching the results as you monitor your blood pressure, your physician may be able to determine whether your pressure reacts negatively to salt.

Our expert nutritionists have designed menus and recipes containing an average of about 2 grams of sodium per day—a good target for those who are trying to control their salt intake. In addition, consideration has been paid to other nutritional factors that may influence blood pressure, such as fats, calcium, magnesium, potassium, and fiber. Also, lists of the sodium and other nutritional contents of various foods have been included to help you follow a low-salt diet.

- How particular foods, like licorice, may raise blood pressure levels significantly in some people

- Relaxation techniques that have proven effective in lowering blood pressure in some patients

- Ways to organize your schedule so that you can deal more successfully with the pressures of our increasingly stressful society

- The alcohol question—specifically, how much is too much?

Research on hypertension has established that excessive consumption of alcohol may contribute to elevated blood pressure. But how much is too much? Most experts agree that "moderate" drinking is all right—but what constitutes moderation? Also, are there people whose blood pressure is "alcohol-sensitive" to the extent that they shouldn't drink at all?

The Active Patient and Antihypertensive Drugs

The first line of attack on mild hypertension usually involves nondrug treatments, including exercise, diet, and stress reduction. Although these approaches continue to be important with higher levels of blood pressure, your physician may also decide that some sort of medication is required.

Some exciting new drugs and drug strategies have emerged in treating hypertension in recent years, and it's essential for you to understand them. Why? You must be in a position to ask the right questions and give the most helpful feedback to your physician—feedback that may lead to a reduction or change in your medication.

To this end, you'll learn the characteristics, operation, and side effects of the major categories of drugs, including:

- Diuretics

- Beta blockers and related medications

- Direct vasodilator (vessel-opening) drugs

- Calcium blockers

- Angiotensin converting enzyme (ACE) inhibitors

The side effects of these drugs vary and may include impotence, increases in cholesterol and triglyceride levels, kidney problems, bad dreams, headaches, constipation, or other problems. By keeping your physician informed about exactly how you're reacting, you'll put him in a better position to minimize the negative effects or even eliminate them entirely by switching you to another medication.

There are also some exciting new strategies that have emerged in the application of both new and old medications. The latest thinking in this field involves paying close attention to matching appropriate drugs to particular individuals, and also adjusting the sequence of moving from one drug to another.

For example, many physicians will begin with a diuretic for patients who are older, black, or obese. But for those who are younger, not obese, and Caucasian, the doctor may select a beta blocker as the drug of first choice.

On the other hand, if a young person is

particularly interested in exercise, beta blockers may not work well because they limit the work capacity of the heart. So with young athletes, another type of drug, such as an alpha blocker or one of the ACE inhibitors, may be chosen first.

An important issue that's directly related to the patient's understanding of drugs is *overmedication*—a condition that the alert and informed layperson can bring to his or her physician's attention before undue discomfort or damage occurs.

In one case, an executive was given diuretics to reduce his blood pressure, which at times had been measured as high as 170/120. Shortly after going on the drug, however, the patient reported feeling lightheaded.

His physician immediately put him on a round-the-clock home monitoring system, and the results showed an average blood pressure of 110/60, with individual measurements that went down even further. These readings were much too low for this man. In effect, the patient had become *hypo*tensive because he was being over-medicated. When his drug intake was reduced, his blood pressure returned to normal and his lightheadedness disappeared.

Clearly, there are many opportunities for collaboration between the patient and physician in achieving control of hypertension. Now, to see how the power of cooperation between the hypertensive patient and his or her doctor can work in more practical terms, let's turn to our first main topic—the meaning of those blood pressure measurements.

2

Demystifying Those Blood Pressure Measurements

Your *true* blood pressure isn't simply one constant set of figures that a doctor can determine with one measurement once a year. Rather, blood pressure readings may vary from hour to hour—or even within a matter of minutes.

Consider a few of the possibilities:

- Many people experience large short-term jumps in blood pressure—up to 30 or 40 points, or even more—as a result of occupational or personal stresses during a typical day. One man I know underwent a 40-point increase after being pricked on the buttocks with a needle!

- The blood pressure of some patients rises much higher due to the "white-coat" phenomenon (or the "cuff syndrome," as it's sometimes called). This reaction refers to the tendency of blood pressure to rise when the person is examined by a physician or in a medical setting.

- Some weight lifters have had an increase in blood pressure to as high as 350/150 during heavy lifting.

- One 75-year-old man, whose pressure was, for his age, a very normal and healthy 120/80 at rest, went to an unusually high 270/100 during exercise on a treadmill.

  Usually, 240/120 is the maximum safe ceiling for a blood pressure rise during maximal aerobic exercise. But in this case, the person consistently experienced this dramatic rise during closely monitored stress tests and then returned to normal—without any ill effects.

What are we to make of these extreme variations in blood pressure? Are they "normal" or "safe"? What is the real meaning of those two mysterious figures that are supposed to reflect our blood pressure?

In fact, all of these extremes in blood pressure may be quite safe and normal. Blood pressure is a very individual matter, and the meaning of *your* particular reading must be determined by your doctor, working cooperatively with you. To facilitate your collaboration with your physician, let's now go into more detail about the possible meanings of your personal measurements.

The Meaning of the Measurements

When you have your blood pressure taken, you'll receive the results in the form of two numbers separated by a slash, such as 120/80. This measurement, by the way, should be read "one-twenty over eighty."

In this case, the first, or upper, number, 120, is known as the *systolic* blood pressure. This systolic figure reflects the force that's exerted against the vessel walls as the blood is pumped during the contracting or beating action of the heart. The second, or lower, number, 80, is the *diastolic* blood pressure. This diastolic reading refers to the pressure level that occurs in your vessels between heartbeats, when the heart muscle is relaxed. Both numbers are expressed in terms of "millimeters of mercury," or mm Hg, because a column of liquid mercury is used in standard sphygmomanometers to measure blood pressure.

Now, about the meanings of these figures for individual patients:

As a basic guideline, blood pressure that is below 140/90 is generally considered normal. But when readings move above 140/90, treatment of some sort, either through diet and lifestyle changes or through doctor-prescribed medications, must be considered.

In my practice, I emphasize nondrug therapies—such as exercise, weight loss, adjustment of diet, and stress-lowering strategies—for systolic blood pressures that range up to 159 and for diastolic blood pressures that range up to 94. These pressures are considered in the borderline or low-mild area of hypertension and may reflect situations where hypertension hasn't yet fully taken hold in a person's life. In these cases, a serious effort to change one's lifestyle can often reverse the progression of high blood pressure.

But pressures that are consistently 160/95 or above (and that means either the systolic *or* the diastolic at these levels) frequently signal the existence of a relatively permanent state of hypertension. In these cases, medications will usually be required in addition to nondrug treatments.

I find that remembering these simple cut-off points can often help patients remember the probable meaning of their blood pressure measurements. Still, there are many other, more detailed, specific schemes for interpreting blood pressure than the shorthand standards I've just suggested. "The 1988 Report of the Fourth Joint National Committee on Detection, Evaluation, and Treatment of High Blood Pressure," for instance, recommends these more extensive classifications and follow-up procedures:

Classification of Blood Pressure in Adults 18 Years of Age or Older

Blood Pressure Range mm Hg (mercury)	Category	Follow-up by physician
1. Diastolic blood pressure:		
<85	Normal	Recheck within 2 years
85–89	High normal	Recheck within 1 year
90–104	Mild hypertension	Confirm within 2 months
105–114	Moderate hypertension	Evaluate or refer promptly to source of care within 2 weeks

Blood Pressure Range mm Hg (mercury)	Category	Follow-up by physician
>115	Severe hypertension	Evaluate or refer immediately to source of care

2. Systolic blood pressure, when diastolic is less than 90 mm Hg:

<140	Normal	Recheck within 2 years
140–159	Borderline isolated systolic hypertension	
>160	Isolated systolic hypertension	If systolic is in 140–199 range, confirm within 2 months. If at or above 200, evaluate or refer promptly to source of care within 2 weeks

The Joint National Committee report also includes these explanatory notes for the above classifications, which I've edited somewhat:

Note 1. The classifications are based on the average of two or more readings on two or more occasions.

Note 2. A classification of borderline isolated systolic hypertension (i.e., systolic of 140 to 159 mm Hg) or of isolated systolic hypertension (systolic at or greater than 160) takes precedence over high-normal blood pressure (diastolic of 85 to 89) for purposes of treatment when both occur in the same person.

Note 3. If recommendations for follow-up of diastolic and systolic blood pressure are different, the shorter recommended time for rechecking and referral takes precedence.

Many physicians—including my special consultant for this book, Dr. Norman Kaplan of the University of Texas Southwestern Medical Center at Dallas, who was a member of the Joint National Committee—accept these classifications as their basic standard.

Like all definitions of hypertension, however, these Joint National Committee figures aren't written in stone. The operative classifications were different as recently as 1980, when the World Health Organization (WHO) recommended that hypertension begin at readings of 160/95.

But more recent studies have demonstrated that serious health risks may accompany even borderline hypertension, down to the lower level of 140/90. So the 1984 Third Joint National Committee elected to begin the designation of hypertension at that lower level.

Before 1984, there were obviously far fewer people who were diagnosed as hypertensive, because the blood pressure levels defining the disease were higher. Under the old 160/95 standard, for instance, 30 million Americans would be classified today as hypertensive, as compared with about 58 to 60 million under the new 140/90 standards. As might be expected, with the more stringent current definitions, doctors today are more likely to begin some sort of treatment at an earlier point than they did in the past.

Will the latest Joint National Committee recommendations on classifying and treating hypertension hold up?

If past history is any indication, they probably won't. The study of hypertension is constantly bringing new information to light, such as the value of exercise and stress-reduction techniques in treating mild hypertension. With this new information, the approaches to treatment and the meanings of various blood pressure levels are subject to constant review and change.

Even today, individual doctors who support the Joint National Committee may still "adjust" or "interpret" these figures according to the special situations faced by persons and groups they treat.

For one thing, informed doctors may be aware that one or more of a particular patient's blood pressure readings are *similar* to those characteristic of certain classifications of people. But that doesn't mean the physician will necessarily treat that patient according to the classification.

A case in point: A number of my patients are subject to the so-called white coat phenomenon, which causes both their systolic and diastolic blood pressure to shoot up 30 or more points when they come into my office for an exam. The mere stress of the visit raises their readings through the roof—even when I take their pressure several times in an effort to get an average reading.

If I chose rigidly to classify these people according to the Joint Committee's criteria, I'd be treating many of them for severe hypertension. But I've learned over the course of several exams that these people aren't really hypertensive. They just have high readings when they're in my office, and then their pressure returns to normal when they leave.

To determine their out-of-the-office readings, I've had a number of them take their own blood pressure through the use of home monitoring devices (which we'll discuss later in this chapter). Then, upon ascertaining that their elevated pressure is due to the surroundings of the medical exam, I'm in a position to classify them, and, if necessary, treat them, differently than I could if I relied only on the measurements taken in my office.

What lesson should we learn from such practical experience? Just this: Classifications such as those suggested by the Joint National Committee are essential to follow as basic guidelines. But the specific treatment, if any, for your blood pressure is a matter for your doctor, working closely with you, to decide.

Even Dr. Kaplan takes a flexible approach to the classifications. He questions, for example, whether everyone whose diastolic (lower) number is in the 85 to 89 range should be labeled as having "high-normal blood pressure." Such a label, he feels, may segregate people unjustly into a "near-hypertensive" category, a designation that might eventually have negative implications for their job promotions or for their insurance status. On the other hand, such a designation might prove helpful if it serves to warn the individual that he or she should make changes in diet, exercise, or lifestyle.

Furthermore, the division of blood pressure classifications into mild and moderate levels may be subject to some interpretation. Some physicians put those with 90 to 100 diastolic pressure into the "mild" classification. Their "moderate" classification then becomes 101 to 114. Anything above that would be regarded as "severe." Doctors who take this approach tend to be more aggressive in prescribing nondrug strategies and medications earlier in order to bring down the high blood pressure.

There are also some other ways to interpret the meaning of blood pressure levels:

The Federal Aeronautics Administration is considerably more lenient than the Joint National Committee, at least when it comes to determining who can fly commercial airliners. To see what I mean, consider the following blood pressure levels, which are regarded as acceptable for pilot applicants when they are tested in a reclining position:

Age 20–29: 140/88

Age 30–39: 145/92

Age 40–49: 155/96

Age 50 and over: 160/98

Clearly, these standards allow those with established high blood pressure to fly airliners. But why is such hypertension allowed?

Probably the main reason is that the FAA places limits on medications for pilots. So the choice has been made to allow blood pressure to be a bit higher, rather than put a cap on it with drugs.

Furthermore, another special dispensation may be available to those applicants of at least 30 years of age whose reclining blood pressure is higher than the maximum allowable for his or her age group. If the applicant undergoes a complete cardiovascular examination and is found to be normal, he or she can *still* qualify at the following blood pressure levels—which are even higher than those for regular applicants:

Age 30–39: 155/98

Age 40–49: 165/100

Age 50 and over: 170/100

When I first heard about these standards, I was shocked. In effect, these guidelines encourage the development of hypertension among one entire occupational group. These pilots may have to choose between their jobs and taking medications in amounts that will keep their hypertension at safe levels. Too often they choose the hypertension—and their employment as pilots.

So, we can see that the FAA has a radically different idea from the Joint National Committee about what is an acceptable level of blood pressure. In somewhat less dramatic fashion, there's also a significant difference of opinion between the American approach, reflected in the Joint National Committee's classifications and recommendations, and the practice of many British doctors.

In a 1987 British report, Dr. J. R. Hampton of the Department of Medicine, University Hospital, Queen's Medical Centre, Nottingham, argued that an "individual with a diastolic pressure of 100 mm Hg or less will certainly not gain any measurable benefit from drug therapy."

Furthermore, Dr. Hampton expressed skepticism about the justification for using medications to treat patients with diastolic pressures that go even higher. In particular, he said he believes "there is little evidence to support the treatment of patients with diastolic pressures up to 109 mm Hg. . . ."

Dr. Hampton acknowledges that treatment of diastolic pressures in the 100 to 109 range may reduce the risk of a stroke, but he says this benefit will "only be achieved at the price of side effects which may make the treatment unacceptable to a patient."

I happen to disagree with Dr. Hampton, as

do the majority of American physicians, because I believe that the risks of serious cardiovascular events or organ damage far outweigh the possible side effects of medications.* In addition, there has been such progress in developing new drugs and in fine-tuning the application of older ones that side effects often can be minimized or eliminated.

But what Dr. Hampton's argument highlights is more important than any reservations I may have about his conclusions: In short, he—along with the FAA officials—points up the many possibilities of interpreting and treating blood pressure readings. This wide range of options can present some perplexing challenges for any physician, and can also be quite confusing for the patient who wants to understand and participate in his or her treatment.

Just how your doctor should go about measuring and evaluating your blood pressure—and how you can assist in this process—is our next concern.

* The 1970 VA Cooperative Study showed that there was a definite advantage in treating moderate hypertension (diastolic blood pressure of 105 to 114 mm Hg), the advantage being primarily in the prevention of stroke and congestive heart failure rather than coronary artery disease.

How Is Your Blood Pressure Measured— and How Do You Know If It's Normal?

Whenever a patient has his blood pressure measured, I like to be sure that he understands these basic principles at the outset:

Principle 1. Don't assume that you know what your blood pressure really is after one reading or even one set of readings.

True blood pressure has to be ascertained over a period of time and in a variety of circumstances. Also, to catch any changes in pressure, regular checks over the years are essential.

What are the practical implications of this principle? Simply this: Your pressure should be checked every time you have a complete physical exam, or *at least once every two years* if your doctor finds in one exam that you're in the normal range.

On the other hand, if your physician determines that your diastolic (lower) reading is in the high-normal range (85 to 89 according to the Joint National Committee's classifications), you should be rechecked within one year.

If your diastolic reading is in the 90 to 104 category, or if your systolic is in the 140 to 199

range, you should come back for another evaluation within two months. If your diastolic is
measured at 105 to 114, or if your systolic is 200
or higher, your physician should evaluate you
further or refer you to special care within two
weeks. Finally, if your diastolic is 115 or above,
your doctor should evaluate you further or refer
you immediately to special care.

*Principle 2. Don't panic if you have one high
reading.*

There are many reasons for one high reading, or one set of high readings—including the
white-coat syndrome, which we will discuss in
more detail shortly. It's true that a person with
one high reading is, statistically, more at risk for
having or developing hypertension; at the same
time, however, *many* people have one high
reading in the doctor's office but then find,
through further testing, that they don't have a
problem.

In addition, high blood pressure is only *one*
risk factor for various cardiovascular problems.
Hypertension alone is certainly a concern, but
not as much a concern if it's all that's wrong with
you. So, if your cholesterol is high or out of
balance, and if you're overweight, if you smoke,
or if you lead a sedentary lifestyle—then high
blood pressure puts you at higher risk than if you
didn't have these other risk factors.

If your blood pressure measurement is high, your physician will likely begin a series of further checks and rechecks to determine the accuracy of the first reading. In the meantime, just relax and wait for the final evaluation to come in.

Remember: *Everyone*'s blood pressure fluctuates to some extent on an hour-by-hour and minute-by-minute basis, depending on the intensity of activity and stress levels. Furthermore, many people experience relatively dramatic rises and drops in blood pressure during the course of a day—but again, that doesn't necessarily mean that these people are hypertensive.

Principle 3. Your average blood pressure is the key to an accurate evaluation.

Your physician should always take at least two to three readings during your physical exam, and then find the average.

The Joint National Committee recommends finding the average of only two readings. But they say that if those two vary by more than 5 mm Hg, additional measurements should be taken.

My special consultant, Dr. Norman Kaplan, recommends a set of three readings for each exam, and I concur with this approach for two reasons: First, taking one extra reading for all exams appears to enhance the accuracy of the final average measurement; second, it is much easier for doctors to make a standard practice of taking three readings, without qualification, rather than to say that in some cases two should be taken and in other cases more may be required.

Now, assume that your doctor finds that your first average blood pressure measurement is sufficiently high to have you come in for a recheck within two months. In such a case, he should take a total of at least three groups of readings during those two months, with two weeks or more between each group. Once again, he'll average all these readings to get a more accurate picture of your blood pressure.

(*Note:* Your doctor may want you to participate in finding your blood pressure average by taking home readings on a home monitoring device. We'll discuss these home gadgets later in this chapter.)

Principle 4. Your risk from high blood pressure is on a continuum.

One of the reasons it's so hard to classify a person according to a blood pressure range or category is that the risks from hypertension—including stroke, kidney failure, and other organ damage—increase gradually, as the average blood pressure level rises.

In other words, a person with a 140/90

reading may have hypertension according to the latest definitions, but he's at a lower level of risk than a person with 150/95; and a person with a measurement of 160/100 is at an even higher risk.

An important corollary of this principle is that you should count it a success when your doctor is able to bring your blood pressure down even a little bit!

A second corollary is that you shouldn't despair or panic if your doctor cannot bring your blood pressure down to normal levels immediately through medications or nondrug means. Because the damage caused by hypertension occurs so slowly, you probably have time for your physician to try a variety of treatments until he finds the right one for you.

A third corollary is that, in general, blood pressure cannot be too low. But there are some exceptions:

- The patient may be in shock, as may occur after a serious accident.

- The patient may have *hypo*tension (blood pressure so low that he or she begins to experience weakness, dizziness, or other problems).

- The patient may be in an advanced state of alcoholism, with the condition known as

Wernicke's syndrome. In this case, systolic blood pressure commonly drops to 50 to 60 mm Hg, with no signs of hypotension.

But aside from these special problems, there's nothing wrong with very low blood pressure. In this regard, I'm reminded of one perfectly healthy woman whose typical average blood pressure readings are about 85/60. No, that's not a misprint! Her readings *are* that low—a systolic of 85 and a diastolic of 60. Some people might have the symptoms of hypotension at these levels, but not this woman. She's completely symptom-free, and she's at a much lower risk for hypertension and its related problems than are those whose blood pressure is 140/90 or above.

With these principles firmly in mind, let's assume that you're ready to go to your doctor's office for a blood pressure reading. Following are the basic guidelines:

- You should avoid smoking, consuming caffeine, or eating before the test.

- Avoid anxiety-producing activities or thoughts. If you're sensitive to stress, these anxieties will show up on the measurement.

- Don't do anything that involves heavy exertion—especially isometric (muscle-tensing) exercises—immediately before the test.

- Avoid becoming chilled or overly cold just prior to the exam. This will cause your muscles to tense and may increase blood pressure levels.

- Urinate before you go into the doctor's examining room. A full bladder may raise your readings.

- Tell your doctor if you are on any medications, including adrenal steroids, estrogens, or over-the-counter drugs such as nose drops. These may elevate blood pressure levels.

- You should be seated, leaning back with your spine relaxed and comfortable against the chair. Your arm should be bared and supported at heart level, either by the chair arm or by some other flat surface. Studies have shown that an arm hanging down at the side, rather than being supported at heart level, can raise pressures by 10 to 12 points.

    Another common mistake that's made in many examining rooms—and that may raise your blood pressure levels significantly—is to allow the patient in effect to do isometric exercises as his blood pressure is being taken. There are several ways this can happen:

First, if the back isn't supported, tension develops in the back muscles. One study revealed that readings were as much as 10 points higher for patients without back supports.

Second, if the arm isn't supported, the muscles in the arm may tense and contribute to a rise in pressure—by as much as 10 percent, according to one report.

Third, any other muscle that is tense will cause a rise in pressure. So, both the physician and the patient should check to be sure that every part of the patient's body is completely relaxed and supported by means other than muscle power.

- Avoid talking while the test is being conducted, as conversation may raise your blood pressure above levels that occur when you're quiet.

- You should rest quietly in the examining chair for at least five minutes before your pressure is taken.

- The cuff of the blood pressure device (the mercury sphygmomanometer) should fit properly. Specifically, the rubber bladder of the device should encircle at least two-thirds of your arm. If the cuff size isn't right—i.e., if the patient's arm is too small, as with a child, or too large, as with a large adult—other sizes should be made available.

- On a first visit, the doctor may measure your pressure while you're standing and also lying on your back (supine). This technique is most common when the patient is elderly or diabetic.

- On an initial visit, the doctor will usually check the pressure in both of your arms, and if there's a difference, he'll choose the arm with the higher pressure. To determine whether both arms are the same, the physician may simply do a quick check of the pulse in each arm; if they are the same, he'll do a formal test on only one arm.

- The doctor must measure both your systolic (upper) blood pressure and your diastolic (lower) pressure.

  He finds these readings by pumping up the inflatable bladder on the cuff device rapidly until your pulse at the wrist disappears. Then, after the pulse disappears, the physician will listen through his stethoscope as he begins to deflate the bladder slowly, at a rate of 2 to 3 mm Hg per heartbeat (or per second).

When he reaches a certain point in this deflation process, the blood will begin to rush back into the closed-off vessels. This flow will cause a kind of tapping or thumping sound in the stethoscope—a sound known as "Korotkoff phase I," named for the well-known hypertension researcher in the early twentieth century.

This first sound signals the point at which the body's blood pressure overcomes the resistance from the cuff on the arm. Most important for purposes of measurement, it's the marker for the systolic blood pressure reading. The physician can tell what number should be assigned to the onset of this sound by checking the mercury level or dial on the sphygmomanometer. So, if the tapping sound begins when the gauge registers "130," then the systolic blood pressure of the patient is recorded as 130 mm Hg (millimeters of mercury).

But this is only the first part of the measurement process. The physician continues to listen to the tapping sounds through his stethoscope until they stop. Precisely at the point that they cease—

known as "Korotkoff phase V"—the physician notes the reading on the mercury level or dial. This figure represents the diastolic blood pressure, or the pressure on the vessels when the heart is at rest, filling up with blood and preparing for the next pumping action.

So, in our hypothetical case, the patient's diastolic number might be 80. His complete reading, then, would be a quite normal 130/80, read as "one thirty over eighty."

In most cases this procedure produces valid results, at least for one set of readings. But there are exceptions, one of which is the condition known as "pseudohypertension."

Pseudohypertension occasionally occurs among people who have rigid or calcified vessels, and especially among older patients. With these people, the inflated cuff-and-bladder device may not be able to collapse the rigid artery until the pressure in the bladder is well above the true systolic pressure inside the artery. The reading on the sphygmomanometer may then be considerably higher than the patient's true blood pressure. The doctor usually recognizes this condition when he continues to feel a pulse in the rigid artery even after the cuff has collapsed the artery farther up in the arm.

One 65-year-old woman had a blood pressure reading of 240/120—a dangerously high level normally requiring immediate medical intervention. But on further examination her physician noticed that there was still a pulse in her arm; the blood vessels were apparently so rigid (calcified) that they remained open even when no blood was flowing into them.

The physician wanted to be certain that her very high readings were not related simply to her rigid vessels. So he took an intra-arterial blood pressure reading by inserting a needle into the woman's arm. This time, the true blood pressure, 180/85, came to light. The systolic pressure was still too high, but it wasn't at a dangerous level; and the diastolic reading was normal.

Another situation that can cause confusion about blood pressure readings is a measurement that is very low—even zero in a few cases!—on the diastolic (lower) reading. Those suffering from anemia or from vitamin B-1 deficiency—and also some otherwise healthy pregnant women, young children, and people who have a great deal of anxiety—may have clear systolic readings, which can be detected easily through the blood pressure device. But the tapping sound of the blood rushing back into the arm may continue far beyond what's considered normal, so that the diastolic pressure comes in at 50 or even lower. (Remember: A doctor determines diastolic blood pressure by listening for the point when the tapping sound in his stethoscope *stops*.)

Sometimes the continuation of the tapping sound may be due to mechanical or technical problems. For example, the physician may be holding the stethoscope on the cuff device too hard over the artery in the upper arm. All the doctor has to do is release the pressure he's applying to the stethoscope, and the tapping will end, thus giving him the diastolic reading.

At other times, a muffled sound may occur and never disappear. In this situation, the physician should note the time when the clear tapping ends and the muffled sounds begin, and take that point to be the diastolic pressure.

On the other hand, there are situations in which these procedural adjustments don't change anything, and the tapping sounds never stop. Consequently, the diastolic pressure appears to be at or near zero—even though the patient seems quite healthy.

Sometimes these very low blood pressure readings are normal for the particular individual—though obviously they are highly unusual when compared with pressures of most people. It is up to the physician to determine whether a patient fits into this unusual-but-healthy category.

Many times, however, other measuring devices may reveal a diastolic pressure that for some reason wasn't picked up by the sphygmomanometer. In one such case, a woman in her fifties had a systolic pressure of 175, but a diastolic pressure of zero. No matter what adjustments the physician made in his equipment and technique, he still ended up with that zero reading.

Finally, he asked her to use a home monitoring device with a digital readout of pressure levels. Probably because the home device detected the movement of blood within the artery under the cuff rather than picking up the Korotkoff sounds, the measurement came out as 175/90. This revealed a hypertensive condition, but one that could be dealt with initially through nondrug treatments. An intra-artery test of her blood pressure later confirmed this reading.

Such home monitoring devices have proved useful time and time again as physicians try to determine the true blood pressure levels of their patients. Used wisely, these gadgets are prime examples of how cooperation between patient and physician can enhance the evaluation and treatment of hypertension.

But under what circumstances should these devices be used? And what guidelines should you keep in mind if you decide to buy one? Let's explore the world of the home blood pressure device a little more closely.

The Home Monitoring Issue: Should You or Shouldn't You?

I believe that *practically everyone* who has a problem with hypertension should purchase and use a monitoring device to measure his or her blood pressure at home, at work, and in other places outside the doctor's office.

The only exception to this view is if your physician feels that using such a device is not in your best interest. For example, some people become obsessed with worry about their blood pressure. Armed with a home monitoring device, they disrupt their daily lives by taking their pressure every few minutes. This approach obviously is not very helpful and may even be counterproductive. These people become so tense about taking their blood pressure that their stress drives up the readings beyond their normal levels!

The main purpose of home monitoring is to enable your physician to get a more accurate overall picture of your blood pressure situation. Typically, when several measurements have been taken at home and then at the doctor's office, the average systolic readings at home are

10 points lower, and the average diastolic readings are 5 points lower.

In some cases the readings at home may be *much* lower—20 to 30 points or more below office measurements. Such readings may be due to the white-coat syndrome—the tendency of some people's pressure to rise significantly in a medical environment.

In other cases, self-monitoring may reveal significant *increases* in pressure over both the doctor's readings and the home readings. One such case was the work-related high blood pressure experienced by "William," discussed in chapter 1.

To sum up, then, home monitoring can be quite useful in at least three situations:

Situation 1. Where a patient has a problem with the white-coat syndrome.

When such patients take their pressure outside the doctor's office, their measurements may be considerably lower.

Situation 2. Where treatment depends on a broader picture of blood pressure in a variety of situations.

As we've seen, a person may be in a state of mild or borderline hypertension during much of the day because of stress at work, but this condition may not show up in the doctor's office. Or there may be higher blood pressure readings at certain times because of physical problems, such as heart or kidney disease. The physician's ability to diagnose may be enhanced by his obtaining a broader picture of blood pressure during the day through home monitoring.

Situation 3. Where the patient is on an antihypertensive medication.

Every patient reacts differently to particular drugs. Some patients' blood pressure will go down with diuretics; others need beta blockers; still others respond best to ACE inhibitors or some other medication. In addition, many patients need a *combination* of two or more drugs to control their pressure.

How is a doctor to know which drug(s) works on a given patient?

The best way is to have the patient try a home monitoring program so that the physician can observe the individual's daily or even hourly reactions to different medications and dosages. With this approach, it's much easier to fine-tune the treatment process. Without it, the interests of the patient won't be as well served, and his or her health may even be jeopardized.

The pressure of one airline pilot was first measured in his doctor's office at a range of

170/110 to 180/120—a level which didn't meet FAA standards for his age. His physician placed him on a rather large dose of a diuretic, but the patient soon began to complain of lightheadedness and excessive fatigue.

Knowing that these were possible symptoms of hypotension—a blood pressure that is too low—the doctor put the pilot on a twenty-four-hour monitoring system. This involved fitting him with an automatic, electronic cuff device that is smaller than a miniature tape recorder. The system contains a built-in microphone that picks up noises inside the artery in the arm, just as a doctor might listen for the tapping sounds with a stethoscope. The systolic and diastolic pressures can thus be recorded by the device.

After certain timing mechanisms have been set, the cuff inflates by itself at regular intervals, from every few minutes to every hour. This particular gadget was set to record the man's pressure every fifteen minutes during the day, and every hour at night. Each time the cuff inflated, the pilot's pressure would be recorded on an electronic memory inside the device, with an indication of the time when the measurement was taken. At the end of the twenty-four-hour period, the doctor hooked up the electronic memory device to a decoder that recorded all of the pilot's pressures over the past twenty-four hours on a strip of paper from the device, like a tape from an adding machine.

The findings? As a result of the medications, the pilot's blood pressure had plummeted from a high of 180/120 in the doctor's office to a low during the day of 105/55—and an average of 115/65. These lower levels produced symptoms of hypotension, which the doctor was able to pinpoint immediately because the patient had used the home monitoring device.

The physician then prescribed a much lower dose of medication, and the pilot's blood pressure moved up to a range that, for him, was more comfortable and appropriate. The lower dose of medication and the resulting lower level of blood pressure meant that he was able to return to full flying status.

Clearly, home monitoring programs are a vital part of the cooperative process between hypertension patients and their physicians. But what specific guidelines should you follow if you plan to purchase and use one of these devices? Here are a few practical points to keep in mind:

- The principles for getting an accurate blood pressure reading in a doctor's office, which were described earlier in this chapter, apply also to home monitoring. In other words, observe these practices: Keep the arm to which you attach the cuff at heart level; be sure that arm is supported on a solid surface; avoid any muscular tension in your body; sit quietly and relax for at least five minutes before you take your pressure.

- In addition, be sure to *follow the particular instructions* provided with your device, as each type is a little different and may require special considerations in application.

  For example, electronic digital readout devices tend to be extremely sensitive. So it's quite important for those using them to place the cuff precisely in the right place over the artery on the upper arm, and also to avoid any arm movements while taking a reading. The wrong cuff position or any motions can cause errors in measurements.

- Be sure to check the accuracy of your device against your doctor's sphygmomanometer. Your physician will guide you in this procedure, but you should be aware of some of the possibilities:

  One way to do this is to take your blood pressure gadget to a special laboratory that tests medical equipment. Your doctor may also have access to equipment that will enable him to make a precise comparison.

Or, for a rougher comparison, your physician might simultaneously check your pressure in one arm with your home monitoring device and in the other arm with his standard mercury sphygmomanometer (provided he knows that the pressure in both arms is the same). When the mercury column registers zero at rest and is clean, the sphygmomanometer tends to be the most accurate device available.

Still another possibility is to take the pressure with each device on the same arm, using one immediately after the other. Again, the accuracy of your instrument can't be ascertained precisely this way, but the comparison should be helpful.

- Generally, the condition of your home equipment should be checked every six to twelve months, unless you use a mercury sphygmomanometer of the type used in a physician's office. These devices are calibrated when they're manufactured, and recalibration is unnecessary as long as (1) the mercury column is precisely at zero when the cuff is deflated and (2) the mercury column is clean.

If you use a mechanical device that requires you to listen through a stethoscope but doesn't contain liquid mercury, a once-a-year calibration for the gadget should be enough, according to the "Revised Statement of the National High Blood Pressure Education Program," issued in December 1985.

However, if you have an electronic digital readout device, the "Revised Statement" recommends that you check it several times a year.

- If you have a traditional device that requires you to listen for the beginning and ending of the tapping sounds that signal systolic and diastolic readings, your doctor should certainly check your accuracy in taking your own pressure.

  Even if you use an automatic digital-display device, you should still have your doctor evaluate your technique to be sure you're following proper procedures. For example, he should watch to be sure you're placing the cuff in the proper place on your upper arm.

- Don't panic or become too concerned if your home monitoring reveals that your blood pressure fluctuates 5 to 20 points during the course of a day. Keep your doctor apprised of these changes, but let *him* interpret the measurements—and understand that it's quite normal for such variations to occur.

• If your physician has instructed you to do home measurements so that he can monitor the effectiveness or impact of your medications, take the readings at the same time each day.

Now, what about specific devices?

Most of the several million people who monitor their own blood pressure do so with one of two types of devices: (1) the mechanical "aneroid" gadget (without liquid mercury), which requires you to listen through a stethoscope and read a gauge dial; or (2) the battery-operated electronic machines that give the pressure readings on a digital display panel.

A study by *Consumer Reports* (May 1987) found that the mechanical aneroid devices were the cheapest ($18 to $30) and, when properly used, the most accurate. In fact, the best ones are usually off by no more than 2 mm Hg.

On the other hand, there are some drawbacks with these mechanical gadgets: They often require skill in manipulating the stethoscope, as well as good hearing (to hear the tapping sounds over the stethoscope) and adequate eyesight (to read the gauge dials).

The easier-to-use electronic models that require the user to pump air into the cuff also cost more—$45 to $89, according to the report. Furthermore, they tend to be less accurate than their mechanical counterparts—being in error by 5 mm Hg or even more, depending on the brand.

The most expensive devices—and also the easiest to use—are the electronic models that have cuffs that inflate automatically when the person presses a button. These cost $70 to $150, but they have the same accuracy problems as the less expensive electronic devices.

Now, with these considerations in mind, following are the *Consumer Reports'* ratings of the major home monitoring devices, of which some may not be available.

Guide to the Ratings

Listed by types; within types, listed in order of estimated quality based primarily on diastolic performance in use tests and on ease of use. Closely ranked models differed little in quality.

1. **Price.** Manufacturer's suggested price. Discounts are sometimes available. + means shipping is extra.

Blood-pressure monitors

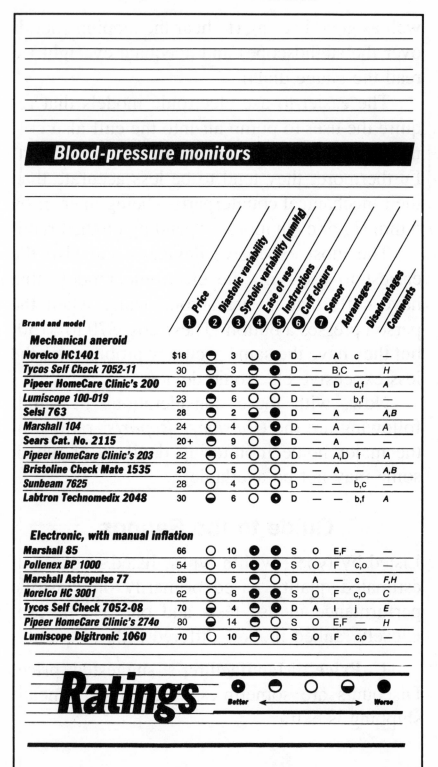

Brand and model	Price (1)	Diastolic variability (2)	Systolic variability (mmHg) (3)	Ease of use (4)	Instructions (5)	Cuff closure (6)	Sensor (7)	Advantages	Disadvantages	Comments
Mechanical aneroid										
Norelco HC1401	$18	◐	3	○	◉	D	—	A	c	—
Tycos Self Check 7052-11	30	◐	3	◐	◉	D	—	B,C	—	H
Pipeer HomeCare Clinic's 200	20	◉	3	◒	○	—	—	D	d,f	A
Lumiscope 100-019	23	◐	6	○	○	D	—	—	b,f	—
Selsi 763	28	◐	2	◒	●	D	—	A	—	A,B
Marshall 104	24	○	4	○	◉	D	—	A	—	A
Sears Cat. No. 2115	20+	◐	9	○	◉	D	—	A	—	—
Pipeer HomeCare Clinic's 203	22	◐	6	○	○	D	—	A,D	f	A
Bristoline Check Mate 1535	20	○	5	○	○	D	—	A	—	A,B
Sunbeam 7625	28	○	4	○	○	D	—	—	b,c	—
Labtron Technomedix 2048	30	◒	6	○	◉	D	—	—	b,f	A
Electronic, with manual inflation										
Marshall 85	66	○	10	◉	◉	S	O	E,F	—	—
Pollenex BP 1000	54	○	6	◉	◉	S	O	F	c,o	—
Marshall Astropulse 77	89	○	5	◐	○	D	A	—	c	F,H
Norelco HC 3001	62	○	8	◉	◉	S	O	F	c,o	C
Tycos Self Check 7052-08	70	◐	4	◐	◉	D	A	I	j	E
Pipeer HomeCare Clinic's 274o	80	◐	14	◐	○	S	O	E,F	—	H
Lumiscope Digitronic 1060	70	○	10	◐	○	S	O	F	c,o	—

Ratings   ● ◐ ○ ◑ ●

Better ←——————→ Worse

Blood-pressure monitors

Brand and model	Price (1)	Diastolic variability (2)	Systolic variability [mmHg] (3)	Ease of use (4)	Instructions (5)	Cuff closure (6)	Sensor (7)	Advantages	Disadvantages	Comments
Electronic, with manual inflation										
Sharp MB-500	55	○	10	◓	◓	S	O	—		c,i,o	—
Sunbeam 7621	65	◒	6	◒	○	D	O	—		b,c	—
Bristoline Check Mate 1735	58	○	12	○	●	S	O	—		b,j,k	H
Sears 2119	45	●	11	◒	◓	D	O	—		b	I
Healthcheck BP-1	50	●	8	◒	◓	D	A	I		g,h,j,o	G
Healthteam 8115	60	●	12	◒	○	D	O	—		b,c,g	—
Electronic, with automatic inflation										
Norelco HC3030	96	◒	11	◓	◓	S	O	—		m,o	C
Marshall 89	131	○	7	◓	◓	S	O	E		k	D
Sunbeam 7650	115	○	8	◒	○	S	O	E		b	—
Sharp MB-600	110	◒	7	◓	◓	S	O	G		m	H
Lumiscope Digitronic 1080	100	○	8	◒	○	S	O	—		m,o	H
Pollenex BP 1500	90	○	11	◒	○	S	O	—		m,o	—
Pipeer HomeCare Clinic's 231	150	◒	9	◓	◓	D	O	H		k	—
Labtron Omron 837	89	◒	9	◓	◓	D	O	—		e,k	—
Panasonic EW250	120	○	8	◒	○	S	A	—		a,o	—
Bristoline Check Mate 1745	94	○	10	◒	○	S	O	—		b,j,k,l	—
Healthteam 8145	120	◒	9	◒	○	D	O	—		b,c,e,h	F
Healthcheck BP-2	70	●	7	◒	◓	D	A	I		g,j,n,o	G

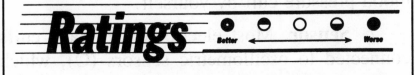

Ratings Better ← ● ◓ ○ ◒ ● → Worse

2. **Diastolic variability.** Use tests compared the pressure each model registered with a nurse's simultaneous reading. Most models were acceptably accurate on average. Our judgment is based on the variability of the readings, a measure of how often and by how much a model's readings differed from the nurse's. The best monitors were seldom off by more than 5 mm Hg. The poorest were off 10 or more mm Hg much of the time, judged too unreliable for home use.

3. **Systolic variability.** Variability of systolic readings is shown for the record, but we gave it little weight. Many doctors feel that systolic pressure is less important than diastolic pressure.

4. **Ease of use.** An overall judgment based on how easy the cuff was to don and inflate, how easy the unit was to operate, and how readable its gauge dial or digital display was.

5. **Instructions.** The clarity and completeness of documentation provided.

6. **Cuff closure.** D-rings (D) are slide bars for looping the cuff and pulling it snug. Cuffs with leaf-springs (S) are curved to approximate arm shape. Either design helps when you don a blood-pressure cuff by yourself.

7. **Sensor.** Most electronic kits have cuffs connected to oscillometric sensors (O), which

calculate pressure from the ebb and flow of blood in the arm. A few have auscultatory cuffs (A), with a built-in microphone that detects the pulse.

Specifications and Features

Except as noted, all have a separate carrying case. All mechanical aneroid models have a stethoscope. Except as noted, batteries are included with all electronic units.

Key to Advantages

A – Stethoscope attached to cuff.

B – Deflation valve easier to use than on other mechanical models.

C – Instruction cassette (supplied) gives sample artery sounds.

D – Cuff marked for left or right arm use.

E – Large, easy-to-read digital display.

F – Batteries last longer than in other models of the same type.

G – Inflation presettings can be more finely adjusted than in most autoinflation units.

H – Voice synthesizer gives pressure readings and instruction.

I – Instruction cassette supplied.

Key to Disadvantages

a – Designed for use on right arm only.

b – Cuff lacks location marker.

c – Plastic fittings judged flimsy; can break in use.

d – Cuff lacks convenient D-ring or spring closure.

e – Automatic inflation or deflation too slow, can cause discomfort.

f – Cuff's inflatable "bladder" too narrow; may give incorrect readings for some.

g – Large error in pulse estimate.

h – Batteries consumed faster than in other models of the same type.

i – Display unit unstable; can tip over when switched on/off.

j – Small digital display less readable than most.

k – Cuff overly sensitive to arm motion; can give incorrect reading.

l – Confusing controls.

m – Automatic inflation too far above preset pressure; can cause discomfort.

n – Pressure may be preset to one value only (180 mm Hg); not appropriate for everyone.

o – Batteries not included.

Key to Comments

A – Gauge may be attached to cuff for reading by second person.

B – Hand-held gauge bulkier to hold than most.

C – Has slide pointer to mark previous readings.

D – Can average last two readings.

E – Has electronic memory to store four previous readings.

F – Fitting broke in use.

G – Self-contained unit without separate carrying case.

H – According to manufacturer, model has been discontinued.

I – Model no longer in catalog, but still available in retail stores.

Another study, done on twenty-three home blood pressure devices, was reported in 1989 in the *Journal of Hypertension*. The investigators gave a passing mark to only twelve of the devices and failed the rest.

Following are two key charts released by those conducting this study. One shows the twenty-three devices that were tested and their salient characteristics; the other lists the passing devices, with notes on their accuracy and other features.

Descriptive Information on Devices Tested

Study in numbers	Device	Manufacturer Distributor	Cost
128/148	Almedic J-410	A	$28.95
126/149	Almedic UA231	A	$159.95
124/143	Almedic UA241	A	$198.00
117/151	Almedic UA251	A	$219.50
127/144	Alsphyg J-300	A	$33.95
123/131	AMG 7-60	B	$29.95
121/132	AMG Health Guard 7-62	B	$34.95
120/147	Astropulse 10^5	C	$67.95
118/141	Astropulse 48	C	$107.90
119/153	Astropulse 77	C	$121.50
137/164	Astropulse 90AC	C	$289.00
110/138	Lumiscope 100-019	D	$18.88
111/115	Lumiscope 100-048[8]	D	$64.95
145/150	Lumiscope 1070	D	$118.88

Descriptive Information
on Devices Tested (continued)

Instructions	Display	Microphone	Stethoscope	D-Ring	Inflation	Deflation
No	Analog	No	Yes[1]	No	Manual	Manual
Yes	Digital	Yes	No	Yes	Auto	Auto
Yes	Printer[3]	Yes	No	Yes	Manual	Auto
Yes	Printer[3]	Yes	No	Yes	Auto	Auto
Yes	Analog	No	Yes[4]	Yes	Manual	Manual
No	Analog	No	Yes[1]	No	Manual	Manual
Yes	Analog	No	Yes[4]	Yes	Manual	Manual
Yes	Analog	Yes	No	Yes	Manual	Semi-auto
Yes	Digital	Yes	No	Yes	Manual	Auto
Yes	Digital	Yes	No	Yes	Manual	Auto
Yes	Printer[3]	No[6]	No	Yes	Auto	Auto
Yes	Analog	No	Yes[7]	Yes	Manual	Manual
Yes	Digital	Yes	No	Yes	Manual	Auto
Yes	Printer[3]	Yes	No	Yes	Manual	Auto

Descriptive Information
on Devices Tested (continued)

Study in numbers	Device	Manufacturer Distributor	Cost
122/154	Precisa 7-69	B	$62.95
163/165	Radio Shack 63-661	E	$59.95
146/156	Sunbeam 7620	F	$49.95
113/140	Taylor 7052-04	G	$52.00
112/130	Tycos 7052-08	G	$69.99
114/155	Tycos 7052-11	G	$39.95
125/139	Winner 858	H	$39.00
135/136	Telelab [9]	I	$1000.00*
133/134	Timex Healthcheck [10]	J	$99.00*

Manufacturer/distributor: A. Almedic, St. Laurent, Montreal, Canada. B. AMG sales (AMG MED). Montreal, Canada. C. Marshall Electronics Inc. Skokie, Illinois, USA. D. The Lumiscope Company Inc. Edison, New Jersey, USA. E. Radio Shack Division. Tandy Electronics Ltd. Barrie, Ontario, Canada. F. Hanson Scale Company (Division of Sunbeam Corp). Shubuta, Mississippi, USA. G. Taylor Instrument Medical Products Division, Sybron Corporation, Toronto, Ontario, Canada. H. Sundex Corporation (Winmed Instruments). Taipei, Taiwan. I. Instromedix Inc. Beaverton, Oregon, USA. J. TMZ Canada Inc. Markham, Ontario, Canada.

Descriptive Information on Devices Tested (continued)

Instruc-tions	Display	Micro-phone	Stetho-scope	D-Ring	Infla-tion	Defla-tion
No	Analog	No	Yes[1]	No	Manual	Manual
Yes	Digital	Yes	No	Yes	Manual	Auto
Yes	Digital	No[6]	No	No[2]	Manual	Auto
Yes	Analog	No	Yes[7]	No	Manual	Semi-auto
Yes	Digital	Yes	No	Yes	Manual	Semi-auto
Yes	Analog	No	Yes[4]	Yes	Manual	Semi-auto
Yes	Analog	Yes	No	Yes	Manual	Manual
Yes	Digital	Yes	No	Yes	Manual	Auto
Yes	Digital	Yes	No	Yes	Manual	Auto

[1]Stethoscope not provided with device. [2]Rigid cuff. [3]All devices with printers also have a digital display. [4]Stethoscope attached. [5]Also has LED display and audible signal to indicate systolic and diastolic pressures. [6]Has microphoneless sensor. [7]Stethoscope provided with device. [8]Also called Almedic UA271 costing $74.95–79.95. [9]Prototypes from USA included in testing. [10]No longer on the market. *Not purchased approx. list price.

Devices Passing the Investigators' Tests (listed alphabetically)

Study ID numbers	Device	Points to note	Diastolic Mean difference corrected (s.d.)	Systolic Mean difference corrected (s.d.)
128/148	Almedic J-410	A B C	1.3 (6.3)	−2.38 (6.10)
124/143	Almedic UA241		0.4 (4.3)	0.67 (4.32)*
117/151	Almedic UA251		−2.6 (6.2)	0.62 (6.69)*
123/131	AMG 7-60	A B C F	−2.8 (6.6)	1.67 (6.81)
120/147	Astropulse 10[1]	F	2.3 (6.3)	4.77 (8.27)
137/164	Astropulse 90AC		−0.6 (5.1)	1.12 (4.73)*
111/115	Lumiscope 100-048[2]		−2.6 (6.2)	−0.38 (4.56)*
163/165	Radio Shack 63-661		−0.6 (7.9)	−3.33 (7.32)*
146/156	Sunbeam 7620	D	−1.1 (7.9)	−3.53 (6.31)*

Study ID numbers	Device	Points to note	Diastolic Mean difference corrected (s.d.)	Systolic Mean difference corrected (s.d.)
113/140	Taylor 7052-04	A	–1.0 (4.4)	0.12 (3.84)
133/134	Timex Healthcheck	E	–4.5 (5.3)	–3.03 (5.46)*
114/155	Tycos 7052-11		–4.0 (5.6)	–2.68 (6.47)*

Points to note: A. no D-ring; B. no instructions supplied; C. stethoscope required but not provided; D. no D-ring but rigid cuff; E. no longer on the market; F. failed performance criteria for systolic readings. [1]Also called Winner 878. [2]Also called Almedic UA271. *Suitable for home use.

Finally, I want to say a word about those stationary automated machines that you may find in public locations, such as pharmacies, airports, or occupational sites. Often these machines require a deposit of money, and certainly they're convenient for many people. But they're usually the *least* accurate of all the devices that you'll find outside your doctor's office.

The "Revised Statement of the National High Blood Pressure Education Program" has reported that the date of the last calibration of these machines is their only measure of reliability. Unfortunately, however, this information often isn't indicated on the devices.

Studies have shown that these machines may be off by 5 to 10 mm Hg or more, for both the systolic and diastolic readings. Furthermore, the "Revised Statement" warns, the "majority of errors are on the high side."

Consequently, I do not recommend these machines as part of your personal monitoring program. Stick to the standard home monitoring devices. They tend to be more accurate, and your doctor can check them against his sphygmomanometer.

The White-Coat Syndrome

A number of my patients have told me that the greatest stress they experience anytime during the year is when they come to my office for an examination.

In many cases, the stress is reflected in a high blood pressure reading, or what physicians call a "pressor effect" on the arteries. The main factor that causes the increase in blood pressure is the presence of the doctor; hence, the term "white-coat hypertension," after the physician's traditional manner of dress.

Furthermore, a number of studies have revealed that in many situations, the *only* place where the patient's blood pressure is high is in the doctor's office!

For example, Dr. Thomas Pickering and several associates, based at the Cardiovascular Center at the New York Hospital–Cornell University Medical Center, conducted research on 292 patients with untreated borderline hypertension. "Borderline," by this group's definition, involved patients with diastolic measurements ranging from 90 to 104 mm Hg.

The investigators reported that 21 percent of the patients who were *thought* to be hypertensive actually weren't hypertensive at all. Readings taken at regular intervals over the course of a typical day with an automatic measuring device showed that their blood pressure levels were normal. These patients provided classic examples of the white-coat syndrome.

In general, these white-coat patients tended to be young, female, and lighter in weight than the other participants in Dr. Pickering's study. Also, unlike many whose blood pressure is sensitive to stress, they didn't show a tendency toward hypertension when they experienced stress at work. In addition, their blood pressure went up more when they were measured by a physician than when a medical technician took the measurement.

Another interesting point: On the average, the highest readings during the *entire day,* for both the borderline hypertensives and for those with more permanent (essential or primary) hypertension, were *measurements taken in the doctor's office.* In more detail, following are some of the results:

When the pressures of the borderline hypertensives were taken by a physician, the average reading was 150/96. Readings taken by medical technicians were lower, averaging 140/95. Measurements made with an ambulatory monitoring device, strapped on the arm during the day and night, varied from a low of 121/79 during sleep to a high of 143/97 at work.

There was a similar response among those with more serious hypertension: When a physician took their readings, they averaged 168/111. With a technician, the average went down to 154/105. And when they wore the ambulatory monitor, the readings ranged from 120/81 during sleep to 152/101 at work.

This white-coat response, then, is a clearly identifiable phenomenon—but what causes it?

There are several possibilities: The main source of the elevated blood pressure may be simple anxiety about seeing a doctor. The results of the Pickering study, which show blood pressure levels going higher during a physician's exam than at any other time of the day, certainly support this conclusion.

But Pickering has also suggested that the rise

in blood pressure may come as a "conditioned response," apart from any particular feelings of anxiety. That is, the patient may be nervous on the first visit or two, and that worry may be reflected in high readings. Then, the anxiety may dissipate. But the patient may still assume, consciously or subconsciously, that he's *supposed* to have high blood pressure when the doctor examines him—and an elevated reading is exactly what the doctor will find.

Finally, another possibility that Pickering has suggested is that in women who have this problem, the response may be "gender specific." In other words, they find themselves confronting the stereotype of the male authority figure when the doctor comes toward them to perform the test—and their blood pressure levels go up as a result.

Whatever the reasons, the white-coat syndrome will remain a significant factor for many patients. But what does it mean in terms of the person's health and the likelihood of developing hypertension in the future?

Dr. Norman Kaplan, in his editorial for the *American Journal of Cardiology*, notes that other studies on white-coat hypertension have revealed systolic increases as great as 70 mm Hg and diastolic jumps as high as 30 mm Hg. He says these responses confirm that "for some patients, the doctor's office may be the only place where the blood pressure is high."

At the same time, Kaplan emphasizes that medical research has shown that those with white-coat hypertension tend to be at little extra risk for either permanent (primary) hypertension or cardiovascular disease. He concludes that there's rarely any need to treat these patients with antihypertensive drugs. The key concern is the long-term level of blood pressure, not occasional high readings in a doctor's office.

The one possible exception, Kaplan says, is the patient who experiences *extremely* high readings, well up into the severe or emergency category. In such cases, the physician conducting the exam must make an on-the-spot decision whether to refer the patient to another source of care or to take immediate countermeasures himself.

Finally, it is true that *on the average,* those who have high readings in the doctor's office are more likely to have problems later. But for treatment purposes, it's important to separate those who experience high blood pressure *only* in the doctor's office from those who have high readings in other environments. In most cases, those who have only white-coat hypertension probably won't need medication.

To sum up, then, the white-coat types without other high readings must be regarded as at considerably lower risk than those who have high readings both in the doctor's office and elsewhere.

A Tale of Two Pressures

The Physician. "All my life, I've tended to get nervous and tense before important events," a physician friend of mine said. "When I ran track in high school and college, I'd always feel the pressure. Many times, I couldn't sleep the night before, or eat properly until after the race had been run."

This tendency to be affected by stress carried over to his medical school years: "I remember when I was in my first year of medical studies, I had to go in for a physical exam, and that made me very tense and nervous."

As a result, his blood pressure reading at that exam was 170/60—quite normal for the diastolic, but well into the isolated hypertension range for the systolic.

The elderly physician taking the measurement helped aggravate the student doctor's anxiety when he said, "Son, you'll be lucky to live to forty!"

Fortunately, that was thirty-five years ago, and my physician friend, who is also my patient, still hasn't developed hypertension. To be certain that he doesn't have a problem in the future,

I've utilized twenty-four-hour monitoring on two occasions, including regular measurements during the eight to ten hours he spends each day at the office. This approach revealed that his average blood pressure was only 116/70.

For people troubled with this white-coat syndrome—or "vascular reactivity," as it's called in medical terminology—two strategies may be of value:

1. Lie down for ten minutes or so before your exam, utilize relaxation techniques, and clear your mind of extraneous thoughts and worries. More often than not, this method will bring your readings down to normal levels.

2. Go out for a fifteen to twenty minute slow jog within one hour of the examination. (Of course, this approach will be of value only for people who are regular joggers.)

The second suggestion, above, may seem questionable, since one of my previous recommendations was to *avoid* undue exertion before an exam. However, slow jogging may be entirely consistent with this guideline—as you'll see from the following explanation:

First of all, the warning against physical activity is directed primarily at *isometric* exercise, which involves stationary or slow-moving, muscle-tensing activities, such as flexing the muscles or weight lifting. Distance running or jogging is an aerobic activity involving the cardiovascular system.

In most cases with aerobic exercise, the systolic pressure goes up and the diastolic stays low during the activity. Then, at the end of the exercise period, the blood pressure tends to fall rapidly—a phenomenon that should help explain why endurance exercises are so helpful in overcoming stress. As I've said in other contexts, "Aerobic exercise is nature's best tranquilizer!"

Why does the cardiovascular system and the body's blood pressure behave this way during aerobic exercise?

There are several possible explanations that are pertinent. First, as I've already said, the systolic reading goes higher during endurance activity because the heart is pumping harder and faster. During those pumping actions, the increased volume of blood coursing through the body puts extra pressure on the vessel walls.

On the other hand, the diastolic pressure (which is measured between beats) isn't usually affected much by aerobic exercise. This is because the vessels become dilated during the forceful pumping action of the heart and then *stay* stretched out when the heart rests between beats. This dilation action minimizes the pressure that the blood exerts against the vessel walls during the between-beats phase.

Finally, when the patient has rested for about ten minutes after an aerobic activity, the vessels remain dilated or stretched, but the pumping of the heart slows down even more. With a normal, resting heart rate, the blood is being pushed less forcefully through the vessels than is the case during exercise. With wider, stretched vessels, and yet a slower heart rate, the blood pressure against the vessel walls may go down to a point even below the person's normal level.

This is a roundabout way of explaining why jogging for fifteen to twenty minutes just before a blood pressure measurement is of value in a well-conditioned patient troubled with the white-coat syndrome.

Another possible benefit of exercise to the "vascular reactor" is the pleasant, relaxed, slightly fatigued feeling that occurs after an endurance workout. Among other things, the exercise probably burns up the tension-triggering hormones that promote constriction of the blood vessels. With fewer of these chemical substances—including the catecholamines and neurotransmitters that are associated with the body's nervous, edgy, "fight or flight" responses—you just don't *feel* as nervous. Lower blood pressure can be a reflection of this more relaxed state.

So, many people do experience these wide variations in blood pressure during the day. But there are others who have much more stable readings—as another of my patients demon-strates.

The Patient. I asked "Larry" to undergo a little experiment for me because I knew that he had relatively stable, unchanging blood pressure readings when he came in for his annual physicals.

While Larry sat in a chair with his arm supported at heart level, his average blood pressure, based on three separate readings, was 112/68. But then we tried a few unusual variations, which I *wouldn't* recommend for anyone who wants to find his or her *true* pressure.

First, Larry sat on the edge of the examining table and pressed down against the tabletop with his right hand (the sphygmomanometer cuff had been placed on his right arm). The result? There was almost no change in his reading—just a slight increase up to 118/70.

Then, Larry clenched his right fist. Still, only a slight increase occurred, this time up to 122/70.

His next assignment was to stand up while his blood pressure was taken. In this position, the systolic was again measured at 122, but the diastolic went up a little higher, to about 80. Such a rise in diastolic pressure is regarded as only a slight shift due to the body's postural change.

Larry also drank some coffee during our experiment, but that had no effect whatsoever on his blood pressure. (In some cases, caffeine can trigger a short-term rise in blood pressure.) Finally, I noted that the stress of being in a "test" situation apparently hadn't affected him either.

When undergoing a stress test, Larry's pressure increased up to normal aerobic-exercise levels, about 190/70. Then the reading dropped down below normal within ten minutes after stopping the exercise. Finally, the measurement returned to his normal 112/68 within thirty minutes.

How would I evaluate Larry's results? He has completely normal blood pressure that is relatively unresponsive to outside stimulation. Physical tension, isometric exercises, caffeine, and stress seem not to affect his measurements appreciably. In short, he's just one more example of how much we may differ from one another in our blood pressure reactions—and how important it is for *each* of us to ascertain how we react in different circumstances.

A person such as Larry has little cause to worry about hypertension or to bother with home monitoring. For those whose pressures are more volatile, however, more attention should be paid to the regular evaluation of blood pressure.

Millions of people occasionally experience

upsurges in their blood pressure levels. Although these individuals don't have hypertension, their periodic high readings *do* put them at greater risk of developing permanent high blood pressure in the future. So it's important to keep close track of their measurements in a variety of daily circumstances and to watch for any unusual changes or trends.

To help you evaluate these and other factors that may bear upon *your* risk of developing hypertension, I'll turn now to a consideration of what I call your Hypertension Risk Profile.

3

What's Your Hypertension Risk Profile?

Risk is *the* major concern for those who have hypertension. Unfortunately, determining the extent to which you, personally, may be at risk can be very complex and confusing. Consider for a moment what's involved:

First, to ascertain your overall risk you must know as much as possible about the health implications of your present blood pressure measurements.

Second, it's important to determine how your lifestyle, diet, and family history may influence your present chances of developing hypertension in the future.

Third, you should know how your blood

pressure may interact with other cardiovascular risk factors—such as elevated cholesterol or cigarette smoking—and thus place you at greater risk for cardiovascular disease.

The best way to determine the degree of danger you may be facing is to design your own personal Hypertension Risk Profile and Hypertension Risk Monitor—a task that requires three separate steps:

Step 1. You must evaluate your risks associated with one or more high blood pressure readings.

Step 2. You must evaluate the hypertension risk factors (other than your initial set of blood pressure readings) that may pose a threat.

Step 3. You must evaluate your vulnerability to the *multiple risk phenomenon* that arises when additional cardiovascular risk factors—including elevated cholesterol, cigarette smoking, diabetes, or abnormal electrocardiogram (ECG) readings—are combined with hypertension.

In the following pages, we'll explore each of these steps in depth, which will give you an idea of your personal Hypertension Risk Profile. Next, I'll provide some guidelines to help you draft your own Hypertension Risk Monitor.

Step 1: Evaluating the Risks of High Blood Pressure Readings

Nearly one-third of the adult American population has been estimated to be at *some* risk for damage to health or for early death as a result of high blood pressure. Specifically—as I'll explain in detail in chapter 4—the possible problems include stroke, kidney disease, and various cardiovascular complications. Yet, not every individual with high blood pressure faces the same degree of danger. To understand how to evaluate *your* risk level, it's helpful first to take a closer look at the huge number of people who are thought to be at some risk—and to differentiate among them.

As I mentioned in chapter 1, a standard estimate accepted by many experts is that there are 58 to 60 million Americans (or about 30 percent of all adults) who have some form of high blood pressure. In this regard, "The 1988 Report of the Joint National Committee on Detection, Evaluation, and Treatment of High Blood Pressure" states:

"As many as 58 million people in the United States have elevated blood pressure (systolic blood pressure . . . of 140 mm Hg or greater and/or diastolic blood pressure . . . of 90 mm Hg or greater) or are taking antihypertensive medication."

But a more detailed analysis of these numbers reveals some interesting variations in risk.

In the first place, the estimate of 58 to 60 million people with high blood pressure is arrived at as a result of only *one* set of initial blood pressure readings. In many cases, later readings have revealed that those who initially tested as hypertensive in fact were *not* hypertensive (e.g., their blood pressure may have increased as a result of the white-coat syndrome).

My special consultant, Dr. Norman Kaplan, who has done in-depth studies on the prevalence of high blood pressure, argues that the current thinking on the number of people at risk for hypertension should be "reinterpreted." (See Kaplan's article, "Hypertension," listed in the bibliography.)

Specifically, Kaplan has fine-tuned the thinking on hypertension in three areas:

- *The prevalence of hypertension.*

It's generally accepted by many physicians that about 60 million Americans have hypertension, with 75 percent of these having mild hypertension (i.e., diastolic readings of 90 to 104 mm Hg).

Kaplan's reinterpretation: At least one-third of those with an *initial* diastolic reading above 95 will have a diastolic measurement below 90 on subsequent measurements! This means that the *real* number of American adults with hypertension, as diagnosed after *more* than one set of readings, is probably closer to 40 million than the 58 to 60 million figure. (On the other hand, only about 50 percent of the "real" hypertensives are aware of their problem. Why? The other 50 percent have never had their blood pressure taken!)

- *Risks based on blood pressure measurements.*

The current thinking is that the risk for developing cardiovascular disease is significantly increased for *all* patients with elevated blood pressure, including those with only one initial set of high measurements.

Kaplan's reinterpretation: Most people with an initial mild hypertension measurement are *not* at high risk for cardiovascular disease. Furthermore, he says, patients who *are* at relatively high risk can easily be identified, and many times the risk can be reduced.

For example, a person who smokes cigarettes, is obese, and has high cholesterol levels *in addition to* mildly elevated blood pressure is at a significantly higher risk for cardiovascular disease than is an individual with mild hypertension alone.

But note: From a statistical viewpoint, an initial high reading *still* signals, by itself, that the person has a somewhat higher potential risk for developing high blood pressure than does the person with consistently normal pressure.

In other words, you may not have hypertension now, even though your initial measurement was high (i.e., later measurements have demonstrated to your physician that you should not be classified as hypertensive). However, that initial high measurement means that, according to various population studies, you are *slightly* more at risk than is the person who has never had a high reading.

Findings by the respected Framingham Heart Study—which has followed the health patterns of thousands of participants in Framingham, Massachusetts, since 1948—support this viewpoint. They show that men with a mildly elevated diastolic reading on a first exam have a greater risk for suffering a coronary event than do those with normal blood pressure measurements.

For example, 170 out of 10,000 men with an initial mild hypertension measurement (in the range of 141/91 to 159/94) had coronary heart disease within eight years, as opposed to 86 out of 10,000 of those with normal blood pressure. Women in the study fared better, but an initial high reading still put them at greater risk: Researchers found that 81 out of 10,000 of those with mild readings developed coronary heart disease, in contrast to 41 out of 10,000 of those with normal measurements.

As for strokes caused by blood clots, 39 out of 10,000 men with mild hypertension on an initial exam suffered later from this disease, as compared with 20 out of 10,000 of those with normal initial hypertension. Again, women faced a lower overall risk for stroke: The study revealed that 16 out of 10,000 with mild hypertension suffered strokes by blood clot, as opposed to 8 out of 10,000 women with normal blood pressure.

Other data used by the life insurance industry to formulate its actuarial tables substantiate these findings. They show that men with a first diastolic measurement in the 88 to 92 mm Hg range were *potentially* more at risk than were those with normal readings. In particular, the men with a mildly elevated diastolic measurement had a death rate more than one-third higher than that of those with lower readings over a twenty-year period.

Clearly, then, an initial mild hypertensive reading will put a person at somewhat higher risk than one with normal blood pressure. But still, it's important for patients not to panic at one high reading or for physicians to plunge into serious treatment before making additional measurements.

- *The treatment of mild hypertension.*

The current wisdom says that the benefits of drug therapy for mild hypertension are clear.

Dr. Kaplan's reinterpretation: The benefits of antihypertensive medications for those with diastolic readings below 100 mm Hg *haven't* been proved conclusively. Consequently, for those who have diastolic readings below 100 *and* who are at relatively low risk otherwise, the emphasis should usually be placed on nondrug therapies.

But remember—when nondrug therapies fail to bring blood pressure readings below 160/95, medications will usually be required. (But only about one-third of hypertensives have made good use of their medications or of nondrug treatments and brought their blood pressure levels under reasonable control, with measurements below 160/90.)

Is There a Difference in Risk Between a High Diastolic and a High Systolic Measurement?

First, let me summarize a few important points about diastolic and systolic measurements.

Over the years, the medical profession has tended to emphasize the diastolic more than the systolic as a diagnostic tool. In fact, if a patient was classified as hypertensive, that designation was based, more often than not, exclusively on the diastolic measurement.

Recent studies, however—including the Framingham reports—have recognized that the *systolic* reading may be even more predictive of later risks than is the diastolic reading.

In this regard, patients in the Multiple Risk Factor Intervention Trial (MRFIT) were evaluated as to links between (1) initial blood pressure levels and (2) subsequent coronary heart disease, stroke, and other causes of death.

As part of this MRFIT study, the initial blood pressures of 317,871 men were taken. Then the researchers tracked the future health of the participants, including, when applicable, the causes and times of their deaths.

The findings, reported in the March 1988 issue of *Circulation,* revealed that during a six-year period, the death rates in men over age 50 were highest among those with isolated systolic hypertension than in any other group. In this study, isolated systolic hypertension was defined as an initial systolic measurement equal to or greater than 160 mm Hg, and a diastolic measurement below 90. Isolated systolic hypertension was *the major determinant* of all causes of death, including coronary heart disease.

A medical examination that reveals isolated systolic hypertension can have special meaning for those in different age groups.

- *Adolescents or young adults* whose systolic is 160 or higher may be at higher risk for developing elevated diastolic blood pressure because of "hyperdynamic circulation," or an excessively strong heart-pumping action and movement of the blood.

  For those with systolic blood pressure of 160 or above (though normal diastolic readings), antihypertensive medications may be in order.

- *Those age 65 or older* often develop some degree of elevation in their systolic pressure, usually because their arteries become more rigid and inflexible. This is a process that occurs primarily because of the hardening of the arteries (buildup of plaque and fatty deposits in the blood vessels as a result of the process of atherosclerosis).

  As I've already mentioned, there's an old rule of thumb that says it's all right to have a systolic blood pressure as high as 100 plus your age. But obviously that rule can't be taken too seriously if we are to follow the latest findings and medical advice on isolated hypertension.

  In other words, if you're 60 years old and your systolic reading is 160, you'd be doing just fine under the old 100-plus-your-age rule. But if we follow the new criteria, a consistent systolic reading of 160 or above at *any* age would require a diagnosis of isolated hypertension and would most likely mandate some sort of treatment.

Furthermore, there's no reason for most older people to develop isolated systolic hypertension. Our surveys at the Aerobics Institute in Dallas show that older people can maintain systolic and diastolic blood pressure levels almost as low as many of those who are much younger.

For example, in a survey of nearly 1,400 men under age 30, the median blood pressure was 120/78. Another survey of more than 3,200 men age 50 to 59 revealed that the median blood pressure was only 125/82. In other words, the readings increased just barely even though the age of those surveyed had approximately doubled! Furthermore, a survey of more than 1,000 men over age 60 showed that their median blood pressure was 132/82.

The men in our surveys were generally fit, maintained healthier lifestyles, and had higher socioeconomic and educational levels than those of the average American.

However, these findings show that you

don't have to settle for a relatively high systolic (or diastolic) reading as you age. In fact, most people can maintain youthful blood pressure readings throughout life— as long as careful attention is paid to diet, exercise, and other antihypertensive life-style practices that I'll be describing in later chapters.

In any case, systolic readings that increase with age are nothing to be complacent about. In the Hypertension Detection and Follow-up Program, deaths from all causes were more than twice as high among those with isolated systolic readings of 160 or above, than for those with normal blood pressure.

On the other hand, treatment of isolated systolic hypertension in older people requires some special considerations. For instance, lowering the blood pressure too quickly may trigger *hypo*tension, signaled by fatigue, dizziness, or even fainting. With this danger in mind, physicians often try to bring down high blood pressure in older people rather slowly—unless the elevated pressure is so high that it poses an immediate threat to health.

Also, there's evidence that as people age into their seventies, the risks for hypertension decrease. Likely, this is due to the fact that those who are most vulnerable to health- or life-threatening problems caused by high blood pressure have already died before age 70.

Still, the risk of hypertension at older ages remains, even though that risk is not as great. Therefore, an effort should be made to reduce high readings.

- For *children,* the following levels have been proposed as the upper limits of normal:

Age/Years	Blood Pressure
15–18	135/90
11–14	125/85
6–10	120/80
below 6	110/75

- Using these limits, we find that less than 3 percent of children in the United States have any form of hypertension, including the isolated systolic form. However, it's important to respond to elevated systolic readings in children because such elevations may be precursors to diastolic hypertension.

- Obviously, then, there are some distinctions that should be made between the diastolic and systolic measurements. But in general, the main message is this: *The risk of cardiovascular diseases and deaths related to hypertension increases steadily as* either *the systolic* or *the diastolic readings rise. Furthermore, if both pressures are too high, the risk of complications may be even greater.*

What does all this tell you about how to evaluate *your* risk from an elevated blood pressure reading—and to develop your own profile? To check yourself, here are the basic points you should keep in mind:

- As you already know from chapter 2—as well as from the preceding discussion on the distinctions between diastolic and systolic pressures—your risk from high blood pressure has to be viewed in terms of a sliding scale: the higher the readings, the higher the risk; the lower the readings, the lower the risk.

- One initial set of blood pressure readings doesn't mean you have hypertension. However, a single high measurement may cause you to be included among the 58 to 60 million people who after at least one reading are in the hypertensive range. Later, however, normal readings may place you among the approximately 20 million people at relatively low risk: These are the ones who have one set of high readings but then have normal measurements afterward.

- If you have one initial set of high blood pressure readings and then have subsequent readings that are normal, you are at *some* risk for later health problems. Consequently, you should pay particular attention to reducing the risk factors and conditions described in the following Steps 2 and 3. But, as I've said, your risk in this situation is relatively low.

- Finally, it's important to keep in mind the basic blood pressure classifications that I included in chapter 2 from The 1988 Report of the Joint National Committee. If your *average* blood pressure measurements consistently fall into one of those hypertension categories, your physician should monitor your blood pressure regularly and take the necessary steps to bring down the readings.

Step 2: Evaluating Other Hypertension Risk Factors

In addition to determining and evaluating your blood pressure readings, it's important for your doctor—with your collaboration—to take a good hard look at a number of other risk factors that may help trigger or aggravate hypertension.

There are at least nine major risk factors that everyone should be aware of and, if possible, take steps to counter: (1) age; (2) genetic influence; (3) ethnic background; (4) gender; (5) salt sensitivity; (6) obesity; (7) alcohol abuse; (8) stress; and (9) a sedentary lifestyle.

There are several other factors that may play some role in high blood pressure measurements—such as fat, potassium, calcium, magnesium, and caffeine—which I'll discuss as well. But the evidence for these influences isn't as solid as that for the main nine, as you'll see in the following explanations.

The Age Factor

Many studies and surveys have shown a tendency for blood pressure to increase with age. As I mentioned earlier, blood pressure in young children is much lower than in adults. (In fact, there also seems to be some relationship between blood pressure and height—the taller a person is, the higher his or her blood pressure may be.)

During early adulthood, however, the blood pressure tends to stabilize.

A gradual rise in pressure may also be seen with advancing age. In the 1985 study by the Subcommittee on Definition and Prevalence, among people 55 years of age and older, at least 50 percent had hypertension.

However, this tendency toward rising blood pressure is less pronounced in people who maintain a healthy lifestyle (such as those evaluated at the Aerobics Institute in Dallas).

The Genetic Factor

There's a definite, powerful genetic component to adult hypertension. A substantial number of people are born with a tendency toward high blood pressure, and there's nothing they can do to eliminate that propensity.

In other words, if one of your parents had high blood pressure, you're about twice as likely to have the problem as someone whose parents had normal blood pressure. There's also a greater likelihood that you'll inherit a tendency toward hypertension if the disease has appeared in your adult siblings. The risks are even greater if high blood pressure has been present in a fraternal twin or especially an identical twin.

The precise genetic mechanism that promotes high blood pressure isn't clear. For instance, some researchers argue that there may be a genetic flaw in the way sodium is carried across cell membranes; others focus on inherited problems in the elimination of sodium from the body; and still others point to excessive sensitivity to stress.

In any case, don't become fatalistic if you have some family history of hypertension. If your parent or sibling has developed hypertension, it doesn't necessarily mean that you will too.

However, the existence of a possible genetic link should alert you to the fact that you're at greater risk than are those with a normal family history. With this knowledge you can begin to *minimize* the genetic component (you cannot eliminate it) by reducing other risk factors, such as a high-sodium diet or a sedentary lifestyle.

The Ethnic and Gender Factors

Certain variations in blood pressure levels occur among different ethnic groups and between the sexes—variations that can make it more likely for you to develop hypertension depending upon these factors.

For instance, hypertension is much more prevalent among blacks than among whites in the United States. According to the National Institutes of Health, about 50 percent of blacks over age 65, as opposed to 40 percent of whites of the same age, have some form of high blood pressure.

Furthermore, the entire population of blacks in the United States has three times the mortality rate from hypertensive diseases that whites have. Blacks tend to develop hypertension at younger ages than whites, and the severity of their hypertension usually is greater than that in whites.

As the population gets older, the proportion of blacks with high blood pressure increases. In the 35 to 54 age group, for instance, there are six times as many deaths among blacks than whites from hypertension-related diseases. Specifically, blacks suffer more deaths from strokes, kidney disease, congestive heart failure, and "left ventricular hypertrophy" (enlargement of the left chamber of the heart).

What causes this higher prevalence of hypertension among blacks?

In part, diet and environmental factors probably play a role. But there are also indications from various studies that, due to certain genetically based cardiovascular traits, blacks may be more predisposed toward hypertension. For example, the systolic blood pressure of blacks tends to rise higher than that of whites in response to certain stress factors, such as exposure to cold and to competitive situations.

Still, there is cause for hope. Deaths associated with high blood pressure, including stroke fatalities, are on the decline among blacks. As the black population becomes more aware of how diet and other factors can aggravate their tendency toward high blood pressure, the death rates from this disease should decrease even more.

Like whites who are at higher risk for hypertension, all blacks should take actions to lower their risk. Following the dietary and other lifestyle guidelines in this book will place blacks in a far stronger position to minimize their risks from high blood pressure. Also, for blacks as well as other ethnic groups, it's essential to have regular physical exams and to become more aware of the antihypertensive drug options, if they become necessary.

There are important differences between the sexes that may have a bearing on your level of risk. However, these variations do *not* mean that you should expect to fare better or worse than the opposite sex at certain ages. Rather, the typical differences between the sexes should be taken only as guidelines to alert you to those times of life when, because of your gender, you may face a greater threat.

In general, during the first part of their lives, white men have higher average diastolic and systolic measurements than do white women.

Then, as the women move into their sixties and seventies, their systolic and then their diastolic pressures catch up to and then exceed those of the men.

The pressures of black women are also lower in the earlier years than are those of black men. But again, with age—on the average, after age 50—both the systolic and diastolic measurements of the women tend to catch up with those of the men.

But note: It's important here to make a distinction between the races. Even though the pressures of black women tend to be below those of all men in the first part of life, they rise above those of white men much earlier than do the pressures of white women. Specifically, both the systolic and diastolic pressures of black women rise above those of white men when the two groups are around age 40. (See p. 6 of Norman M. Kaplan's *Clinical Hypertension*.)

So, what's the significance of the differences in blood pressures between men and women?

Usually, women suffer fewer complications from the same levels of high blood pressure than do men. As a result, some experts have suggested that it might be appropriate to define hypertension for women at higher levels of systolic and diastolic pressure than we do for men.

To account for the variations in blood pressure at different ages between men and women, my colleague Dr. Norman Kaplan has suggested that the definition of hypertension might be restated this way:

- Hypertension for men under 45: greater than 140/90

- Hypertension for men over 45: greater than 150/95

- Hypertension for *all* women: greater than 150/95

Using the prevailing, standard hypertension definition of 140/90, researchers have found that the prevalence of the disease in each racial group is consistently lower for women than for men up until the late fifties or early sixties. After that, hypertension rates for women tend to exceed those of men.

No one knows for sure why young women have less hypertension than young men but then have higher rates than men after they pass through their fifties. However, it's been suggested that during the years of regular menstruation, the volume of fluid in women tends to stay relatively low because of the menstrual blood loss. As a result, the pressure within the circulation system remains low. When they pass through menopause, however, they no longer have this natural means of reducing fluid content. As a result, they retain more, and the larger volume causes their blood pressure to rise. *Note:* No studies are available on the impact on blood pressure of women who have had hysterectomies or ovariectomies.

The risk factors we've discussed so far—genetic background, race, and gender—cannot be changed. But risks associated with these factors *can* be reduced by those who pay close attention to the factors that *are* controllable. The following risk factors fall into this controllable category.

The Salt Sensitivity Factor

About half of those with hypertension are salt-sensitive. That is, their blood pressure rises when they consume excessive amounts of sodium and drops when they reduce their sodium intake.

   Note: A distinction should be made between salt and sodium. Sodium is a component of salt: it comprises 40 percent of a given amount of salt, with chloride making up the other 60 percent. So, if you consume 5 grams of salt you're taking in 2 grams of sodium. In this book, I'll be referring to specific amounts of sodium rather than salt, unless noted otherwise.

   (To convert grams of sodium into grams of

salt, multiply the number of grams of sodium by 5/2. If you know the amount of salt and want to find the amount of sodium, multiply the grams of salt by .40.)

By some estimates, about half of all people with hypertension are salt-sensitive. That is, if you give them salt, their blood pressure goes up, and if you reduce their salt intake, their pressure goes down.

Is it possible to tell who is salt-sensitive and who isn't?

Unfortunately, there's no easy test for identifying sensitivity to salt. However, patients who are willing to experiment with their physicians may be able to get a fairly accurate reading on their own sensitivity. Here's the way such an informal experiment might be conducted:

First, your physician takes your blood pressure. Then you cut your sodium intake by one-half for one entire week. In other words, if your typical daily sodium consumption is around the national average of 4 to 5 grams per day, you reduce that to 2 to 2.5 grams. At the end of that week, your physician takes your blood pressure once more.

If either your systolic or diastolic pressure has dropped by 5 mm Hg or more, there's a fairly good chance that you're salt-sensitive. The more your measurements drop during this test period, the more salt-sensitive you're likely to be.

Obviously this is not a rigorous, scientific test. But it will provide you and your physician with some idea of the effect that salt intake has on your blood pressure. If you conduct this test several times during the course of a year and continue to come up with similar results, you can confirm your initial findings.

One patient, a 68-year-old man, noticed that his systolic pressure had been increasing steadily each year until it reached the 170/80 range. This level of blood pressure—a clear case of isolated systolic hypertension—put him at a greater risk for stroke and other vascular complications. His physician decided to make one last major effort at a nondrug approach before prescribing any drugs.

The doctor noted that the patient was a "high salter"—he ate very salty foods and also consumed liberal amounts of table salt. Knowing that many people tend to get more sodium-sensitive as they grow older, the doctor put his patient on a low-sodium diet of about 2 grams per day—the amount used in the menus later in this book.

Also, he increased the patient's potassium and calcium intake, since sodium restriction could result in a calcium deficiency. (Many foods such as milk and cheese that are high in sodium tend also to be high in calcium.)

After this sodium reduction, the patient's blood pressure dropped almost immediately to 155/78. The systolic was still higher than the physician wanted, but it was in a much safer range. Also, he felt that with an exercise and stress-reduction program in addition to the diet, it might be possible to reduce the systolic pressure further.

In general, I recommend that everyone cut sodium intake—especially those who are hypertensive or at the risk for hypertension. Here are some other thoughts and facts you might keep in mind as you move in this direction:

- Some researchers have found that near-total restriction of sodium will reduce the blood pressure of almost all patients hospitalized with hypertension. But, of course, it's not practical for those eating normal meals outside a clinical setting to achieve this kind of reduction.

  The most workable sodium-restricted diets—which may reduce high blood pressure in about half of all hypertensive patients—involve the consumption of about 2 grams of sodium per day. As I've said, this is the target we've set for our diets in this book.

- Elderly hypertensive patients and those with kidney-related hypertension have been found in certain studies to respond best to sodium restriction.

- Probably, sodium restriction lowers blood pressure by reducing fluid volume in the body and by reducing calcium in the cells.

- There is currently no standard definition of sodium sensitivity. In some cases, this sensitivity has been defined as a drop in average blood pressure by at least 10 mm Hg, following a special medically induced diuresis, or increased excretion of urine.

  In other cases, those studying the phenomenon have provided participants with an extra salt "load" and then measured how much, if at all, their blood pressure rises.

  In still other cases, researchers have defined a sodium-sensitive response as a 5 mm Hg drop in average pressure after the consumption of a low-sodium diet. In the experiment I suggested earlier to determine your own salt sensitivity, I assumed a 5 mm Hg drop in pressure as the appropriate standard.

- Both blacks and whites display greater sodium sensitivity as they grow older.

The Obesity Factor

Alice, a 40-year-old homemaker, found that her weight had gradually crept up over the years. Finally, she hit a high of 162 pounds—40 pounds over her ideal weight of 122. As often happens with obese people, her blood pressure increased, to a high of 160/100.

Her doctor expected that a weight reduction and exercise program might, by itself, lower her blood pressure to normal limits. So he placed her on a reduced-calorie regimen and encouraged her to walk vigorously for at least twenty minutes a day, three to four times a week.

To help motivate Alice, her physician encouraged her to buy a home device and monitor her blood pressure regularly. At first she reported the results to him weekly, and they were both extremely happy with the results. After the first month, she had lost about 15 pounds and her readings were down to 150/95.

But then disaster struck: She went on a two-week family vacation, during which she broke her diet and regained several pounds. When she came home, the pressures of returning to her regular daily life disrupted her diet and exercise program still further. Before long she was almost back up to her original heavy weight and high blood pressure.

Then, after a stern session with her doctor,

she really "got religion." She went back on her diet and stayed on it, and she also resumed the light walking regimen she had neglected. At the end of five months, Alice had dropped those 40 excess pounds, and a medical exam at that time revealed that her blood pressure reading was 130/85—within the normal range.

With such a significant weight loss, it's quite possible that *many* people could experience a decrease of 10 to 20 points or more in systolic and diastolic measurements. Conversely, those who remain obese—generally defined in this context as those who are 15 to 20 percent or more above their ideal body weight—are at higher risk for hypertension.

Important scientific investigations bear out these conclusions. In the Framingham Heart Study, for instance, patients who were 20 percent or more over ideal weight were eight times more likely to become hypertensive.

On the other hand, research on the overall risks associated with obesity has revealed that the hypertension in obese people is less dangerous than hypertension in those who aren't overweight. In this regard, one group of researchers reported in 1987 in *Hypertension* that over the nine-to-fifteen–year period covered by the study, obese men with high blood pressure had much lower rates of coronary mortality than nonobese men.

Does this line of research mean we can now relegate obesity to a relatively minor position as a risk factor for hypertension and its complications?

By no means! A major reason why we must continue to be concerned about obesity is that risk seems to be determined by *where* the fat occurs on a person's body.

A number of findings—including a 1987 report in the *Journal of the American Medical Association*—have revealed that upper-body obesity (defined as excess fat in the abdomen and chest) is more often associated with hypertension than is lower-body obesity, located mainly in the hips and thighs.

In the *JAMA* report, Dr. Paul T. Williams and several colleagues found that in 76 middle-aged men, diastolic blood pressure increased linearly with increasing waist girth (when compared to hip girth). Specifically, the diastolic pressures of these men rose from an average of about 66 to more than 80 mm Hg as their waist-to-hip girth ratio increased.

In another study of 227 Cooper Clinic patients (men, ages 30 to 59), chest, waist, and hip (gluteal) measurements were compared with both systolic and diastolic blood pressures. The percentage of body fat was determined by underwater weighing and measurements of skinfold thickness.

Our investigation revealed that neither body weight nor percentage of body fat correlated as highly with blood pressure readings as did the girth (waist) measurements. Also, men with large chests and/or hip girths tended to have higher blood pressure levels. The researchers concluded that "body trunk largeness," and not simply a relatively high proportion of body fat, is one of the major contributors to hypertension.

Excess upper-body fat has been associated with a multitude of other threats to good health, including:

- Diabetes

- Hypertriglyceridemia (excessive levels of triglycerides, a fatty substance in the blood)

- Low levels of HDL ("good") cholesterol, which is associated with protection against atherosclerosis (the build-up of fatty deposits in the blood vessels)

- Coronary heart disease

To sum up, then, obesity is definitely a risk factor for hypertension and its various complications and related illnesses. But upper-body obesity (from the abdominal area on up) apparently poses a greater risk than excessive fat on other parts of the body. So, those who are fatter in the upper part of the body should regard themselves as at greater risk than those with lower-body fat.

When it comes to reducing this risk factor, however, there's no point in attempting any sort of spot reduction for upper-body fat. No weight-loss program has been shown to be totally effective in this area.

Instead, using a weight-loss diet of the type included later in this book, you should work to reduce your overall calorie consumption. Then, you can expect your *overall* weight to decrease—and your upper-body fat with it.

What kind of blood pressure decreases can you expect with such weight loss? Here are some of the possibilities that have emerged in various studies on the subject:*

- In a study in Israel reported in 1978 in the *New England Journal of Medicine,* 79 of 81 hypertensive patients stuck to a four-month diet and lost an average of more than 20 pounds. They also experienced a decrease in blood pressure averaging 30 mm Hg on their systolic readings and 20 on their diastolic.

* *Note:* More complete citations for sources mentioned throughout the text but not in the "References" section may be found in Norman Kaplan's *Clinical Hypertension* (Baltimore: Williams & Wilkins, fourth edition, 1986).

- Researchers E. Reisin and several colleagues, writing in the *Archives of Internal Medicine* in 1983, concluded that weight loss—especially rapid weight loss—may produce immediate declines in blood pressure. Furthermore, they noted that this drop in blood pressure occurred with or without sodium restriction in their diets. Dr. M. H. Maxwell and his team of investigators reported essentially the same thing in their article in the August 1984 issue of the *Archives of Internal Medicine*.

- Other studies have noted that weight loss has produced a wide range of drops in systolic and diastolic readings. These have included a decline of 52/32 (systolic/diastolic) in the Dahl study in 1958; 30/21 in the Maxwell study in 1984; 37/23 in a Reisin study of 1978; and 33/16 in the Fletcher investigation of 1954. (See Kaplan, *Clinical Hypertension*, p. 149.)

Nobody knows exactly how obesity contributes to hypertension or how weight loss produces a drop in blood pressure. But one possible answer is that with an increase in weight, blood volume and the force with which the heart pumps blood (stroke volume) also increase. Rises in blood volume and stroke volume are often associated with hypertension.

Another possibility is that when a person gains weight, there's a tendency for insulin secretion to increase as well. (Insulin, a hormone produced in the pancreas and released into the bloodstream, facilitates the body's metabolism and use of sugar.)

Note: High levels of insulin are more common in those with an excess of upper-body fat.

The insulin, in turn, increases the absorption of sodium in the kidneys and reduces sodium excretion through the urine. This process may promote the expansion in volume of the body's fluids. The more fluids we retain, including blood, the higher our blood pressure is likely to be.

There are a number of ways that obesity may contribute to the development of hypertension, but the definitive explanation awaits further research. In the meantime, the main thing you should know is this: Being overweight will put you at greater risk for high blood pressure and may in fact be the *primary* factor contributing to hypertension.

The Alcohol Factor

John, an aggressive businessman in his late thirties, worked six and sometimes seven days a week under considerable stress. Although he was under substantial pressure at work, he didn't feel sick or unhealthy, so he was quite surprised when he discovered during a routine medical exam that he had high blood pressure.

His physician informed him that his average measurement after three readings during the exam was 150/95. "But I want you to come in for several other blood pressure measurements over the next month or two," the doctor said. "That way, we can determine for sure whether you really *do* have high blood pressure."

Unfortunately, the later exams confirmed the original reading: John's blood pressure was indeed too high. But, as the doctor told him, the elevated readings weren't anything to worry about and might well be brought down through nondrug therapy.

During an ensuing conversation, the doctor learned some things that he felt might be quite helpful in reducing John's blood pressure without medications. Most important, he discovered that John was a heavy drinker.

"I really need a few drinks at night to relax," John said. "I get stressed out during the day at work." Specifically, he consumed two to three cocktails and two four-ounce glasses of wine each evening.

In addition to this drinking, John usually drank alcoholic beverages during his frequent business lunches. It was common for him to have a couple of beers or a couple of martinis on those occasions.

When he and his physician calculated his total alcohol consumption on a typical day, they discovered that he was ingesting nearly four ounces of ethanol (pure alcohol) per day. Furthermore, on occasional weekend binges at parties, his intake was even higher.

The physician explained that, according to the latest research, those with hypertension who drink should consume *no more than one ounce of ethanol per day*. That is the amount contained in two ounces of 100-proof whiskey, eight ounces of wine, or twenty-four ounces of beer.

John wasn't happy about this news. But he was even less happy about the fact that he had hypertension. Under his doctor's guidance, he decided to cut down his drinking to no more than one ounce of alcohol per day.

When he returned for a blood pressure check the next month, his measurements had dropped from 150/95 to a quite normal 130/84. With further nondrug treatments, such as an exercise and weight-loss regimen he had started, he had every reason to expect his blood pressure and his level of risk for hypertension to decline even more.

In general, most experts say that it's wise to consume no more than two ounces of alcohol per day—preferably, no more than one ounce per day. There are estimates that excessive alcohol consumption may be the key factor in causing the disease in 10 percent of male hypertension patients and 1 percent of female hypertension patients.

Also, those who stop drinking entirely can expect a fairly speedy response in their blood pressure levels. Research on heavy drinkers has revealed that 80 percent of patients who have high blood pressure when they enter alcoholic rehabilitation programs end up with normal blood pressure *within thirty to sixty days* after they stop drinking. Furthermore, they experience this decline in blood pressure without the use of medications.

In general, the average hypertensive drinker who stops or reduces his alcohol intake below one ounce per day can expect to experience a drop in blood pressure.

Should you drink at all?

If you don't drink alcoholic beverages now, I don't recommend that you start. Consuming an average of only one ounce of ethanol per day has been found to increase diastolic blood pressure by an average of 2 mm Hg.

As you may have heard in other contexts, there have been reports that drinking one to two ounces of ethanol per day will help protect against coronary heart disease. These studies have concluded that those who drink moderate amounts of alcohol, generally defined as 1 to 2 ounces per day, seem to have some protection against heart attacks and to have a lower overall incidence of strokes.

In this vein, Japanese medical researchers like to tell this story:

Shigechiyo Izumi was reportedly the world's oldest man—at least the oldest in possession of an official birth certificate. His personal drinking habits? He drank slightly more than one ounce of alcohol a day until he finally died in 1986 at age 120. This amount of alcohol is almost precisely the same as the amount found by various researchers to be most protective against coronary heart disease.

One possible moral to this story, according to the Japanese, is that it may demonstrate that sake, the strong, favored alcoholic drink of the Japanese, is the "best drug"—or, to put it in the original, *Sake hyaku yaku no chyo!* (See p. 171 of Kikuo Arakawa's article in *Seminars in Nephrology.*)

Unfortunately, the alcohol issue can't be disposed of quite so easily. For example, women who drink even moderate amounts have a higher incidence of strokes involving hemorrhages.

Furthermore, as far as hypertension is concerned, there is some clinical evidence that certain individuals may be alcohol-sensitive. In other words, drinking *any* amount of alcohol, no matter how small, will drive up their blood pressure significantly.

One patient who came into our clinic was typical of a number of alcohol-sensitive patients we've encountered. Everything about her lifestyle seemed in order: She was on a low-sodium diet, she was at her ideal weight, and she was pursuing a regular aerobic-exercise program. Still, her blood pressure was elevated at a consistent measurement of 145/93.

We continued to monitor her pressure at regular intervals, fully expecting to place her on medication eventually. But first, at the suggestion of our nutrition department, she was asked to stop drinking the one glass of wine she typically consumed each evening. Almost immediately, her blood pressure dropped to normal.

This woman's response confirmed that she was an alcohol-sensitive person who could easily move in and out of a hypertensive classification simply by having one small drink. She provided a classic example of the fact that in some people, alcohol, even in small quantities, can elevate blood pressure.

My conclusion as far as alcohol as it relates to hypertension: If you don't drink now, don't start. If you do drink, limit it to the equivalent of no more than one ounce of pure alcohol per day, as is contained in two average-size drinks of wine, beer, or whiskey.

The Stress Factor

Don, a stockbroker in his early forties who was under considerable stress at work, had consistently mild hypertension of 150/93. No matter what his physician recommended—including low-sodium diets, exercise, and restriction of alcohol intake—Don's blood pressure remained slightly elevated.

Finally, the doctor recommended that Don try some relaxation therapy. The approach they chose involved setting aside two to three times a day to go through a routine of twenty to thirty minutes of muscle-relaxing and deep-breathing exercises.

Don would sit quietly during these sessions and relax each of his major muscle groups, beginning with his feet and ending with his neck, shoulders, and head. As he was going through this procedure, he would concentrate only on his breathing, being sure to inhale and exhale steadily and slowly. When outside thoughts—such as those involving work or family problems—threatened to interrupt, he would simply turn away from them and focus once more on his breathing.

The first session was scheduled just after he rose in the morning; the second, at lunchtime; and the third, when he was at home at night. Sometimes he even worked a fourth session in during his commute home on the train.

The result? His blood pressure dropped to 138/84 within a few weeks.

In recommending antistress relaxation therapy, physicians and therapists often suggest that patients try it only twice a day, for ten to twenty minutes per session. Harvard cardiologist Dr. Herbert Benson calls the calming effect in the sympathetic nervous system the "relaxation response." He has used this approach to lowering blood pressure with considerable success, as described in his books *The Relaxation Response* and *Your Maximum Mind*. (See full citation under chapter 10 section of "References.")

Frequently, patients resist *any* relaxation therapy in their daily schedules because they feel they just don't have the time or discipline for it—especially if it involves setting aside time each day.

But Don was motivated. He was health oriented and didn't want to use medications. Also, he had shown considerable discipline and interest in following low-sodium *and* low-cholesterol diets, and in embarking on a regular aerobics exercise program. Furthermore, he had tried, with some success, a number of other self-help programs related to the stresses of his work.

So he was ready to try not only two sessions a day but three or four if necessary. By making this relaxation therapy the foundation of each day's activities, he found that he could stay "looser" and more relaxed when crises occurred at work. Consequently, he was able to reduce the impact of the stress in his life, and his blood pressure declined accordingly.

When we experience stress—such as the pressures which produce fear, anger, or anxiety—the sympathetic nervous system automatically increases its production of various secretions, including the hormone epinephrine (also known as adrenaline) from the adrenal gland.

Among other things, epinephrine produces what's known as the "fight-or-flight" response to stress. This involves such physical changes as an increase in heart rate, increased perspiration, and a feeling of being "on edge." In addition, this hormone constricts the blood vessels and raises blood pressure.

Unfortunately, the work of epinephrine doesn't end with the initial response to a stressful situation. Rather, the impact of the hormone often *continues* to keep the blood pressure higher than normal after the event that triggered the initial reaction. An hour or more later, both the systolic and diastolic measurements may be elevated into the hypertensive range. Furthermore, most experts now believe that continued exposure to epinephrine may cause permanent hypertension in some people.

What evidence do we have that sustained

rises in blood pressure resulting from stress may produce hypertension? Here are the results of a few of the studies that have led us to consider this possibility:

- Studies of air traffic controllers have revealed that their stressful occupation is associated with the development of hypertension at a rate 5½ times as high as that among pilots who were comparable in physical attributes. (On the other hand, one study revealed that over a ten-year period, the air traffic controllers had a lower rate of hypertension than similar men in the population at large.)

- When people residing in small, quiet, secure communities move to higher-pressure urban environments, their blood pressure measurements tend to rise to hypertensive levels. Researchers have concluded that there's a major link between hypertension and the trauma of being uprooted from one's home.

- Men exposed regularly to noise have been shown to have higher blood pressure and an increased incidence of hypertension.

Although research is still being done to understand the link between stress and hypertension, the present indications are that there *is* a definite connection. So, stress is now regarded as a definite risk factor for the disease.

In later chapters we'll go into more detail about what you can do to counter the stress risk factor. For now, just be assured that the experience of Don, described above, isn't an isolated case.

To sum up, stress *can* be managed. It's not stress that causes problems, but rather, the way stress is handled.

The Sedentary Lifestyle Factor

The relationship between physical fitness and hypertension comes across fairly clearly in this statement from a report by M. L. Slattery and D. R. Jacobs in the *American Journal of Epidemiology:*

"Results from this study suggest that middle-aged men with lower levels of physical fitness . . . are at greater risk of dying of coronary heart disease, cardiovascular disease, and all causes. . . . This greater risk is largely due to higher blood pressure levels."

This conclusion reflects a generally accepted truth about hypertension: the more physically fit you are, the less likely you are to suffer from hypertension. By the same token, the more sedentary you are, the greater your risk of developing high blood pressure.

In general, the kind of physical training that helps lower blood pressure is endurance or aerobic exercise, such as distance running, jogging, cycling, or vigorous walking. This exercise should be done at least three to four times a week, for twenty to thirty minutes per session. But muscle-tensing exercises, such as weight lifting, tend to raise blood pressure and should be avoided by those who are at risk. This rise in pressure occurs as the result of a bodily reflex when the heart rate increases and the blood vessels constrict during this sort of exercise.

Exactly how effective is the endurance-exercise approach to lowering blood pressure?

"Hypertension," the 1988 Consensus Conference on Exercise, Fitness, and Health held in Toronto reported: "Individuals with essential hypertension can decrease their resting systolic and diastolic blood pressure by approximately 10 mm Hg with endurance exercise training."

This conference went on to caution that those with blood pressure measurements higher than 160/105 should add exercise to their programs *only* after beginning therapy with antihypertensive medications, under a doctor's care.

However, I believe that uncontrolled hypertension—i.e., blood pressure of approximately 175/110 or higher while on medications—is a clear contraindication to exercise. Vigorous exercise by those with such severe hypertension could further raise the pressure to a level that possibly could cause a stroke!

In chapter 8, I'll be going into this exercise issue in more detail. As part of that discussion, you'll be provided with a special exercise program that has been proven to lower the blood pressure levels of many people.

Other Possible Hypertension Risk Factors

Although a number of other risk-related issues have been studied, numerous questions about many of them remain. Following is an overview of these concerns, with some comments about the general directions in which medical research is pointing.

- *High creatinine levels.* Creatinine is a substance produced when muscle tissue is broken down by the body, transported by the blood, and excreted in the urine. If the levels of creatinine in the blood are high, that's an indication that the kidneys aren't able to clean the blood properly.

  According to a study reported in May 1989 in the American Heart Association's journal *Hypertension,* the levels of creatinine in the blood—which can be detected by a simple blood test—are a good predictor of stroke and heart attack among hypertensives.

Specifically, the researchers found that hypertensive patients with high levels of creatinine in their blood were five times as likely to die of stroke or heart attack as those with low levels. Furthermore, the creatinine measurements were better predictors of cardiovascular death than were such risk factors as high cholesterol, smoking, a history of heart disease, or diabetes.

Note: A normal creatinine level is 1.2 to 1.5 mg/dl. Those with high blood pressure should have their creatinine tested at least once a year, and if it's elevated, they should seek more intensive treatment or take other precautions against heart disease, as directed by their physician. Very likely, a high creatinine level indicates some kidney malfunction, which *may* be able to be reversed or controlled.

- *Caffeine.* Caffeine may have a temporary "pressor effect," in the sense that for a short period, it may raise blood pressure by as much as 5 to 15 mm Hg. This increase may occur within fifteen minutes of drinking two to three cups of coffee, but then the blood pressure usually drops back to normal within two hours.

  There's no solid evidence that consumption of caffeine causes permanent hypertension. But one 1983 study in France did show a slight permanent blood pressure increase in those who drank five or more cups of coffee per day.

- *Smoking.* Like caffeine, smoking may temporarily raise blood pressure. But regular smokers don't experience a permanent increase in their measurements. Even though cessation of cigarette smoking will not lower blood pressure, it's the single most important thing in improving cardiovascular health.

- *Fats.* In a 1989 study reported at the American Heart Association's Council for High Blood Pressure Research, a clear relationship was shown between blood lipids (particularly cholesterol and triglycerides), and hypertension. Dr. Roger Williams, of the University of Utah, reported that one-third of hypertensives had increased LDL cholesterol; and two-thirds had decreased or abnormally low HDL cholesterol. One-half of the hypertensives had elevated triglycerides. As for *polyunsaturated* fats, a Finnish study reported an antihypertensive effect by (1) reducing the total fat consumption (from 108 to 50 grams per day) and (2) increasing the ratio of polyunsaturated to saturated fats (from 0.27 to 0.98). Both the systolic and diastolic pressures fell significantly in those on the low-fat regimen. The hypertensives on this diet experienced a decrease in systolic/diastolic measurements of 13/10 mm Hg; those with normal blood pressure on the diet also declined by 7/5 mm Hg.

As for *monounsaturated* fats—such as those found in olive oil—the picture is at least as promising. A study by researcher Paul T. Williams of the Stanford Center for Research in Disease Prevention reported: ". . . increased consumption of monounsaturated fat is related inversely to resting blood pressure, although causality remains to be determined."

So, the greater the proportion of monounsaturated fats in your diet, the lower your blood pressure is likely to be.

As the report above indicates, the cause for this effect isn't yet known, and more research is needed. But, as of now, the benefits of reducing saturated fats while increasing polyunsaturated and monounsaturated fats, seem to apply to hypertension, as to cardiovascular disease and cancer.

- *Vegetarianism.* Vegetarian diets have been associated with lowered blood pressures in some studies. In one report, hypertensives on a vegetarian diet for six weeks experienced an average drop of 5 mm Hg in their systolic measurements.

  The reason for this is not entirely clear, but there is probably a connection with the higher amounts of polyunsaturated fats (vs. saturated fats), and also with the increased levels of potassium and fiber in vegetarian diets.

- *Dietary fiber.* At least three studies have demonstrated that a high-fiber diet (30 to 45 grams per day), taken either alone or in combination with a low-fat, low-sodium regimen, may lower blood pressure by 5 to 10 mm Hg.

- *Potassium.* A 1987 report by Kay-Tee Khaw and Elizabeth Barrett-Connor, published in the *New England Journal of Medicine,* said that "clinical, experimental, and epidemiologic evidence suggests that a high dietary intake of potassium is associated with lower blood pressure."

  Over twelve years, the researchers followed 859 men and women, ages 50 to 97, in Southern California. After investigating twenty-four stroke-associated deaths in the participants, they affirmed "the hypothesis that a high intake of potassium from food sources may protect against stroke-associated death." They noted further that an increase of daily potassium in one extra serving of fresh fruit or vegetables "was associated with a 40 percent reduction in risk." Furthermore, the intake of potassium in this study apparently had a beneficial effect independent of the participants' blood pressure levels.

In another study, patients with normal blood pressure were placed on a diet severely deficient in potassium. A significant increase in blood pressure occurred in nearly all of them.

The research goes on. But, the indications are that extra potassium may protect against hypertension and stroke.

- *Calcium.* Even though diets deficient in calcium have not been shown to cause hypertension, oral calcium supplements may benefit certain patients with mild to moderate hypertension.

  In a study with hypertensives and normotensives taking 1,000 mg of either calcium carbonate (Oscal) or calcium citrate (Citrical) daily for eight weeks seems to have been effective in the hypertensives:

They had a 3.0 mm Hg decrease in their supine (lying on the back) systolic pressure; a 5.6 mm Hg decline in their standing systolic reading; and a 2.3 mm Hg drop in their standing diastolic pressure.

In normotensive patients, neither standing systolic nor diastolic pressure, nor supine systolic pressure, changed with the calcium supplement. However, supine diastolic pressure did decrease by 3 mm Hg.

The authors of this study, D. A. McCarron and C. O. Morris, concluded that treatment with 1,000 mg per day of oral calcium for eight weeks represents a safe, well-tolerated, nonpharmacologic intervention that lowers blood pressure in selected patients with mild to moderate hypertension.

Unfortunately, these results have not been readily confirmed by other authors. Overall, calcium supplements have produced an inconsistent response in various studies. In fact, in some hypertensives, calcium may actually *increase* blood pressure! (L. M. Resnick, *Annals of Internal Medicine*.)

These, then, are the major and minor risk factors that are often associated with the development of hypertension. As we've already seen, any one of them may be the key factor that triggers a rise in blood pressure. So, it's important to pay attention to *each* of these factors and do your best to reduce their impact in your life.

But now there's another level of risk related to hypertension—and another step you must take in evaluating the threat that this disease may pose to you. That's the *multiple* risk to health that occurs when hypertension is combined with other cardiovascular risk factors.

Step 3: Evaluating the Multiple Risk Phenomenon

In attempting to ascertain the true role of hypertension as a risk factor in your life, it's important to think about it as both an *individual* threat and a *combined* threat, linked with other risk factors.

As an individual threat to your health, hypertension is, to put it mildly, awesome. William B. Kannel, Professor of Medicine at the Boston University Medical Center and a researcher with the Framingham Heart Study, puts it this way: "Systolic or diastolic hypertension at any age in either sex contributes powerfully to cardiovascular disease." (*American Heart Journal,* 1987, p. 213.)

In more specific terms, Dr. Joseph Stokes, Dr. Kannel, and other Framingham researchers formulated a table showing the impact of age and various risk factors on cardiovascular diseases in men. Below is a copy of this table.

The investigators devised the table with a scale of quantitative rankings: A minus rating means there's relatively little association between a risk factor and a disease. A plus rating shows a greater association. An award of three minuses indicates the strongest inverse or negative relationship between a risk factor and protection from a disease. In contrast, four pluses indicates the strongest positive relationship or ability to cause a disease. Anything in between these two rankings indicates degrees of risk that vary between the extremes.

How did hypertension fare in the rankings? The researchers reported:

"Systolic blood pressure contributes more consistently and more significantly to the risk of development of all manifestations of cardiovascular disease than do any of the other standard risk factors. . . . It is also the most important risk factor for stroke and TIAs [transient ischemic attacks, which are "small strokes" that are often precursors of major strokes]." (Joseph Stokes, et al., *Circulation,* June 1987, p. 66.)

Using the plus-minus ranking system, the study group gave high systolic blood pressure three pluses for all age groups as a risk factor for coronary heart disease. The risk was even greater for stroke and transient ischemic attacks

The Effect of Age on Selected Risk Factors for Men with Various Manifestations of Cardiovascular Disease[A]

30 Years of Follow-up in the Framingham Study (Source: Circulation, vol. 75, suppl. V, June 1987, p. 71)

Risk factor	CHD		Stroke and TIA	
	Age 35–64	*Age 65–94*	*Age 35–64*	*Age 65–94*
Systolic blood pressure	+ + +	+ + +	+ + + +	+ + +
Cholesterol	+ + +	±	−	−
Glucose	−	+ +	−	±
Metropolitan relative weight	+ +	±	−	−
Cigarette smoking	+ + +	−	+ + +	±
Hematocrit	±	±	+ + +	±
Limited vital capacity[B]	−	±	±	+
Heart rate	−	+	±	±
LVH/ECG	+	+ +	+ +	+ +

[A]Multivariate model includes the risk factor identified as well as age, systolic blood pressure, serum cholesterol, glucose intolerance, number of cigarettes per day, and LVH.

[B]Inverse relationship.

The Effect of Age on Selected Risk Factors for Men with Various Manifestations of Cardiovascular Disease[A] (continued)

30 Years of Follow-up in the Framingham Study (Source: Circulation, vol. 75, suppl. V, June 1987, p. 71)

Intermittent claudication		Total CVD	
Age 35–64	Age 65–94	Age 35–64	Age 65–94
+ + +	+	+ + +	+ + +
+ +	+	+ + +	−
+ +	+ +	+ +	+ +
− − −[B]	±	+	±
+ + + +	−	+ + +	±
+ +	+ +	±	±
−	±	+	±
±	−	+	+
−	−	+	+ +

Note:
   CHD = Coronary Heart Disease
   CVD = Cardiovascular Disease
   LVH = Left Ventricular Hypertrophy

in the 35 to 64 year age group: hypertension received the top ranking of four pluses for these conditions. In the 65 to 94 year age range for strokes and TIAs, hypertension was given three pluses.

Finally, in the 35 to 64 year age group, hypertension received three pluses as a risk for intermittent claudication (i.e., pains, usually in the legs, which are directly the result of athero-sclerosis or obstruction of blood vessels). In the 65 to 94 year age range, hypertension got one plus for intermittent claudication.

Overall, using this risk-factor ranking system, high systolic blood pressure received a risk ranking of three pluses in the 35 to 64 year age range, which was equal to the rating given to both high cholesterol and to cigarette smoking. Furthermore, the systolic measurement was given a three-plus rating overall for the 65 to 94 year age group—a level that made it the *greatest* threat of all in this age category.

To sum up, when all age groups are taken into account, *hypertension seems to be the most important risk factor of all for your cardiovascular health.*

The preeminent position of hypertension as a risk factor becomes especially important when you combine it with other risk factors. This combination produces what I call the "multiple effect" or the "multiple risk phenomenon."

The data provided by the Framingham Study illustrates this point. The study investigated the probability of a person with one or a combination of several risk factors developing coronary artery disease over an eight-year period. Then, they devised a profile for a 40-year-old man to show the impact of five risk factors (see the accompanying chart):

1. Elevated systolic blood pressure (195 mm Hg)

2. Cholesterol of 335 mg/dl

3. Glucose intolerance (the condition that could lead to diabetes)

4. Cigarette smoking

5. Abnormalities in the electrocardiogram (the ECG, which measures electrical impulses in the heart); or left ventricular hypertrophy (enlargement of the left chamber of the heart)

What the researchers found was that, as could be expected, the 40-year-old man with normal measurements or evaluations in each of these five categories had a very low risk of coronary disease. But as one or more of the risk factors were added, the risk increased exponentially.

For example, when only the cholesterol was elevated (from a normal 185 mg/dl to 335), the man's risk increased fourfold. As additional risk factors were added, the risk went up even more.

Now, assume that the man has *all* the high-risk factors: He has diabetes, he smokes, and he has high blood pressure and elevated blood cholesterol. In that case, his risk would increase 100-fold! (Levy and Kannel, *American Heart Journal,* pp. 270–71.)

To state the issue in terms of the patient's chance of having a major cardiovascular event:

If our 40-year-old man has systolic blood pressure of 195 but is otherwise at low risk, his chance of having a major cardiovascular problem in the next eight years is 4.6 percent. But if he has high blood pressure *and* is at high risk with all the other factors, his chance of a big cardiovascular event within eight years leaps up to 70.8 percent. (Norman Kaplan, *Annals of Internal Medicine.*)

By rearranging these risk factors somewhat and taking a 45-year-old man as an illustration, we get another view of how this multiple risk phenomenon works.

We'll assume that this patient has no family history of cardiovascular disease, his weight is normal, his ECG result is normal, he has a normal-sized heart, and he doesn't have diabetes.

Now, let's consider the multiple impact of only three risk factors: (1) cigarette smoking; (2) elevated total cholesterol of 310 mg/dl; and (3) elevated systolic blood pressure of 165 mm/Hg.

First, suppose our patient has none of these three risk factors. That is, he doesn't smoke, his serum cholesterol is 185, and his systolic blood pressure is 120. In this case, he has only a 1.8 percent chance of suffering a coronary event within the next six years.

Next, assume that he smokes, but that all the other risk conditions stay normal. Now he has a 2.7 percent chance of a coronary event in six years.

If he smokes *and* has elevated total cholesterol of 310, his chance of a coronary event in six years hops up to 8.8 percent.

Finally, if he smokes *and* has elevated cholesterol *and* has elevated systolic blood pressure of 165, his chance of a coronary event goes up again, this time to 14.5 percent. (See p. 5 of "Hypertension: The Patient at Risk," by William Kannel et al.)

As you can see, adding one or more of these risk factors doesn't increase one's risk simply by equal, stair-step increments. Rather, the risk factors build upon one another to produce together a total risk that far outstrips the risk that any of them can produce alone.

Also, as I've already indicated, the experts have concluded that hypertension must be placed at the top of the list of the risk factors that play a role in this multiple risk phenomenon. So, controlling hypertension assumes even greater importance as you consider how to reduce your cardiovascular risk.

The Three Steps to Evaluate Your Risks from Hypertension and Formulate Your Personal Hypertension Risk Profile

Clearly, the evaluation of the risks from hypertension can be a complex matter.

There's no simple way to set up a point chart or table that tells you, in effect, "This is my risk." Instead, as you formulate your personal Hypertension Risk Profile, you and your physician must identify and evaluate such diverse factors as:

- The relative impact of various levels of systolic and diastolic pressure

- The interrelationship between the different lifestyle, nutritional, and genetic influences

- The impact of the multiple risk phenomenon

As complex as these factors can be, one fact about evaluating your risk for hypertension is rather simple: If you find that you are at high risk from *any one* of the factors or conditions I've discussed, take action now to correct that factor.

I've heard patients say, "Well, *only* my systolic pressure is a little elevated," or, "My *only* problem is I love salty foods," or, "The *only* things I have to worry about are some mild hypertension and a slightly elevated cholesterol level. Otherwise, I'm okay."

But as we've seen, it's *not* okay to ignore or downplay the impact of even a single factor or condition related to hypertension. It may take only one or two of these factors to put a person on the track that leads to a major cardiovascular event, such as a stroke.

The accompanying checklist will help you in evaluating your risks. Because any one of the items listed in this "Hypertension Risk Monitor" may be decisive in triggering hypertension, it's important that you monitor all of them—and overlook none.

Hypertension Risk Monitor

Step 1. Enter your blood pressure measurements below. Then, using the hypertension classifications on pages 30–31, indicate the extent to which you may be at risk from these measurements. When you have your blood pressure checked in the future—or approximately every three to six months if you check your pressure at home—make a new entry.

Your Current Blood Pressure Measurements: _____

Extent of Risk: _____

Step 2. Indicate below with a checkmark whether you are at significant risk for one or more of these hypertension risk factors. If you determine during later evaluations that you are no longer at significant risk, remove the checkmark.

I've indicated what aspects of these factors might put you at risk, but to do a proper evaluation of your situation, you'll have to refer back to the in-depth discussion of these factors earlier in this chapter.

Risk factor	*Check if at significant risk*
Genetic factor (family history of hypertension)	_____
Ethnic factor (black race)	_____
Gender factor (male sex)	

Risk factor	*Check if at significant risk*
Excessive sodium intake (more than 2 grams per day)	_____
Obesity (more than 15% above ideal weight)	_____
Excessive alcohol use (more than 1 ounce per day—see explanation earlier in this chapter)	_____
High stress lifestyle	_____
Sedentary lifestyle	_____

Step 3. Check below to indicate the other significant coronary risk factors in your life. Remember: The fewer of these risk factors you have, the lower—in *geometrical* or exponential terms—your overall cardiovascular risk will be.

Risk factor	*Check if at significant risk*
Smoking	_____
Elevated total cholesterol (above 200 mg/dl)	_____
Diabetes (fasting blood sugar above 120 mg/dl)	_____

Risk factor	*Check if at significant risk*
Abnormal electrocardiogram	_____
Left ventricular hypertrophy (enlarged left chamber of the heart)	_____

Your goal: Eliminate or minimize as many as possible of the risk factors that you've checked. There may be some you can't get rid of, such as the genetic influence, but by eliminating others, you'll reduce the risks associated with those you can't change—and your chances for avoiding or controlling hypertension will increase.

It should be clear by now that the effective management of hypertension must center on evaluating and dealing with *all* three of the steps we've discussed, and with *all* of the risk factors or conditions within those steps. To this end, resolve to work closely with your physician to correct each problem or element that may be contributing to a higher risk for hypertension. It's only by keeping the entire picture of hypertension in view that truly effective control can be achieved.

4

How Hypertension— The Silent Killer— Builds in Your Body

Hypertension has been called "the silent killer" because it does its deadly work over the course of many years—often without any external symptoms.

Exactly how does hypertension build in the human body?

High blood pressure occurs in a "closed system" involving several parts of the body:

1. The heart, which acts as a pump to push blood through the organs and tissues

2. The blood vessels, which constrict and open up according to various processes they undergo and signals they receive

3. The kidneys, which manage the volume of fluid in the vessels

4. Various brain, nerve, and hormonal functions

These four physical networks play an ongoing role in determining your blood pressure levels. Unfortunately, this inner system sometimes malfunctions, causing blood pressure to drift too low or too high.

When blood pressure becomes excessively low, *hypotension* may occur. As we'll see later in this chapter, this problem may promote fatigue, dizziness, or fainting.

On the other hand, *high* blood pressure, or hypertension, may usher in even more severe challenges to health. At first, there are usually no noticeable symptoms. It's only at the later stages of the disease that severe morning headaches or organ malfunctions may begin to occur.

For decades, uncorrected high blood pressure may gradually and quietly place unbearable strains on various tissues and organs, such as the brain, blood vessels, kidneys, and heart. The final result may be strokes, advanced vessel disease, heart attacks, kidney problems, and eventually death.

Fortunately, however, these dire results aren't inevitable. Physicians now know that blood pressure can be controlled in a number of ways:

- Altering the pumping action of the heart
- Dilating the blood vessels
- Adjusting the action of the kidneys
- Influencing the operation of various hormones and nerve functions

The drug and nondrug programs described in this book can go a long way toward helping you lower your blood pressure and reduce the risks to your life and health. But to be an effective, active patient—one who is prepared to cooperate to the fullest with a physician—you need a basic understanding of what's going on in your body.

In particular, you must have a grasp of the physical mechanisms by which certain treatments can help control your hypertension—and also why a combination of treatments may be necessary. That will put you in a better position to ask pertinent questions and to respond intelligently to your doctor's directions.

How Hypertension Develops in Your Body

I sometimes think of the body's blood pressure system in terms of the way a manual bicycle pump works.

As I mentioned at the beginning of this chapter, the key elements in producing blood pressure are the heart, the blood vessels, the kidneys, and the brain-nerve-hormone network. In grasping how these four factors interact, it may be helpful to think of them this way:

- The *heart* reminds me of the combined action of my hands, my arms, and the pump in forcing air into a bicycle tire. After placing my feet on the metal flanges at the base of the pump to steady it, I grasp the horizontal handle and thrust the plunger of the pump steadily and rhythmically down and up, down and up. The faster I pump, the more air pressure I force into the tire—and the more quickly pressure inside the tire rises.

  The heart has often been described as a pump: Beat by beat, it pushes blood out into the blood vessels, then relaxes, and then once again pushes the blood out. The faster and more forcefully it works, the more pressure there is in the circulatory system.

- The *blood vessels,* which come in varied shapes and sizes, make me think of two things: the pump's rubber tubing, which snakes out from the metal casing of the pump, and the bicycle tire itself, into which my pumping action forces the air. The tension exerted by the air inside the tire helps determine the tire pressure, just as the tension exerted by the blood inside the vessels influences blood pressure levels.

- The *kidneys* bring to mind the valve on the bicycle tire. The ingoing air is pumped through this valve into the tire, and any excess air in the tire can be released through the same channel.

  The work of the kidneys is similar, as they excrete sodium and water in response to elevations in the blood pressure. This decrease in the volume of fluids in the body brings down the blood pressure.

- The *brain-nerve-hormone network* makes me think of myself as a young bicycle owner. I was always squeezing the tires to check the pressure, or patching up places where I had found a leak—or buying a new tire if an old one seemed beyond repair.

The tension of the peripheral blood vessels is also regulated by a kind of "bicycle owner"— the body's automatic (sympathetic) brain and nervous systems, and the various hormonal secretions that help tighten or loosen the vessels.

In a properly working bicycle, the air pressure in the tires has to be adjusted periodically for top performance: If the pressure is too low, the rubber may wear down prematurely; if the pressure is too high, the bike may provide too rough a ride, control may be more difficult, and flats may occur.

Tire trouble will be most likely to develop in such circumstances as these:

1. The pumper may fail to work the tire pump correctly.

2. The air valve in the tire may develop a leak, or may trap too much air in the tire if it isn't used to release excess pressure.

3. As the tire ages, it may become perforated or otherwise defective.

4. The bike owner may fail to check the pressure regularly or otherwise monitor the condition of the tire.

Blood pressure problems may arise in much the same fashion. Consider this scenario of what may happen over the lifetime of a typical hypertensive person, whom I'll call Liz:

As a child and young adult, Liz didn't have hypertension, but she did have a number of risk factors that bore watching: She was overweight; she had a family history of hypertension—both her father and grandmother were on antihypertensive medications; and her blood pressure always measured higher than that of the average person her age. (A number of studies have indicated that children with higher-than-average—

though not hypertensive—measurements are at higher risk of becoming hypertensive as they grow older.)

As a result of these factors, Liz was at higher risk than the average young person. Still, medical examinations revealed that she was staying in the normal range for an adult while she was in her early and middle twenties: Her typical measurement was about 135/88.

After Liz passed age 30, however, her pressure gradually moved up into the mild hypertensive range. She began to have periodic readings above 140/90. By the time she was in her early forties, her measurements, without medication, consistently ranged from 140/90 to 150/95.

At no point did Liz complain of any symptoms. The silent, damaging work of hypertension proceeded without a single signal to alert Liz or anyone else that something was amiss in her body. The only way she could monitor her blood pressure was to have regular measurements.

Liz's case was typical of that of many people who develop hypertension. Certain risk factors identified her as likely to develop permanent hypertension later in life. And sure enough, as she grew older, her measurements marched steadily upward.

In most cases, hypertension develops this way. The patient may have higher than average but *not* hypertensive readings at first, along with a number of other risk factors. Then, as the person ages, the measurements move up gradually until sometime between ages 30 and 50, a diagnosis of permanent hypertension is confirmed.

Typically, after the condition has become "fixed," it may take another ten to twenty years for organ damage to occur. There will frequently be no symptoms whatsoever until, finally, a stroke or kidney malfunction occurs.

There may be some exceptions to this asymptomatic feature of hypertension, but they're often hard to interpret. A 1973 report in the *New England Journal of Medicine* investigated possible symptoms of patients with hypertension. The researchers found that among those who had diastolic pressures of 90 to 99 mm Hg *and* who reported symptoms, the percentages broke down this way:

- 21 percent had headaches
- 21 percent experienced fainting
- Lower percentages had dizziness, tinnitus (noises in the ears), nosebleeds, or other ailments

Those with diastolic pressures greater than 100 reported the same symptoms in almost the same percentages.

But the most startling finding concerned people with diastolic pressures below 90—i.e., those with normal diastolic pressure. Those who reported symptoms had the *same* physical problems in almost the same percentages as those who were hypertensive! So, clearly, symptoms are not the best indicators of blood pressure levels.

Morning headaches and some of the other symptoms cited above have been associated with hypertension. But no one should rely on such symptoms, or a lack of symptoms, to make a guess about his or her blood pressure! The *only* way to ascertain whether your blood pressure may be building toward permanent hypertension is to take measurements with a blood pressure device.

But now let's return to Liz. What was going on inside her body as hypertension silently built up over the years?

Was Anything Wrong with Liz's Heart Pump?

Even as a young child, the output of her heart (her "cardiac output"*) was greater than normal.

* Cardiac output is determined by multiplying the stroke volume, or amount of blood pumped by the heart with each beat, times the number of heartbeats per minute.

That is, her heart beat harder and faster than that of the normal child. After Liz reached adulthood, her cardiac output fell, but at the same time her blood pressure rose gradually to hypertensive levels.

There is great uncertainty and disagreement about the role that an overactive heart plays in the development of hypertension. A slightly more rapid heartbeat is fairly common before the pressure goes up. Typically, however, the volume of fluids and blood plasma in the body is *less* in hypertensives than in those with normal blood pressure. This fact argues against attaching much blame for high blood pressure to increased blood volume.

On the other hand, there are studies that show that even when the cardiac output or fluid volume of hypertensives is low, often it is still too high for the person's level of blood pressure. In other words, the higher one's pressure is (because of extra tension in peripheral blood vessels), the lower the blood volume needs to be. Yet, with hypertensives, the blood volume is frequently greater than necessary.

In addition, those with high blood pressure tend to have more fluid in the spaces between the body's tissues, and also a greater amount of fluid inside the body's cells. In effect, the increased cardiac output may *force* more fluid out of the mainstream of the vessels and capillaries and into these areas.

Finally, as the cardiac output continues to rise over the years, a process known as *autoregulation* may occur. Specifically, as too much blood circulates through the body, an overabundance of nutrients triggers a mechanism that says, in effect, "Enough is enough! I'm full and I don't need any more!"

In physiologic terms, the blood vessels reduce the flow of incoming blood through constriction, so that the supply of blood and nutrients moves into balance with what the body actually needs. This constant constriction of the vessels in response to the increased cardiac output may cause the vessels to thicken and become more rigid—and permanent hypertension may result.

To sum up, then, Liz's increased cardiac output reflected a high pulse rate and a slightly elevated volume of blood and fluids in her body at an early age. Over the years, her blood vessels, responding to this excess heart action, tightened up to control the influx of blood. As the tightening or constricting process occurred, some of the excess blood and fluids spilled over into the spaces between the tissues in her body and also into her cells.

With this vessel constriction and related mechanisms, the volume of blood in her vessels dropped to a level less than that of those with normal blood pressure. But at the same time, her blood pressure, responding to these various internal mechanisms, went steadily upward.

How Well Did Liz's Kidneys Manage Sodium?

Let's recall my analogy of the valve on the bicycle tire—the point at which air can be admitted into the tire or released if there's too much.

The valve is analogous to the kidneys, which regulate the volume of fluid and blood in the vessels. The kidneys do this mainly by controlling the level of sodium, a key ingredient in determining the fluid and blood volume (i.e., the more sodium, the more volume; the less sodium, the less volume).

Now, with this picture of the pump, valve, and tire in mind, let's turn again to the events taking place in Liz's body.

In people with normal blood pressure, the volume of the body's fluids shrinks as blood pressure rises. This shrinkage occurs because the kidneys automatically excrete sodium and water and thereby bring the pressure back down to normal.

But in those with high blood pressure—such as Liz—there may be a flaw in this kidney mechanism. Consequently, the body retains too much sodium and water; the blood and fluid volume stays too high for the blood pressure level; and the blood pressure remains at hypertensive levels.

My consultant, Dr. Norman Kaplan, suggested the following scenario to explain how blood pressure *may* rise because of a flaw in the way the kidneys handle sodium. But it's important to caution that research in this area is still developing, and there is still controversy over the precise role of sodium and the kidneys in the development of hypertension.

Event 1. Liz takes too much sodium into her body through her diet. For example, she consumes the average American's amount of 10 grams of salt per day (or 4 grams of sodium).

Event 2. Because of a genetic defect, her kidneys retain a bit too much of this sodium, which enters (with water) into the bloodstream.

Event 3. The fluid volume of her body increases to excess levels.

Event 4. A "natriuretic hormone," which specializes in the excretion of salt, intervenes to get rid of the excess salt. (Evidence for this hormone has been accumulating, but as yet there's no certainty that it exists.)

Event 5. An internal "sodium pump," which transports sodium among the body's cells, reduces its activity because of the work of the salt-excreting hormone in Event 4.

Event 6. Other mechanisms that are supposed to transport sodium among the body's cells—including a kind of "hookup" between sodium and potassium—are also flawed. So, the movement of salt among cells is impeded even more.

Event 7. Excess sodium begins to build up within the body's cells because of a decrease in the activity of the sodium pump and other defects in sodium transport.

Event 8. As sodium builds up within the cells, this process encourages the concentration of calcium within the cells.

Event 9. The extra calcium inside the cells of the vessel walls causes the vessels to contract. In those with normal blood pressure, this intracellular calcium is relatively low, while in those with hypertension, it's high. (Keep this in mind when we discuss calcium channel blockers as a way to treat patients with hypertension.)

(*Note:* Paradoxically, as mentioned earlier, there are studies that show that for some people, *increasing* consumption of calcium in the diet may actually *lower* blood pressure—though no one knows the mechanism by which this occurs.)

Event 10. The vessel walls become thicker as a result of the contractions they undergo. Consequently, they are more likely to provide stronger resistance against blood flow and volume.

In addition, the stronger, thicker vessels may become more responsive to stress hormones that the body releases. This increased sensitivity to stress can further aggravate high blood pressure.

Event 11. As the vessels become permanently thicker and more resistant, the blood pressure rises—and hypertension ensues.

Clearly, some complicated events are going on in Liz's body! And those events become even more difficult to understand and evaluate when we recognize that there is considerable scientific uncertainty about many of the steps of this sodium-handling process.

A similar kind of complexity confronts us when we delve into the internal brain-and-nerve network that is at work in hypertension.

Was There a Flaw in Liz's Sympathetic Nervous System?

The sympathetic nervous system is the part of the brain-nerve-hormone complex that controls involuntary actions in the body, such as the contraction of blood vessels.

The sympathetic nervous system is supposed to work automatically, like the increasing tension in a bicycle tire as air is pumped into it. But sometimes the system doesn't operate in quite the way that we hope and expect.

Liz's situation is typical. Her sympathetic nervous system works overtime to produce catecholamines—hormonal secretions that are associated with stress and elevations of blood pressure.

Her body produces excessive amounts of the hormone epinephrine (adrenaline). Any release of this substance, which produces the anxiety-inducing fight-or-flight response, causes a rise in the blood pressure that may last for an hour or longer. Many experts believe that excessive production of it, consistently throughout a person's life, may contribute to permanent hypertension.

Furthermore, there are links between the action of the sympathetic nervous system and the work of the kidneys—links that may very well promote high blood pressure.

For example, the catecholamine hormones may tighten the arterioles, or small arteries in the kidneys. This action contributes to the problems with intercellular transport of sodium and promotes the accumulation of sodium and calcium within individual cells.

Also, the difficulties caused by an overactive sympathetic nervous system—and the body's extrasensitive response to stress—may call into action another, related system, the "renin-angiotensin system."

Don't be put off by this rather esoteric name. You need to understand something about this important network *now* if you hope to grasp the operation of some of the newest and most important kinds of antihypertensive medications.

Liz's Renin-Angiotensin System and Its Role in Her Hypertension

As we've seen, some extremely complicated biological maneuvers going on inside Liz are contributing to her hypertension. But the situation becomes still more involved as we take into account her body's hormones and other chemicals and secretions.

These secretions exert an impact on her blood pressure in their own right, and they also interact with other processes that are going on in the kidneys, circulatory system, and nerve-brain network. With such complexity, our relatively simple analogy of the bicycle pump becomes less helpful—unless we begin to talk about the composition of the rubber in the tires or perhaps the action of the air molecules inside a tire!

Renin is an acid (an enzyme) that is secreted by the kidneys and acts on a larger protein in the bloodstream to split off a small portion of itself, which circulates as an inactive hormonelike substance called "angiotensin I." By itself, angiotensin I doesn't have any effects. But it has tremendous potential, as we will see in following its progress through the body.

As the angiotensin I moves through the bloodstream, it comes into contact with an enzyme that splits off another small portion and immediately converts it into angiotensin II, a powerful constrictor of the blood vessels (i.e., a "vasoconstrictor").

As we'll discuss in chapter 5, this angiotensin converting enzyme ("ACE") is especially important in the treatment of hypertension. Recent clinical strategies have focused on medications that *inhibit* the work of the converting enzyme (these drugs are classified as "ACE inhibitors").

With the converting enzyme rendered inoperative, the inactive angiotensin I can't be converted into the active, vessel-constricting angiotensin II. The result is that the vessels, which would have been constricted by the angiotensin II, instead remain dilated. With this dilation, less force is exerted by the blood against the vessel walls, and the blood pressure level falls.

Angiotensin II is a key factor in constricting blood pressure and inducing hypertension. Therefore, it might seem that the level of renin, which is the necessary first step in the production of angiotensin I and II, would be a good marker for the disease.

Unfortunately, the level of renin in Liz's blood, or in anyone else's, isn't much help in this regard. Patients with low, normal, or high levels of renin may *all* have primary hypertension. So, trying to identify a person's renin status probably won't be helpful in evaluating his or her level of risk for hypertension.

But in exploring the potential for controlling hypertension, scientific studies and clinical experience *have* identified at least four key junctures or signposts in the winding, tortuous route of the renin-angiotensin system:

Signpost 1: The kidney's production "factory" of the enzyme renin.

Renin output tends to be stimulated by the action of the sympathetic nervous system, including the release of the catecholamine hormones. Obviously, the body must have renin to produce angiotensin I and II, and ultimately to constrict the blood vessels and raise the blood pressure. So, using medications to *block* the nerve network's stimulation of the "renin factory" may reduce the output of renin and ultimately of angiotensin II—and thereby reduce blood pressure.

Signpost 2: Renin moving about in the bloodstream.

Renin is important mostly because of its

potential to produce the vessel-constricting angiotensin II. But there still may be a chance to deal directly with the renin in controlling hypertension. This can be achieved by making the renin inert through medications.

Considerable research is going on in an effort to find a generally usable drug in this area. But presently the main medications available are being employed on an experimental basis.

Signpost 3: The meeting between angiotensin I and the converting enzyme.

An important function in determining the body's blood pressure is the introduction of the inactive angiotensin I to the angiotensin converting enzyme (ACE). As a consequence of this encounter, the angiotensin I—much like Cinderella with her fairy godmother—can be transformed into the active, vasoconstricting angiotensin II.

Medications that attack or neutralize the converting enzyme in effect remove the "fairy godmother" in the scenario, and the appearance of angiotensin II becomes impossible. As you know, without the angiotensin II, there tends to be less constriction of the blood vessels, and blood pressure stays lower.

Signpost 4: The active work of angiotensin II.

Even after angiotensin II has appeared as a

result of an encounter with the converting enzyme, the work of the angiotensin II must still be done effectively if the vessels are to be tightened up and the blood pressure elevated.

If the angiotensin II doesn't work properly—for example, if its operation is blocked by medication—the vessels will remain unconstricted, and blood pressure will stay lower.

In addition to the work of these major systems and networks in the body, there are other factors that may play a role in the development of high blood pressure. Some of the major ones, discussed in some detail in chapter 3, are obesity, alcohol abuse, and sedentary living.

In the last analysis, however, no one really knows what *causes* at least 90 to 95 percent of the cases of high blood pressure. Certainly one or more of the factors we've just discussed may contribute to high blood pressure in any given patient, such as Liz. But *most* patients—and that means millions upon millions—are in the category of those whose hypertension is of unknown origin. This condition is what the medical community calls "essential" or "primary" hypertension.

On the other hand, what *is* known is the devastating and often deadly work that the silent process of hypertension can eventually do. Now, let's take a closer look at the challenges to health that Liz may be facing unless she brings her hypertension under control.

Where Is Your Hypertension Heading?

Just as no one knows the exact cause of most cases of hypertension, no one can predict precisely what complications and problems may ultimately occur. But various surveys and clinical studies have revealed quite clearly some of the possibilities and even probabilities that may accompany this illness.

For one thing, we know beyond doubt that there is *some* chance of damage to health or of death with even mild or borderline levels of hypertension. Of course, the risk rises alarmingly as the systolic and diastolic pressures increase.

A quick overview of the outlook for untreated hypertension is sobering, to say the least. Those with uncontrolled (primarily unmedicated) high blood pressure—in contrast to those with controlled high blood pressure—are *three times* as likely to suffer from coronary heart disease; *six times* as likely to develop congestive heart failure; and *seven times* as likely to have a stroke!

A closer look at the statistics shows that no group is immune to this scourge. For example, women between 45 and 74, with diastolic pressures of 100 to 104, have twice the risk of developing heart disease as women with readings of 75 to 79. Furthermore, women with higher pressures have almost three times the risk of suffering a stroke as do those with normal readings.

Obviously, there are many different ways of dissecting and interpreting statistics. But as far as hypertension is concerned, they all lead to one ominous conclusion: High blood pressure is the major risk factor for the half a million strokes, including the nearly 200,000 stroke deaths, that Americans suffer annually. It's also a contributing factor in the 1.5 million heart attacks and the more than half a million deaths from heart attacks each year.

In addition, hypertension is a big risk factor for congestive heart failure; kidney disease; aneurysms (a weakening and ballooning of the wall) in the aorta, the large artery leading from the left ventricle of the heart; and diseases of the peripheral blood vessels.

To get an idea of the relative risks from these complications of hypertension, consider a few further findings:

- In a long-range 1955 study, researcher G. A. Perera monitored 500 untreated hypertensive patients, who had diastolic pressures of 90 mm Hg or higher until their deaths. The average age of onset of hypertension in these patients was 32 years, and their average survival time was twenty years.

Among other things, Perera found that 74 percent of these patients had enlargement of the heart (as determined through an x-ray procedure); 50 percent had congestive heart failure; 12 percent suffered from stroke; and 42 percent experienced the appearance of protein in the urine, which is often an indication of kidney disease. *Note:* This study was conducted before there were medications capable of lowering the pressures. People with hypertension were simply watched through their lifetimes.

- The Veterans Administration Cooperative Study Group on Antihypertensive Agents of 1967, 1970, and 1972 also revealed a variety of complications arising from untreated hypertension. During an average monitoring period of only 1.3 years per patient, the researchers found these problems in people with rather severe high diastolic pressures (115 to 129 mm Hg):
  - Nearly 25 percent suffered from cerebral hemorrhage, severe congestive heart failure, or kidney disease.

• Ruptured aortic aneurysms afflicted 6 percent.

• Another 9 percent experienced heart attacks (myocardial infarctions), blood clots in the brain, mild congestive heart failure, or "mini" strokes (TIAs, or transient ischemic attacks).

To sum up, within only three years, nearly 40 percent of these patients with fairly marked high diastolic readings experienced severe health problems!

This same VA study *also* found that even those with untreated diastolic readings that were somewhat less elevated (in the 90 to 114 range) faced the possibility of serious complications. In this group, who were monitored for an average of 3.3 years, 10 percent died of strokes, ruptured aneurysms, heart attacks, or unknown causes.

Overall, 15 percent of those under age 50 with fairly mild hypertension had serious hypertension-related health problems; 27 percent of those ages 50 to 59 had such health problems; and 63 percent of those 60 or older had illnesses linked to their hypertension.

By far, the worst danger to all groups— a danger that accelerated with age—was strokes.

- The Australian Therapeutic Trial, reported in *The Lancet* in 1980, followed 1,600 adults with diastolic pressures of 95 to 109 mm Hg for an average of three years.

The investigators reported that during the three-year period of the study, there was no unusual increase in deaths or in health problems among the 80 percent of untreated patients whose diastolic pressures averaged less than 100 mm Hg. Excess health complications were observed *only* in those whose final diastolic blood pressure was higher than 100.

These findings may offer some comfort to those with mild diastolic elevations in blood pressure. But don't become complacent or jump to any hasty conclusions! My consultant, Dr. Norman Kaplan, puts the Australian study in perspective this way:

"For now, the Australian Trial data can be taken as indicative of a relatively benign course *over a short period* for patients who are free of known cardiovascular disease and whose DBP [diastolic blood pressure] remains below 100 mm Hg. This conclusion in no way denies the long-term risks of even minimally elevated blood pressure. . . ." (Norman Kaplan, *Clinical Hypertension*, p. 130.)

There have been a number of other clinical trials and studies, but they all point in the same general direction as do those I've already mentioned. In short, *any* level of high blood pressure will increase your risk for a wide variety of health problems, including damage to important bodily organs and early death.

But exactly *how* does high blood pressure produce these horrendous results? To answer this question, let's examine more closely what hypertension does to blood vessels.

How Hypertension Affects Blood Vessels

Although no one knows precisely how damage to the blood vessels occurs with hypertension, the experts accept several factors as particularly threatening:

- *A high rate of increase in blood pressure.* If blood pressure goes up quickly and forcefully in response to stimuli like stress, that will likely do more damage than if it goes up more slowly and gradually. In fact, various studies suggest that if the rate of rise in pressure stays relatively low, even high blood pressure and a high pulse rate won't necessarily cause vessel damage.

The rate of increase makes such a difference because when the blood pressure goes up quickly and violently, the turbulent blood flow is more likely to damage the vessel walls, weaken them, and make them more vulnerable to plaque buildup or rupture.

- *Deterioration of the inner walls of blood vessels.* With higher levels of pressure, including periodic fast and forceful increases in pressure, the inner walls of the vessels tend to be stripped of their natural tissue linings. As a result, they may become rougher and may lose the ability to release hormones and other secretions that keep the vessels loose and relaxed.

- *The promotion of atherosclerosis.* After vessels sustain injury from violent blood flow and from the pressure-induced stripping-away of vessel lining tissue, the damaged muscles and cells in the vessel walls replace themselves. But this replacement process sets the vessels up for further problems: notably, the potentially deadly work of atherosclerosis.

   Atherosclerosis—plaque buildup in the vessels as a consequence of fatty deposits such as cholesterol—narrows vessel walls and makes them less elastic.

This process may cause vessel blood flow to become blocked off entirely if a clot lodges in a narrowed area. When such blockage occurs in the coronary arteries, which carry blood to the heart, oxygen and nutrients stop flowing to the heart tissue, and a heart attack results.

- *Fibrous (scar) tissue growth in damaged vessels.* These growths cause the vessel walls to thicken and become more rigid, which may aggravate increases in vessel pressure.

- *Small aneurysms in the smaller arteries of the brain.* An aneurysm, as I've already noted, is a weakening and ballooning of the vessel wall. The aging process and increased pressure on these weak spots may eventually cause them to rupture. The ensuing hemorrhage will cause blood to damage the surrounding tissue. If an aneurysm ruptures in the brain (or intracranial area), a stroke will occur, with loss of brain function and perhaps death.

With any patient who has long-standing hypertension, there is an increased risk that tiny aneurysms will develop in the brain's arterioles, or smaller arteries. Constant high blood pressure pushing against these aneurysms may eventually cause one or more of them to leak, with a resulting "small" stroke.

These forms of damage and deterioration of the blood vessels in various parts of the body put the hypertensive person at considerably greater risk for serious organ damage or death. As I've already indicated, the usual mechanisms through which this occurs include (1) a rupture or bursting of the damaged area or (2) a blockage (occlusion) of blood flow to tissues supplied by the vessels.

The parts of the body at most serious risk from these complications of hypertension include the brain (with stroke being the greatest danger); the kidneys; the peripheral blood vessels; and the heart.

In the kidneys, like many other organs, damage from hypertension typically occurs at a slow pace, often taking ten to twenty years to become evident. Finally, when the damage is extensive, "azotemia" or "uremia" (a poisoning of the body due to poor functioning of the kidneys) occurs. This process signals the onset of the final serious phase of the disease, which can lead to death.

Before we leave this subject, let me note this final point: Although there is no disagreement about the importance of hypertension as a cardiovascular risk factor, there has been some dispute about the extent to which hypertension *per se* contributes to coronary artery disease.

For example, "The 1988 Report of the Joint National Committee on Detection, Evaluation, and Treatment of High Blood Pressure" questions the use of antihypertensive medications by those with coronary artery disease:

"Taken as a whole, findings from clinical trials suggest that benefits of antihypertensive treatment on the incidence of either fatal or nonfatal myocardial infarction [heart attack] or on mortality related to coronary artery disease are modest at best."

As a result, the report suggests, more careful attention should be paid to controlling other cardiovascular risk factors, such as smoking, high cholesterol levels, and diabetes mellitus.

On the other hand, experts such as Dr. Dean Mason, Chief of Cardiovascular Medicine at the University of California at Davis, emphasize the importance of hypertension as an independent coronary risk factor—and the importance of managing it with appropriate treatment.

Citing a large study done across the United States under the direction of the Hypertension Detection and Follow-up Program, the National Institutes of Health, Mason notes that treatment of patients with an initial diastolic blood pressure of 90 to 104 mm Hg "resulted in an overall 26 percent decrease in deaths from cardiovascular complications during the five-year study period. . . ." (Mason and Cutler, 1980 Pfizer monograph, p. 1.)

Mason says further that, according to N.I.H. investigations, antihypertensive therapy resulted in 46 percent fewer deaths from heart attacks (myocardial infarction), as well as 45 percent fewer deaths from stroke.

Yet when you look at the combined results of several large, long-term antihypertensive studies, it appears that deaths from strokes can be reduced by 38 percent, while there is only an 8 percent decrease in deaths from heart attacks. (Dr. William Kannel made this point during a presentation at a hypertensive conference in August 1989 in Dallas, Texas.)

What conclusions should we draw from these observations?

First, we must recognize that much remains to be understood about the relationship between this condition and coronary artery disease. The uncertainty among experts arises from their desire to be conservative in their conclusions.

Second, the link between hypertension and such complications as stroke or kidney disease is *definitely* better established than the link between hypertension and coronary artery disease.

This may be due to the fact that hypertensive medications such as hydrochlorothiazides (Dyazide, Aldactazide and Hydrodiuril), which are used by most of these studies, can cause a significant increase in the triglycerides and also both the total and low-density lipoproteins (LDLs, or "bad" cholesterol). These increases raise the risk of coronary artery disease. (See Thomas Pollare, et al., "A Comparison of the Effects of Hydrochlorothiazide and Captopril on Glucose and Lipid Metabolism in Patients with Hypertension," *The New England Journal of Medicine*, Vol. 321, Sept. 28, 1989, pp. 868–873.)

Third, hypertension seems to loom as a more ominous factor when it's accompanied by other risk factors, such as smoking and high cholesterol, than when it stands alone. In this regard, you'll recall the "multiple phenomenon" discussed in chapter 3.

Whatever the uncertainties or qualifications, though, high blood pressure *must* be included among the "big three" coronary risk factors, along with smoking and high cholesterol. The present evidence absolutely dictates this conclusion.

To sum up: Hypertension is present in more than 50 percent of patients with coronary artery disease and heart attacks; in more than 75 percent of patients with various cerebral vascular events, including strokes; and in more than 90 percent of patients with dissecting aortic aneurysms.

When combined with cholesterol levels greater than 150 mg/dl, hypertension clearly accelerates atherosclerosis and its devastating consequences. Conversely, those with lower blood pressures can expect to have fewer such problems. (See William C. Roberts, "Frequency of Systemic Hypertension in Various Cardiovascular Diseases," *The American Journal of Cardiology*, Vol. 60, Sept. 18, 1987, pp. 1E–8E.)

5

Designing a
Personal Drug Program

When should antihypertensive drug treatment begin?

In general, nondrug treatment should be used with mild or borderline hypertensives—often this solution is enough. Patients in this category include those whose average blood pressure ranges from 140/90 to 159/94 mm Hg. When average measurements reach 160/95 or higher, drug therapy along with the nondrug approach usually becomes necessary.

But are there any circumstances under which medications should be prescribed for those in the mild range of 140/90 to 159/94?

About 40 percent of those having diastolic

readings of 90 or above are in the range of 90 to 94. So the answer to this question has broad implications for a large number of people—as many as 25 million Americans.

Most physicians feel that nondrug approaches should be used with mild hypertensives for at least several months, perhaps for a year or more, in an effort to bring down the measurement *without* drugs. (Non-drug treatments—which include dietary changes, exercise, relaxation techniques, and special lifestyle adjustments—are discussed in depth in chapter 8 and subsequent chapters of this book.) In situations where these efforts fail to produce normal readings, however, opinions begin to diverge.

Some experts say that drugs should eventually be used if vigorous nondrug efforts fail to bring the pressures down below 140/90.

Another view, which I concur with, is that doctors should *continue* to use the nonpharmacologic approaches alone, even if the pressures never reach normal levels. However, it is generally recommended that these physicians keep a close watch on their patients to be certain that mild hypertension doesn't creep up to moderate or higher levels of 160/95 or more.

"The 1988 Report of the Joint National Committee on Detection, Evaluation, and Treatment of High Blood Pressure" summed up the second position this way: "Physicians who elect not to use drug therapy for patients in the 90 to 94 mm Hg range should monitor their patients closely, since some will progress to higher levels of blood pressure that clearly warrant antihypertensive drug therapy."

Furthermore, patients with the following risk factors may have to go on drug therapy, even when their blood pressure is in the 140/90 to 159/94 range:

- Being a male
- Having elevated cholesterol or other lipids, such as triglycerides
- Being a smoker
- Having existing damage to kidneys, heart, or other vital organs
- Showing abnormalities in electrocardiograms (ECGs), either while resting or during exercise
- Suffering from diabetes mellitus
- Being obese
- Drinking excessive amounts of alcohol
- Living an exceptionally high-stress lifestyle
- Having a family history of heart disease

If you have one or more of these risk factors and your blood pressure is mildly elevated, your physician will have to determine whether you should continue with a nondrug approach or start on medications. With the decision to begin medications, an entirely different range of considerations about treatment comes into play.

An Introduction to the Major Antihypertensive Drugs— and How They Work

Any discussion of antihypertensive medications must begin with some thoughts on *compliance*.

Getting patients to make a commitment to take their drugs regularly is a major ingredient in the success of any medication program. Studies have shown that up to half of those who begin antihypertensive drug therapy will stop using their medications in less than one year!

Furthermore—according to the National Health and Nutrition Examination Surveys, 1960–62 and 1976–80—only about four out of five hypertensives on drug therapy have their blood pressure under control. A major reason: Patients go on and off their medications improperly, because either they don't understand their doctors' instructions, or they forget to take them, or they decide to take their treatment into their own hands.

Why is there so much noncompliance with drug therapy?

- Patients with hypertension typically don't have any symptoms, so they convince themselves that they really don't need medications.

- The patient's social or family life may somehow discourage compliance. For example, the person may become forgetful because of a preoccupation with business or marital problems; or constant travel or other disruptions of the daily routine may make it hard to stay on a regular medication program.

- The side effects of the medications, such as impotence, headaches, bowel disturbances, or fatigue, may discourage a patient from taking them regularly.

- The patient may have a bad relationship with his physician, and a failure to comply may seem a way to rebel against the doctor's authority.

- Some other aspect of the treatment process—such as frustration or anger at long waits in the physician's office—may discourage the patient from keeping or making appointments.

Whatever the reason, it's important for patients not to "play doctor" and discontinue their medications without their physicians' advice. As we'll see shortly, there are some circumstances when hypertensive patients can stop taking their drugs. But this must be done *only* under strict guidelines and a doctor's close supervision.

Now, let's take a look at the three major categories of antihypertensive medications:

1. The fluid volume reducers (often called the "volume depleters")

2. The inhibitors of sympathetic nervous system secretions (the "adrenergic inhibitors")

3. The vessel openers ("vasodilators")

Each of these three types of drugs can be related back to my simple illustration of the bicycle pump.

The first type, the fluid volume reducers, lower blood pressure by eliminating extra fluids that are pressing on the vessel walls. Similarly, pressure in the bicycle tires can be reduced simply by reducing the amount of air in the tires, perhaps by releasing the air through the valve stem.

The second type of medications, the adrenergic inhibitors, may operate through a variety of channels, including slowing down the rate at which the heart pumps blood through the vessels. With the bike pump, you can reduce the buildup of pressure by pumping slowly or less frequently.

The third kind of drugs, the vasodilators, lower blood pressure by causing the vessels to loosen up and expand in diameter. The wider and less resistant the vessels become on the inside, the less pressure the blood is able to exert on the vessel walls. A concomitant drop in overall blood pressure will then occur.

Once more, the bicycle analogy applies. Suppose you change from a skinny, small-volume tire to a larger-volume one, yet keep the same amount of air in the large tire as you had in the smaller one. Of course, you'll end up with lower overall pressure than you had with the smaller tire. The same result would occur if you could somehow stretch the inside of the small tire while keeping a constant volume of air in it.

Probably, you are wondering which of these three major types of drugs you should be using. To determine that, it's necessary to look more closely at the specific types of drugs in each of the three categories and see in greater detail just how they work.

First, we'll explore the characteristics of the different drugs. Then, we'll examine their side effects and also the strategies that may be employed in administering them to patients.

As we proceed with this discussion, you'll probably want to refer periodically to the accompanying chart listing the various antihypertensive drugs and recommended daily doses. This listing has been reproduced from page 1028 of "The 1988 Report of the Joint National Committee On Detection, Evaluation, and Treatment of High Blood Pressure."

Antihypertensive Drugs and Recommended Daily Doses

	Dosage Range, mg/d*	
Type of Drug	*Usual Minimum*	*Usual Maximum*
Diuretics		
Thiazides and related sulfonamide diuretics		
Bendroflumethiazide	2.5	5
Benzthiazide	12.5–25	50
Chlorothiazide	125–250	500
Chlorthalidone	12.5–25	50
Cyclothiazide	1	2
Hydrochlorothiazide	12.5–25	50
Hydroflumethiazide	12.5–25	50
Indapamide	2.5	5
Methyclothiazide	2.5	5

Antihypertensive Drugs and Recommended Daily Doses (continued)

Type of Drug	Dosage Range, mg/d*	
	Usual Minimum	*Usual Maximum*
Metolazone	1.25	10
Polythiazide	2	4
Quinethazone	25	100
Trichlormethiazide	1–2	4
Loop diuretics†		
Bumetanide‡	0.5	5
Ethacrynic acid‡	25	100
Furosemide‡	20–40	320
Potassium-sparing agents		
Amiloride	5	10
Spironolactone	25	100
Triamterene	50	150
Adrenergic inhibitors		
β-Adrenergic blockers§		
Acebutolol	200	1200
Atenolol	25	150
Metoprolol	50	200
Nadolol	40	320
Penbutolol sulfate	20	80
Pindolol‡	10	60
Propranolol hydrochloride‡	40	320

Antihypertensive Drugs and Recommended Daily Doses (continued)

Type of Drug	Dosage Range, mg/d*	
	Usual Minimum	*Usual Maximum*
Propranolol, long-acting	60	320
Timolol‡	20	80
Centrally acting α-blockers		
Clonidine‡	0.1	1.2
Clonidine TTS (Patch)‖	0.1	0.3
Guanabenz‡	4	64
Guanfacine hydrochloride	1	3
Methyldopa‡	250	2000
Peripheral-acting adrenergic antagonists		
Guanadrel sulfate‡	10	100
Guanethidine monosulfate	10	150
Rauwolfia alkaloids		
Rauwolfia (whole root)	50	100
Reserpine	0.1	0.25

Antihypertensive Drugs and Recommended Daily Doses (continued)

Type of Drug	Dosage Range, mg/d*	
	Usual Minimum	*Usual Maximum*
α-Adrenergic blockers		
Prazosin hydrochloride‡	1–2	20
Terazosin hydrochloride	1–2	20
Combined α-β-adrenergic blocker:		
Iabetalol‡	200	1800
Vasodilators		
Hydralazine‡	50	300
Minoxidil‡	2.5	80
Angiotensin-converting enzyme inhibitors		
Captopril‡	25–50	300
Enalapril maleate	2.5–5	40
Lisinopril	5	40
Calcium antagonists		
Diltiazem hydrochloride¶	60	360
Nitedipine§	30	180
Nitrendipine	5	40
Verapamil¶	120	480

Antihypertensive Drugs and Recommended Daily Doses (continued)

	Dosage Range, mg/d*	
Type of Drug	*Usual Minimum*	*Usual Maximum*
Verapamil SR (long-acting)	120	480

*The dosage range may differ slightly from the recommended dosage in the *Physicians' Desk Reference* or package insert.

†Larger doses of loop diuretics may be required in patients with renal failure.

‡This drug is usually given in divided doses twice daily.

§Atenolol, metoprolol, and acebutolol are cardioselective: pindolol and acebutolol have partial agonist activity.

‖This drug is administered as a skin patch once weekly.

¶This drug is usually given in divided doses three or four times daily.

1: The Volume Reducers

Medications that reduce the volume of the body's blood and fluids are known as "diuretics." These are by far the most-used type of antihypertensive drug, with an estimated 60 million prescriptions being filled annually in the United States.

Most diuretics work this way:

About 5 ounces of fluid per minute pass through the average person's kidneys. That means about 216 quarts of fluid are filtered through our kidneys every day.

Note: The function of the kidneys is to remove impurities, waste products, and some water from the bloodstream. As part of this filtering process, the kidneys act to excrete those wastes as urine.

Despite the huge volume of fluids that circulate through the kidneys each day, we excrete only about one to two quarts of that fluid daily. The rest of the fluid that passes through the kidneys goes right back into the circulatory system.

The purpose of diuretic drugs is to shrink by a small amount the volume of fluids circulating through the blood vessels. They achieve this by blocking the reabsorption of sodium back into the system, so that the sodium exits the body through increased urination.

Surprisingly, it doesn't take the elimination of a very large volume of fluid to lower blood pressure significantly. The typical diuretic will cause a patient to urinate about one extra quart of fluid per day for about three days. In other words, the body loses about three quarts in those three days.

As the patient continues to take the diuretic, the fluid volume creeps back up over the next few weeks until it stabilizes at a point about two quarts lower than the premedication level. This represents a decrease of about 5 to 8 percent in the body's total volume of fluids. If the person goes off the drug entirely, the fluid volume will quickly return to its premedication level.

What happens to the blood pressure during diuretic treatment?

With lower fluid volume, the pressure on the blood vessels is less, and the cardiac output goes down. Furthermore, the resistance or tightness of the peripheral blood vessels eventually decreases. As a result of these physical responses, the blood pressure declines.

For most patients, the diastolic or systolic measurements or both will begin to drop immediately. Within four weeks the readings typically decline by an average of about 10 mm Hg. Certain types of patients, including blacks, obese persons, and the elderly, often find that the decreases with the use of diuretics are even more dramatic.

According to the 1962 Veterans Administration Cooperative Study and other studies conducted during the same period, administration of thiazide diuretics can cause decreases in systolic and diastolic pressures that range from 8/4 mm Hg to 19/11 mm Hg.

Often, those who go on diuretics will get quite thirsty at first—a signal that their bodies want more liquids and sodium. So they'll increase their intake of fluids. Simultaneously, their frequency of urination will increase, with many people finding that they need to get up more often at night to go to the bathroom. In a short time, though, the body adjusts to less sodium and a lower volume of fluids, and the thirstiness and excessive urination decline.

In the following discussion of the characteristics of specific diuretics, you may want to refer back to the chart on pages 194–198, which lists different types of drugs and their recommended doses.

- *Thiazides.* These operate by blocking the reabsorption of sodium and chlorides back into the bloodstream. There are a number of different types of thiazides, as you can see from the chart, but hydrochlorothiazide is the most popular. This drug was the one used in the HDFP and MRFIT studies and in many other investigations into the relationship between blood pressure and cardiovascular disease.

  Usually, an adequate pressure-lowering response can be reached with relatively low doses of these drugs. For example, when hydrochlorothiazide is taken alone, a dose of 25 mg, twice a day, will result in the maximum possible antihypertensive impact for most people.

- *Loop diuretics.* These tend to be stronger than the thiazides and are often reserved for patients with more resistant hypertension, which doesn't respond to the milder drugs.

  The loop diuretics—so-called because they prevent reabsorption of sodium in that part of the kidneys known as the loop of Henle—may eliminate as much as 20 percent of the salt filtered through the kidneys. In contrast, the thiazides eliminate only about 5 to 8 percent of the kidney-filtered sodium.

  To act properly, however, loop diuretics must be able to enter strategic parts of the kidneys. If there is any blockage, such as by a high acid concentration or reduced blood flow, these drugs may be ineffective.

  The loop diuretics now in use are furosemide (Lasix) and bumetanide (Bumex).

- *Potassium-sparing diuretics.* These include spironolactone, triamterene, and amiloride, which act to reduce the loss of potassium that often occurs with diuretics.

In other words, when the sodium is washed out through the urine, potassium also tends to be lost.

With excessive loss of potassium, the condition known as hypokalemia (too little potassium in the body) may result. The consequences of this condition may include impaired kidney function; heart problems, including irregular heartbeat; inadequate dilation of the blood vessels with exercise and heat; or a decline in glucose (blood sugar) tolerance, which may indicate the presence of diabetes. In the worst cases, there may be paralysis, severe muscle pain, and even death.

The prime candidates for the potassium-sparing drugs are those who naturally experience heavy loss of this mineral with normal diuretics. These medications are also in order for those very few patients with the condition known as aldosteronism—which is caused by a tumor in the adrenal gland and involves too high a loss of potassium from the blood. Those suffering from aldosteronism may experience very low potassium levels that may lead to paralysis, along with very severe hypertension. Aldosterone, by the way, is a hormone secreted by the adrenal gland, which regulates the metabolism of sodium and potassium.

2: The Sympathetic Nervous System Inhibitors

These drugs—known among doctors as "adrenergic inhibitors"—lower blood pressure by acting in a number of different ways on the sympathetic nervous system.

The sympathetic nervous system controls the body's automatic nerve responses that trigger such events as changes in blood pressure, perspiration, and heartbeat. This system is influenced by the presence of such hormones and neurotransmitters as epinephrine (adrenaline), and norepinephrine (noradrenaline).

Epinephrine and norepinephrine—which are often lumped together under the term "catecholamines"—have an impact on blood pressure only when they are bound or locked into "receptors" on the surface of the vessel cells. Then, when the hormones are "hooked up" to the cells, they send signals to the vessels that cause them to relax or to tighten up. The result is a rise or a fall in blood pressure.

Researchers have recently discovered a variety of different receptors, which have been classified under the general categories of "alpha" and "beta" receptors. Sometimes the alpha and beta receptors work against each other; sometimes they work together.

For example, certain beta receptors may increase the action of the heart; dilate coronary arteries or other arteries; or increase the force of the heart's contractions during its pumping action. In contrast, alpha receptors may constrict the blood vessels of the bronchial tubes.

The sympathetic or adrenergic inhibiting drugs may act on these receptors to block their responses. Or they may interfere in other ways with the sympathetic nervous system and thus help to bring about lower blood pressure.

Let's consider some specific sympathetic nervous system inhibitors that work on the peripheral vessels:

- *The peripheral inhibitors.* These drugs, which have been around longer than most other antihypertensive medications, block the movement of norepinephrine from the nerve endings to the blood vessels. As a result, there is a decrease in the ability of the vessels to tighten up. Also, the heart rate may decrease with this medication.

  Reserpine (Serpasil) is the most popular of these drugs. Years of treatment have demonstrated that small doses may be adequate to achieve the maximum possible results. When the drug is used alone, doses of 0.25 may be prescribed. But when reserpine is combined with a diuretic, doses as small as 0.05 mg per day may be appropriate.

The overall impact when reserpine is used by itself is to reduce blood pressure by an average of only 3/5 mm Hg. But when combined with a diuretic such as a thiazide, pressure has been shown to drop by an average of 14/11 mm Hg.

Some other peripheral adrenergic inhibitors have been prescribed mostly in the past, though they are still sometimes used as a last resort for highly resistant hypertension. These include guanethidine (Ismelin) and guanadrel (Hylorel).

- *Drugs that act on the central brain stem.* Known as "central alpha agonists" or simply "central agonists," these drugs stimulate activity of the alpha receptors in the brain stem (the central nervous connection between the brain and spinal cord). The term *agonist* in this context simply means "stimulator."

  The stimulation of the alpha receptors causes a *decrease* in the activity of the sympathetic nervous system. As far as blood pressure is concerned, there are two results: (1) the resistance or tightness of the blood vessels is reduced; (2) the pumping action of the heart declines somewhat.

The final result with many patients is lower blood pressure.

The most common drugs in this category include methyldopa (Aldomet); clonidine (Catapres); guanabenz (Wytensin) and guanfacine (Tenex). Of the four, my consultant Dr. Norman Kaplan regards the third, guanabenz, as the most attractive. Two reasons: Studies have shown that it can lower blood cholesterol by 5 to 10 percent, and it causes little retention of bodily fluids.

In addition to the beneficial impact on high blood pressure, clonidine (Catapres) has also been used effectively to help people break the cigarette smoking habit.

• *The alpha blockers.* These block the action of the alpha receptors in the vessel tissues and thus reduce the resistance or tightness in the vessels. Also, they have no effect on cardiac output.

Alpha blockers may be particularly useful for young people who want to maintain a high level of physical activity, as it allows them to engage in vigorous exercise without having to worry about full heart action and unimpeded blood flow. In addition, alpha blockers may actually increase blood volume; consequently, some of the dehydrating tendencies of diuretics can be avoided, which is especially important to athletes who train in hot weather.

Currently, two alpha blockers are on the market—prazosin (Minipress) and terazosin (Hytrin). Others that may be available soon are indoramin and doxazosin.

If your physician prescribes prazosin or terazosin, you should be alert to several features of these drugs. First, an initial dose may lower your blood pressure precipitously, especially if you're already on a diuretic. The result may be that your blood pressure dips so low that you experience the condition known as hypotension: feelings of fatigue, dizziness, and faintness. (We'll discuss these hypotensive symptoms in more detail in chapter 6.)

Overall, though, the benefits of alpha blockers such as prazosin usually far outweigh the negative characteristics for most patients. In addition to allowing full physical activity, this drug lowers total cholesterol and tryglyceride levels. Furthermore, with many patients, it raises levels of HDL (high-density lipoprotein) cholesterol. HDL, as you are probably aware, is the "good" cholesterol, which is generally regarded as protective against atherosclerosis and cardiovascular disease.

Finally, the alpha blocker Minipress (prazosin) has sometimes also been of help in reducing the size of benign prostate enlargement.

- *The beta blockers.* These drugs—which are the second most popular among all antihypertensive medications,* next to diuretics—produce multiple effects on the circulatory system. Most of these effects work to reduce blood pressure.

  First, pure beta blockers, without any additional medication, block or inhibit the beta receptors in the heart, which are normally part of the mechanism that raises the heart rate. With the activity of these beta receptors reduced by the drug, a cap is placed on the maximum heart rate. The final result is a lowering of blood pressure.

  Second, beta blockers block the production of renin in the kidneys. As you know from chapter 4, the release of renin is the first in a series of steps that leads to the appearance of angiotensin II, the powerful vasoconstrictor that increases vessel resistance and raises blood pressure. With-

*Over 30 million prescriptions written in 1988.

out a full supply of renin, blood pressure tends to stay lower.

Third, these drugs *may* reduce the release of norepinephrine, decrease the activity of certain alpha receptors, and, as a consequence, lower blood pressure. This issue is still under study, however.

Beta blockers are frequently the most effective drugs for young, white patients but are less helpful for the elderly and blacks. One reason that has been suggested for this difference is that blacks and the elderly on average have lower renin levels. As a result, the impact of the medication is reduced.

Extremely active young people, such as athletes, will probably find beta blockers unacceptable. The reason: By reducing the maximum heart rate (i.e., putting a governor on the heart rate), the medications place a limit on the degree of cardiovascular fitness that can be achieved. With a regulated lower heart rate, athletes are unable to perform at those high levels of physical activity that require a heart pumping at maximum or near-maximum rate.

On the other hand, it *is* possible for those on beta blockers to achieve some training effect and to maintain a reasonable level of physical fitness, even though they may not reach the standards of top athletes. In chapter 8, which deals with exercise for hypertensives, I'll provide a formula to show you how to determine your target heart rate during exercise if you're trying to keep fit while on beta blockers.

Beta blockers may also create problems for those in very cold climates because the drugs may constrict peripheral blood vessels. With less blood flowing to the arms and legs, feet and hands may become uncomfortably cold.

With all these drawbacks and qualifications, you may ask, "Why should *anyone* go on beta blockers?"

There are a number of reasons: These drugs can be quite helpful in protecting patients who have suffered one heart attack and may be in danger of a second. By lowering the heart rate, less stress is placed on the heart.

Also, these medications sometimes can relieve or improve certain painful or serious health conditions, such as migraine headaches, angina pectoris, and glaucoma. Those who are prone to anxiety reactions, including a racing heart and extreme nervousness, may benefit from the slower heart rate imposed by these drugs.

The many beta-blocker drugs all operate within the general framework I've described, but they do have a relatively wide range of variation in the way they work. For example, some, like atenolol, metoprolol, and acebutolol, are better at reducing the heart rate than at tightening up the peripheral blood vessels. As a result, they may be more appropriate for those patients who aren't worried about limiting the output of their heart muscle but who *are* concerned about getting cold hands or feet!

Another concern about beta blockers is the extent to which they are soluble in fats or lipids in the bloodstream. Those that are most lipid-soluble may not be as effective for some people because the liver grabs them and removes them from the bloodstream before they can have an impact. Consequently, less soluble beta blockers like nadolol and atenolol may be better for many patients.

There's also the so-called intrinsic sympathomimetic activity (ISA) issue with beta blockers. This ISA response, which involves complex interactions in the sympathetic nervous system, allows the blood pressure to fall. But even with a significant drug-induced drop in blood pressure, the ISA response may result in little or no decrease in heart output or rate, or drop in renin levels.

The beta blocker pindolol, and to some extent acebutol, have these ISA characteristics. They may be particularly suitable for patients who suffer from excessively slow heart rates or who have cold hands and feet. Also, because these ISA beta blockers have fewer negative side effects, such as a tendency to reduce the "good" HDL cholesterol, they are often preferred over other beta blockers.

- *The combination alpha-beta blockers*. Research into the properties of alpha and beta blockers has produced at least one drug, labetalol (Normodyne or Trandate), with qualities of both.

  This medication causes the blood pressure to decrease by opening up the blood vessels, while at the same time maintaining a relatively normal heart rate. On the other hand, labetalol is quite soluble in fats, so that only about a quarter of it becomes available for use by the body when it's taken orally. The liver in effect "gobbles" most of it up!

  Usually, physicians prescribe this drug for those with moderate or severe hypertension—but not for mild hypertension. Also, they may inject it intravenously into patients who need a fairly fast drop in very high blood pressure.

3: The Vessel Openers

The vessel-opening drugs, known as the "vasodilators," act directly or indirectly on the walls and tissues of the arterioles (small arteries) to decrease vessel tension and resistance.

One drug that acts directly on the vessels in this way is hydralazine (Apresoline). This medication actually *relaxes* the muscles of the vessel walls and thus decreases their tension. With less tension in the arterioles, blood pressure decreases.

However, as the arterioles relax, an opposing set of reactions is triggered elsewhere in the body to compensate: Heart rate goes up; the kidneys release more renin; veins elsewhere in the body tighten up; and catecholamine production is increased. Also, the kidneys tend to retain extra sodium and encourage a rise in fluid volume in the body. The final result may be an interference with the pressure-lowering properties of the drug.

To offset these negative responses, physicians almost always *combine* hydralazine with other drugs—such as beta blockers to lower heart rate, or diuretics to decrease fluid volume. With particularly severe hypertension, a combination of three types of drugs can be quite effective.

In the 1962 Veterans Administration Cooperative Study, for instance, hydralazine plus a thiazide diuretic produced an average reduction in systolic blood pressure of 11 mm Hg and a decrease in the diastolic of 12 mm Hg. But when .25 mg of the drug reserpine was added twice a day, the combination produced an average decrease of 23/21 mm Hg.

Similarly, three other drugs—a diuretic, the beta blocker propranolol, and hydralazine— were used by researcher R. Zacest and his colleagues in a 1972 study, reported in the *New England Journal of Medicine*. In this investigation, average blood pressures in hypertensives with highly resistant forms of the disease dropped by an average of 44/31 mm Hg!

This direct-acting vasodilator, hydralazine, seems most beneficial for patients with difficult, hard-to-control cases of hypertension, and for certain older individuals whose vessels have become relatively insensitive to the action of other drugs.

An even more powerful direct-acting vasodilator, minoxidil, may be prescribed for those whose high blood pressure can't be brought down by other, less potent medications. Usually, minoxidil, like hydralazine, has to be given with other drugs that offset increased heart rates and increased retention of fluids.

An interesting aside about minoxidil: It's long been known that one of the side effects of this drug is the increase in the body's production of hair. For women, the extra hair growth is usually bothersome and often makes the drug completely unacceptable. But for men, this effect is sometimes welcomed, since new hair may begin to grow on previously bald or thinning pates. As has been mentioned in the popular press, some people are now applying minoxidil externally to their heads, and in many cases some new hair growth has been noted. (The trade name for the hair-growing variation of minoxidil is Rogaine.)

New Drugs Bring New Hope: The Calcium Blockers and the Converting Enzyme Inhibitors

These two types of drugs are considered vessel openers, or vasodilators, as are the ones we just discussed. But these medications act *indirectly* by influencing chemicals, secretions, or other substances in the body, which in turn open up the vessels. We've already discussed much of the physiology involved with the operation of these drugs in chapter 4; but more needs to be said about the action of specific medications.

- *The calcium blockers.* Also called "calcium entry blockers," "channel blockers," or "calcium antagonists," these medications bring down blood pressure by inhibiting the entry of calcium into the muscle cells of the blood vessels. Calcium in these cells is required for the vessels to contract. Conversely, a limitation on the calcium reduces the vessels' ability to contract.

  In other words, every time *any* muscle in the body contracts, it's necessary for calcium to enter into the muscle cells from outside fluids (the "interstitial" fluids that surround and bathe each cell). In addition, some calcium necessary for contraction is already in the cellular structure.

  The calcium-blocking drugs keep out the fluid-transported calcium. Also, these medications promote more relaxation or distension of the muscles lining the walls of the blood vessels.

  Another key point about the physiology at work here: The muscle cells have "channels," which are openings through which the calcium enters. These drugs plug up those channels and keep out the necessary calcium.

The four calcium-blocking drugs now available are verapamil (Calan or Isoptin), diltiazem (Cardizem), nifedipine (Procardia), and nicardipine (Cardine). Verapamil lowers blood pressure a bit more slowly than the other three; in fact, nifedipine is so fast that, taken orally or put under the tongue, it can lower blood pressure significantly in less than twenty minutes!

These drugs are particularly effective with older people and blacks, and somewhat less helpful for some younger people. On the other hand, athletic young people who are on nifedipine find no interference with their heart rate or ability to achieve levels of cardiovascular conditioning.

Note: The latest research suggests that in general, calcium channel blockers have advantages over beta blockers and diuretics for many hypertensive patients who want to pursue a vigorous exercise program. The best of the calcium channel blockers may be nifedipine and diltiazem, rather than verapamil, because the first two permit the heart of the exerciser to contract at maximum levels.

Overall, about two-thirds of the patients who take calcium blockers find that these medications can control their hypertension. The declines can mean the difference between hypertension and normal or near-normal blood pressure: In one 1983 study of patients with an average blood pressure of 161/100 on the first visit to the doctor, pressures dropped an average of 16/10. In this study, the patients took 20 mg of nifedipine twice a day.

Nifedipine and nicardipine also have been effective when used in combination with diuretics and beta blockers. However, experts caution that using the other two calcium blockers (verapamil and diltiazem) with beta blockers may create problems. One reason: Like the beta blockers, these two calcium blockers also tend to lower the heart's ability to contract. The double-edged impact of both sets of drugs may thus be too much for the patient's well-being.

- *The converting enzyme inhibitors.* In chapter 4, we considered in detail the operation of these drugs, which are also known as "angiotensin converting enzyme (ACE) inhibitors."

To sum up, they intervene in the kidneys in this sequence:

- The kidneys produce the enzyme renin.

- The renin releases the passive hormone angiotensin I.

- The *active* hormone angiotensin II is formed through the work of a "converting enzyme" in the blood cells, which transforms the angiotensin I.

The angiotensin II, in turn, acts in two direct ways to raise blood pressure:

1. It constricts the blood vessels.

2. It stimulates the adrenal glands, which cause the kidneys to absorb more sodium and thus retain more fluids. With tighter vessels and a higher fluid volume, blood pressure goes up.

The ACE inhibitors—which are the fastest-growing of the new drugs, even though they've been in use for only about five years—interrupt this process by blocking the action of the converting enzyme. Without the converting enzyme, the passive angiotensin I can never become angiotensin II. So the ACE drugs eliminate a major factor in constricting the vessels and raising blood pressure.

Presently, three ACE inhibitors are on the market—captopril (Capoten), enalapril (Vasotec) and lisinopril (Prinivil or Zestril). Physicians have learned to administer relatively low doses of captopril because at first, higher doses produced a number of severe side effects, such as impairment of kidney functions, loss of taste, rashes, and leukopenia (an excessively low number of white blood cells, which may lead to bone marrow disease).

These days, the typical doses for captopril are 12.5 to 25 mg two to three times daily, though in some cases of severe hypertension the daily doses may still reach 200 mg per day. In the past, the worst side effects occurred with even higher doses of 400 to 600 mg daily.

These ACE inhibitors are being used increasingly as the first drug of choice for many with hypertension, including mild hypertension. A current disadvantage is their expense: They cost 50 to 60 cents per pill, in contrast to the diuretics, which may be purchased in generic form for as little as 3 cents per pill or capsule. As prices go down in the future, the use of the ACE inhibitors is likely to widen.

Up to this point, I've said relatively little about the negative aspects of these drugs. But the issues of side effects and consequences of interactions with other drugs are extremely important in helping physicians and patients design successful medication strategies.

The Side Effects of the Antihypertensive Drugs

Almost every medication carries with it some unwanted impact on the body. These side effects may emerge in a number of ways:

- Simply as bothersome physical manifestations, such as fatigue

- As deeply disturbing changes in a person's ability to function, such as sexual impotence

- As negative changes in the emotions, such as depression

- As permanent threats to health or even to life

The accompanying comprehensive chart on side effects will provide both patients and physicians with a good reference point for a consideration of possible adverse reactions to drugs. This chart comes from "The 1988 Report of the Joint National Committee on Detection, Evaluation, and Treatment of High Blood Pressure."

Now I'll explain more completely, in layman's terms, some of the most common side effects of the major antihypertensive drugs included on the chart. We'll consider these medications in order, in each of the three major drug categories.

Adverse Side Effects of Antihypertensive Drugs*

Drugs	Selected Side Effects†	Precautions and Special Considerations
Diuretics‡		
Thiazides and related sulfonamide diuretics	Hypokalemia, hyperuricemia, glucose intolerance, hypercholesteremia, hypertriglycaridemia, sexual dysfunction, weakness	May be ineffective in renal failure; hypokalemia increases digitalis toxicity; may precipitate acute gout; may cause an increase in blood levels of lithium
Loop diuretics	Same as for thiazides	Effective in chronic renal failure; hypokalemia and hyperuricemia as above

Adverse Side Effects of Antihypertensive Drugs* (continued)

Drugs	Selected Side Effects†	Precautions and Special Considerations
Potassium-sparing agents	Hyperkalemia	Danger of hyperkalemia or renal failure in patients treated with ACE inhibitor or nonsteroidal anti-inflammatory drug; may increase blood levels of lithium
Spironolactone	Gynecomastia, mastodynia	Interferes with digoxin immunoassay
Triamterene Amiloride	. . . .	Danger of renal calculi . . . .

Adverse Side Effects of Antihypertensive Drugs* (continued)

Drugs	Selected Side Effects†	Precautions and Special Considerations
Adrenergic inhibitors β-Adrenergic blockers§ Acebutolol Atenolol Metoprolol Nadolol Penbutolol sulfate Pindolol Propranolol hydrochloride Timolol	Bronchospasm, peripheral arterial insufficiency, fatigue, insomnia, sexual dysfunction, exacerbation of congestive heart failure, masking of symptoms of hypoglycemia, hypertriglyceridemia, decreased HDL cholesterol (except for pindolol and acebutolol)	Should not be used in patients with asthma, COPD, congestive heart failure, heart block (> first-degree), and sick sinus syndrome; use with caution in insulin-treated diabetic patients and patients with peripheral vascular disease; should not be discontinued abruptly in patients with ischemic heart disease

Adverse Side Effects of
Antihypertensive Drugs* (continued)

Drugs	Selected Side Effects†	Precautions and Special Considerations
Centrally acting adrenergic inhibitors		
Clonidine	Drowsiness, sedation, dry mouth, fatigue, sexual dysfunction	Rebound hypertension may occur with abrupt discontinuance, particularly with prior administration of high doses or with continuation of concomitant β-blocker therapy
Guanabenz	As above	As above
Guanfacine hydrochloride	As above	As above

Adverse Side Effects of
Antihypertensive Drugs* (continued)

Drugs	Selected Side Effects†	Precautions and Special Considerations
Methyldopa	As above	May cause liver damage and Coombs-positive hemolytic anemia; use cautiously in elderly patients because of orthostatic hypotension; interferes with measurements of urinary catecholamine levels
Clonidine TTS (Patch)	As above: localized skin reaction to the patch	. . .

Adverse Side Effects of
Antihypertensive Drugs* (continued)

Drugs	Selected Side Effects†	Precautions and Special Considerations
Peripheral-acting adrenergic inhibitors		
Guanadrel sulfate	Diarrhea, sexual dysfunction, orthostatic hypotension	Use cautiously because of orthostatic hypotension
Guanethidine monosulfate	Same as for guanadrel	Same as for guanadrel
Rauwolfia alkaloids	Lethargy, nasal congestion, depression	Contraindicated in patients with history of mental depression; use with caution in patients with history of peptic ulcer

Adverse Side Effects of
Antihypertensive Drugs* (continued)

Drugs	Selected Side Effects†	Precautions and Special Considerations
Reserpine	Same as for rauwolfia alkaloids	Same as for rauwolfia alkaloids
α, Adrenergic blockers Prazosin hydrochloride	"First-dose" syncope, orthostatic hypotension, weakness, palpitations	Use cautiously in elderly patients because of orthostatic hypotension
Terazosin hydrochloride	As above	As above

Adverse Side Effects of Antihypertensive Drugs* (continued)

Drugs	Selected Side Effects†	Precautions and Special Considerations
Combined α-β-adrenergic blocker: Labetalol	Bronchospasm, peripheral vascular insufficiency, orthostatic hypotension	Should not be used in patients with asthma, COPD, congestive heart failure, heart block (> first-degree), and sick sinus syndrome; use with caution in insulin-treated diabetic patients and patients with peripheral vascular disease
Vasodilators	Headache, tachycardia, fluid retention	May precipitate angina pectoris in patients with coronary artery disease

Adverse Side Effects of Antihypertensive Drugs* (continued)

Drugs	Selected Side Effects†	Precautions and Special Considerations
Hydralazine	Positive antinuclear antibody test	Lupus syndrome may occur (rare at recommended doses)
Minoxidil	Hypertrichosis	May cause or aggravate pleural and pencardial effusions; may precipitate angina pectoris in patients with coronary artery disease

Adverse Side Effects of
Antihypertensive Drugs* (continued)

Drugs	Selected Side Effects†	Precautions and Special Considerations
ACE Inhibitors Inhibitors	Rash, cough, angioneurotic edema, hyperkalemia, dysgeusia	Can cause reversible, acute, renal failure in patients with bilateral renal arterial stenosis or unilateral stenosis in a solitary kidney; proteinuria may occur (rare at recommended doses); hyperkalemia can develop, particularly in patients with renal insufficiency; rarely can induce neutro—

Adverse Side Effects of
Antihypertensive Drugs* (continued)

Drugs	Selected Side Effects†	Precautions and Special Considerations
		penia; hypotension has been observed with initiation of ACE inhibitors, especially in patients with high plasma renin activity or in those receiving diuretic therapy
Calcium antagonists	Edema, headache	Use with caution in patients with congestive heart failure; contraindicated in patients with second- or third-degree heart block

Adverse Side Effects of
Antihypertensive Drugs* (continued)

Drugs	Selected Side Effects†	Precautions and Special Considerations
Verapamil	Constipation	May cause liver dysfunction
Diltiazem hydrochloride	Constipation	May cause liver dysfunction
Nifedipine	Tachycardia	. . .
Nitrendipine	Tachycardia	. . .

*Sexual dysfunction, particularly impotence in men, has been reported with the use of all antihypertensive agents.

ACE indicates angiotensin-converting enzyme; HDL, high-density lipoprotein; and COPD, chronic obstructive pulmonary disease.

†The listing of side effects is not all-inclusive, and health practitioners are urged to refer to package insert for a more detailed listing.

‡See pages 194–198 for a list of these drugs.

§Sudden withdrawal of these drugs may be hazardous in patients with heart disease. See pages 194–198 for a list of these drugs.

The Volume Reducers: Diuretics

The thiazides and related drugs. Common side effects include:

- Hypokalemia (too little potassium, which may cause irregular heartbeat and other problems)

- Hyperuricemia (overproduction of uric acid, which may trigger an attack of gout)

- Glucose intolerance (an inability of the body to metabolize, use, and store sugar— as seen in diabetes mellitus)

- Hypercholesterolemia (elevation of blood cholesterol)

- Hypertriglyceridemia (elevation of the blood fats known as triglycerides)

Loop diuretics. These drugs display the same side effects as the thiazides.

The potassium-sparing drugs. All of them— amiloride, spironolactone, and triamterene— may produce hyperkalemia (excessive amounts of potassium in the blood, a toxic condition that occurs usually with kidney impairment). Also, spironolactone may cause enlargement of the male breasts (gynecomastia) or pain in the breasts of young women (mastodynia).

The Sympathetic Nervous System Inhibitors (The Adrenergic Inhibitors)

Drugs that inhibit the peripheral nerves (as in the arms and legs). Taking guanadrel may result in "orthostatic hypotension" (blood pressure that's too low when the person is standing) and diarrhea. The side effects for guanethidine are similar.

Reserpine and the rauwolfia alkaloids may produce tiredness, aggravation of depression, irritation of peptic ulcers, or nasal congestion.

Drugs that inhibit the central nervous system. Guanabenz, guanfacine, methyldopa, and clonidine may cause tiredness, dry mouth, or sleepiness. Also, methyldopa may result in liver damage or disorders of the body's immune system.

Alpha blockers. Prazosin or terazosin may trigger palpitations of the heart, general feelings of weakness, or standing hypotension.

Beta blockers. Possible side effects include excessively slow heart rates (bradycardia); insomnia; strange dreams; excessive fatigue; elevated triglyceride counts; declines in the "good" HDL cholesterol; depression; and aggravation of angina pectoris pains. These negative effects can be minimized in those drugs with the ISA factor, such as pindolol and acebutolol.

Combined alpha-beta blockers. People on

these medications, including labetalol, may experience headaches, tiredness, dizziness, nausea, or asthma.

The Vessel Openers (Vasodilators)

The direct-acting vessel openers. Hydralazine may produce excessively fast heart rates (tachycardia), headaches, excessive retention of fluids, and angina pains in those with coronary heart disease.

Taking minoxidil may result in excessive hair growth (hypertrichosis) and too much fluid retention.

The indirect-acting vessel-openers. The ACE inhibitors captopril, enalapril, and lisinopril may cause hypotension; coughing; localized swelling, especially around the face (angioneurotic edema); excessive retention of potassium (hyperkalemia); rashes; or loss of taste (dysgeusia).

The ACE inhibitors may also lead to kidney failure in patients with existing kidney problems; the appearance of protein in the urine (proteinuria), which may signal kidney disease; and sometimes a decrease in the white blood cells (neutropenia), which is a factor in bone marrow disease.

The second group of indirect-acting vessel openers, the calcium blockers, can have a variety of adverse side effects:

- All may cause headaches, dizziness, and flushing.

- More specifically, verapamil may produce flushing, swelling (edema), and constipation.

- Nifedipine and nicardipine may result in local swelling and flushing.

- Diltiazem may cause nausea and can trigger complications in patients with heart problems, such as congestive heart failure.

Now, with a better knowledge of how the major antihypertensive drugs work and also of their side effects, we can discuss some of the strategies physicians may employ in treating patients.

Guidelines for Designing a Personal Drug Strategy

There is a fairly uniform way of determining one's blood pressure status: First, the doctor or patient straps a measuring device on the upper arm and proceeds to find the systolic and diastolic readings. These two numbers are then compared with standard ranges of pressure, and the person is classified as normal or as having mild, moderate, or severe hypertension.

However, even though measurements may

be done the same way, there are many kinds of high blood pressure. Three people, for instance, may all have readings of 160/100 mm Hg. But they may each respond differently to certain medications.

The blood pressure of the first person may decrease to normal almost immediately with a thiazide diuretic. The pressure of the second may not respond at all to the diuretic, but may be reduced to normal with a beta blocker. And the pressure of the third may go down with both the diuretic and the beta blocker, but the side effects may be such that only an ACE inhibitor is appropriate.

For example, this third person may be a young athlete who finds that the diuretic produces dehydration and that the beta blocker places too low a limit on his heart rate. The ACE inhibitor, in contrast, lowers blood pressure without either of these adverse consequences.

In light of such considerations, what guidelines can physicians use to work with their patients in designing an appropriate antihypertensive drug program?

The stair-step diagram I've reproduced here provides a good, basic approach to developing a drug strategy.

Step-Care Therapy

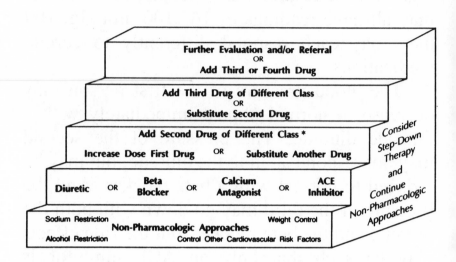

Individualized step-care therapy for hypertension. For some patients, nonpharmacologic therapy should be tried first. If blood pressure goal is not achieved, add pharmacologic therapy. Other patients may require pharmacologic therapy initially. In these instances, nonpharmacologic therapy may be a helpful adjunct. ACE indicates angiotensin-converting enzyme; asterisk, drugs such as diuretics, β-blockers, calcium antagonists, ACE inhibitors, α-blockers, centrally acting α$_2$-agonists, rauwolfia serpentina, and vasodilators.

As you can see, the first "step" in this approach to treatment—which experts call "step-care therapy"—is to try nondrug techniques to lower pressure. *All* patients should be involved in the nondrug approach, though many with high or resistant hypertension may also be placed on medications at the beginning of treatment.

The second step includes the prescription of drugs that most experts today feel could qualify as "first choice" medications (i.e., those that can be tried before any other drug). These include diuretics, beta blockers, calcium antagonists, or ACE inhibitors. Most patients with mild hypertension find that their blood pressure can be managed with only one drug.

Diuretics are still the first drug of choice, and beta blockers are in second place. But some of the newer drugs, such as the alpha blockers and ACE inhibitors, are gaining in popularity because of their minimal side effects and effective action.

The choice of one drug over another will depend on the lifestyle the person wants to maintain, on the side effects he or she experiences, and, most important, on which drug *works* in lowering blood pressure.

The third step involves adding a second drug of a different classification, increasing the dose of the first drug, or substituting a second drug for the first. When I refer to drug "classifications" here, I have in mind the three major classifications into which we've already divided the drugs: the volume reducers, the inhibitors of the sympathetic nervous system, and the vasodilators.

Usually, if a drug other than a diuretic has been selected as the first choice, a diuretic will be used in this second step. One of the reasons for this is that even if the first drug has succeeded in lowering blood pressure somewhat, there may still be a tendency for the body to retain too much fluid. The diuretics, with their volume-depleting powers, can correct this problem and further help reduce the pressure.

Still, physicians may continue to avoid prescribing diuretics at this stage because of a patient's particular problems or reactions to these medications. For example, diuretics may aggravate gout, diabetes, or existing heart problems.

Sometimes, a physician may elect simply to increase the dose of the first drug. An argument in favor of this is that it's easier for some patients to discipline themselves to handle one medication, but more than one drug may create confusion or other noncompliance problems. On the other hand, there is frequently a trade-off: Increasing the dose often won't help lower the blood pressure much, and there may be a decided increase in side effects.

Finally, if the choice is to use a second drug at this third step, the physician must become particularly sensitive to possible interactions between medications. To get an idea of the possibilities, consult the following chart.

Drug Interactions in Antihypertensive Therapy

Diuretics

Diuretics can raise lithium blood levels by enhancing proximal tubular reabsorption of lithium.

Nonsteroidal anti-inflammatory agents, including aspirin, may antagonize antihypertensive and natriuretic effectiveness of diuretics.

Angiotensin-converting enzyme (ACE) inhibitors magnify potassium-sparing effects of triamterene, amiloride, or spironolactone.

ACE inhibitors blunt hypokalemia induced by thiazide diuretics.

Sympatholytic agents

Guanethidine monosulfate and guanadrel sulfate: Ephedrine and amphetamine displace guanethidine and guanadrel from storage vesicles. Tricyclic antidepressants inhibit uptake of guanethidine and guanadrel into these vesicles. Cocaine may inhibit neuronal pump that actively transports guanethidine and guanadrel into nerve endings.

These actions may reduce antihypertensive effects of guanethidine and guanadrel.

Hypertension can occur with concomitant therapy with phenothiazines or sympathomimetic amines.

Monoamine oxidase inhibitors may prevent degradation and metabolism of released norepinephrine produced by tyramine-containing foods and may thereby cause hypertension.

Tricyclic antidepressant drugs may reduce effects of clonidine and guanabenz.

β-*Blockers*

Cimetidine (Tagamet) may reduce bioavailability of β-blockers metabolized primarily by liver by inducing hepatic oxidative enzymes. Hydralazine, by reducing hepatic blood flow, may increase plasma concentration of β-blockers.

Cholesterol-binding resins, i.e., *cholestyramine* (Questran) and *colestipol* (Colestid), may reduce plasma levels of propranolol hydrochloride.

β-Blockers may reduce plasma clearance of drugs metabolized by the liver (e.g., lidocaine, chlorpromazine, coumarin).

Combinations of calcium channel blockers and β-blockers may promote negative inotropic effects on the failing myocardium.

Combinations of β-blockers and reserpine may cause marked bradycardia and syncope.

ACE inhibitors

Nonsteroidal anti-inflammatory drugs, including aspirin, may magnify potassium-retaining effects of ACE inhibitors.

Calcium antagonists

Combinations of calcium antagonists with quinidine may induce hypotension, particularly in patients with idiopathic hypertrophic subarotic stenosis.

Calcium antagonists may induce increases in plasma digoxin levels.

Cimetidine may increase blood levels of nifedipine.

(From "The 1988 Report of the Joint National Committee . . .", *Archives of Internal Medicine.*)

The fourth step in drug therapy includes adding a third medication of a different classification. Or, the doctor may substitute a second drug, in case he merely increased the dose of your first drug in the preceding step.

About one in ten patients needs more than two drugs to bring down blood pressure to manageable levels. In general, when three drugs are required, the doctor will choose one from each of the three main classifications—a diuretic, a sympathetic nervous system inhibitor, and a vasodilator.

The fifth and final step calls for further evaluation by the physician; referral of the patient to a specialist or a special facility; or the addition of a third or fourth drug to the medication regimen.

Now, suppose that at the second or perhaps the third step, you find that your blood pressure is well under control—in the normal range, below 140/90 mm Hg. Will you have to stay on drugs all your life, or is there any chance you can get off drug therapy entirely?

Is It Possible to Stop Drug Treatments?

One patient who was on a thiazide diuretic experienced a decline in his blood pressure from a beginning average of 162/97 down to the normal range (below 140/90) over a period of about two months. With this improvement, he became convinced that his hypertension had been "cured." Also, he had become frustrated because the medication had caused some degree of impotence. So he decided, on his own, to stop taking the medication.

As often happens in such cases, the man's

blood pressure increased within a week, back up to the moderate hypertensive level where he had started. He learned the hard way that a patient *must not* take his drug treatment into his own hands.

Fortunately, however, this incident opened up a productive dialogue between this patient and his physician. The doctor had been unaware of the problem with impotence because the patient had failed to tell him about it. But when the doctor learned why the man had decided to go off the diuretic, he simply prescribed another medication—an ACE inhibitor, which typically causes fewer difficulties with the sexual function.

As the patient used the ACE inhibitor, he found, as his physician expected, that his sexual capacity remained normal. In short, this collaboration between patient and physician produced a very desirable result.

Although this particular patient erred in going off his medication before consulting his doctor, his expectations about the possibility of discontinuing drugs weren't all wrong. Certainly, in most instances those who go on hypertensive medications must expect to stay on them indefinitely—probably for the rest of their lives. But in a significant minority of cases, it's possible to reduce drug doses or even to go off therapy completely—with blood pressure still under control.

Encouraging findings along these lines have emerged from the VA Cooperative Study Group of 1975 and also from a study by researcher L. J. Maland and several colleagues, which was reported in 1983 in the journal *Hypertension.*

The first of these investigations revealed that 15 percent of those with moderate hypertension after a period on therapy could then go off the drugs completely for at least a year, with no return of high blood pressure. The second study found that an even higher proportion, 25 percent, could completely stop drugs for a full year.

What guidelines should you follow in stepping down or stepping off therapy? Here are a few suggestions:

1. *Don't* stop taking medications on your own. Act only with the advice and approval of your physician.

2. *Don't* try going off your medications for a day or so at a time—say, to regain sexual potency you may have lost as a result of the drugs. Antihypertensive medications are designed to be taken regularly, not at intervals of your own choosing.

3. Expect to be on medications for at least a year, and probably longer, before you even consider stopping them.

4. Expect to "step down" gradually on your medication, not to go off it abruptly. Typically, doctors recommend that patients who have been doing well drop their doses by a few milligrams and then doctor and patient watch to see what happens. If all goes well, the doctor may elect to reduce the medication further.

5. Feel free to question your doctor about the possibility of stepping down or stepping off drugs. If he or she seems unreasonably negative about the idea, perhaps you should consult another physician.

6. Vigorously pursue nondrug treatments—such as a low-salt diet, limited alcohol intake, regular aerobic exercise, and stress-reduction techniques. It's highly unlikely that any hypertensive patient will ever be able to stop drug therapy without simultaneously taking nondrug measures to keep hypertension under control.

7. Recognize that *most* people who begin drug treatment can never stop it successfully. Certainly, many reduce their dosages, and most who are disciplined about taking their medications live quite normal lives. But only a minority can eliminate it entirely.

Remaining on antihypertensive medications is certainly no tragedy. In the long run, it's much better to find and stay on a good medication than to become frustrated, throw all drugs aside, and suffer the long-term consequences of uncontrolled high blood pressure. In the final analysis, those who have their blood pressure *under control* are the ones who enjoy the longest, healthiest lives.

6

About Hypotension

Although hypertension typically has no symptoms until major damage has been done to the body, hypotension—excessively low blood pressure—usually *does* have symptoms, such as fatigue, dizziness, or fainting.

How low a reading is too low? It's difficult to generalize, because a measurement that causes symptoms of hypotension in one person may not do so in another individual.

By most current standards, the average normal blood pressure reading for adults is 120/80 mm Hg. The National Institutes of Health consider readings down to 110/70 safe for most people. However, these numerical guidelines are not definitive of what's "safe" or "unsafe," nor of what's "healthy" or "unhealthy." For example, I've encountered a number of people whose "normal" systolic readings were 100 mm Hg or even lower and whose diastolic measurements dipped well below 70.

But these are the exceptions. In general, if a patient not on antihypertensive medication has measurements of 100/70 or below, I'll want to know more about his health—and whether he is experiencing symptoms of hypotension.

In contrast to the hypertensive whose blood pressure is under control *without* drugs, some patients on medications may be "normal" only when their diastolic pressure stays around 85 mm Hg or a bit higher.

One case that comes to mind was an executive whose blood pressure levels ranged from 170/110 to 170/120. He was given a beta blocker to lower his blood pressure, but then he began to complain of lightheadedness.

His physician put him on a twenty-four-hour blood pressure monitoring system, and the man's average blood pressure dropped to an average of 117/75. Such systolic and diastolic readings would be considered normal for many people. But for this patient, blood pressure in this range produced symptoms of hypotension.

Suspecting that the antihypertensive drug was causing the hypotensive reaction, the physician eased up on the dosage. The patient's blood pressure then rose to an average of 130/85, and he no longer felt lightheaded.

Why should this patient experience a symptom of hypotension at a level of 117/75, while others with even lower readings have no symptoms?

The answer is simply that the circulatory systems of some people have become adjusted to higher pressures than those of other people. We're all special individuals, with special needs, whether the issue is blood pressure, food consumption, or the optimum amount of sleep.

To return to our bicycle illustration, imagine two different bikes with different tire sizes. The bicycle with the big tires needs a greater volume of air to give the owner a good ride, while the one with smaller tires needs less air. Also, the recommended pressure in one set of tires will probably be different from the recommendation for the other set.

In the case of our executive, his body *needed* a higher level of blood pressure for him to feel well and to function properly. His inner network of heart pump, resistance in blood vessels, and blood volume was such that at a pressure of 117/75, his brain simply wasn't getting enough blood; thus, his symptom of lightheadedness. With reduced medication, the executive's blood pressure rose to a more comfortable level, and he felt much better.

However, overmedication is just one among many possible causes of hypotension—as you'll see in the following discussion.

What Causes Hypotension— and What You Can Do About It

Unlike our typical approach to hypertension, the treatment of hypotension usually begins with an investigation of certain symptoms, including dizziness; fainting or lightheadedness when sitting or standing up; nausea on sitting; fatigue; drowsiness; headaches; and weakness.

When a patient complains of such problems, his or her doctor may explore several factors that can trigger hypotension. The potential causes of this condition—which will help determine the treatment—run the gamut from overmedication, to circulation problems associated with aging, to serious organic or cardiovascular distress or damage. The following discussion of some of these causes will give you an idea of the range of possibilities.

First Cause of Hypotension: Overmedication

Those on these antihypertensive medications should be especially careful about "orthostatic" (standing) hypotension:

- The sympathetic nervous system inhibitors guanadrel and guanethidine

- The alpha blockers prazosin and terazosin

- The combined alpha-beta blocker labetalol

On the other hand, large doses of practically *any* antihypertensive medicine can precipitate a steep drop in blood pressure, with resulting hypotension.

Older people are particularly vulnerable to this problem. Often they grow accustomed to functioning at higher levels of blood pressure. Their organs and circulatory systems adjust to some degree of hypertension, and a significant reduction in pressure with antihypertensive drugs may trigger symptoms of hypotension.

Why use drugs that may cause hypotension? Sometimes, a powerful antihypertensive drug such as guanethidine (Ismelin) will be prescribed after other drugs have failed to produce results. With guanethidine, the drop in blood pressure tends to be steep and immediate. One of the major side effects is postural hypotension.

Another illustration of how drugs may produce hypotension is the impact of the medications prazosin (Minipress) or terazosin (Hytrin). The side effects of these drugs, as listed by the 1988 Joint Committee, may include fainting after only one dose; "orthostatic" (standing) hypotension; weakness; and heart palpitations.

The committee provides this warning about prazosin and terazosin: "Use cautiously in elderly patients because of orthostatic hypotension." ("The 1988 Report . . .")

Alpha blockers such as prazosin are particularly effective in combating severe hypertension and chronic kidney failure. However, as Dr. Norman Kaplan notes on p. 217 of his book *Clinical Hypertension,* "In the presence of renal [kidney] failure, the hypotensive action is enhanced."

To alleviate the problem of drug-induced hypotension, the physician may cut back on the drug dosage. For example, with prazosin many physicians recommend that the initial daily dose be limited to 1 mg, administered at bedtime. This can minimize the effects of hypotension, including dangers such as falls. Then, dosages can be increased gradually to a level where the drug lowers blood pressure *without* causing hypotension.

However, even small doses of a very strong medication may produce some symptoms of hypotension. In such cases, the doctor may suggest that the patient wear special elastic stockings or panty-hose-type supports that cover both the legs and abdomen. With these devices, pooling of blood in the lower extremities is reduced, and thus blood pressure can be kept at higher levels in the rest of the body.

A related issue is that overmedication with antihypertensive drugs *may* cause serious or even fatal cardiovascular problems. However, don't be alarmed by this, because in most cases, when drugs are carefully and sensitively administered, there's no danger. In fact, there's generally a much *greater* danger for hypertensives who refuse to take their prescribed medications.

On the other hand, in a number of major clinical studies using high doses of drugs, medical researchers have found *no significant decrease* in coronary deaths among participants who were on antihypertensive medications. Even more disturbing, in four out of the nine major studies dealing with this issue, there was actually an *increase* in deaths.

The MRFIT project (the Multiple Risk Factor Intervention Trial, 1982, 1985), for instance, followed the cardiovascular health of thousands of men, ages 37 to 54, over a six-year period. More than 2,500 with various levels of hypertension were given relatively high doses of the diuretic hydrochlorothiazide. Approximately an equal number were *not* given any special additional care for hypertension.

The results: *More* of the mild hypertensives who started with known coronary artery disease (angina or a prior heart attack) and who were on a diuretic drug died of cardiovascular heart disease or other causes than did those who

received no special antihypertensive treatment!
(For purposes of this study, "mild hypertensives" were defined as patients with initial
diastolic pressures of 90 to 94 mm Hg.)

Deaths among those in the more moderate 95
to 99 diastolic range were about the same for
both the specially treated and the "normal care"
groups.

But as diastolic blood pressure increased to
levels of 100 mm Hg or higher, deaths became
more common among the normal-care patients,
as opposed to those specially treated with the
high dosages of diuretics. In other words, the
antihypertensive medications clearly helped those
with the higher blood pressures.

So what are we to conclude from this?

Although those with the most serious cases
of high blood pressure were helped by the drugs,
the high-dosage diuretic treatments did more
harm than good for patients with mild hypertension and underlying heart disease.

According to a 1987 medical editorial in
Acta Medica Scandinavica, referring to various
studies on the link between antihypertensive
medication and death rates: "All these analyses
point in the same direction, i.e., that lowering
BP [blood pressure] too much might precipitate
cardiovascular complications, especially myocardial infarctions [heart attacks]."

What's the reason for the higher death rates

among the mildly hypertensive patients who were treated with diuretics?

Most experts, including those who conducted the study, aren't sure at this point—but they have provided us with some solid possibilities:

To begin with, the key to any meaningful interpretation of the data from the MRFIT project and similar studies is recognizing that the participants on special treatment used *rather large doses of the diuretic*. Typically, the doses of hydrochlorothiazide were about 75 mg per day, whereas most experts recommend a maximum of 50 mg daily and a usual dose of 12.5 to 25 mg.

It's possible that the high dosages of diuretics administered in these trials could lead to serious health problems, including death, for a number of reasons:

- *Reason 1*. Large doses of *any* antihypertensive drug, including diuretics, may cause a drop in blood pressure below the comfortable or safe level for a given individual. The result may be hypotension, where too little blood is flowing to the heart, brain, or other organs.

   How low does the blood pressure have to go with those who are "normally" hypertensive to cause a dangerous hypotensive reaction?

Even a relatively moderate decrease in diastolic pressure below the normal limit of 90 mm Hg may create problems. We saw this phenomenon in the case of the executive who had been overmedicated. So, for many people with high blood pressure—and especially for those with other coronary risk factors, such as fat-clogged blood vessels or angina pains— the diastolic reading may only have to go below about 85 mm Hg for hypotensive symptoms to occur.

The consequences may be quite serious: A drop in blood pressure due to antihypertensive medication may shut down much of the flow of blood to the brain and trigger a "mini-stroke" (a transient ischemic attack, or TIA).

TIAs typically involve many of the symptoms of a full stroke, with paralysis, loss of brain function, or other disabilities. But, unlike a regular stroke, TIAs usually debilitate the person only for a few minutes or hours, with full recovery often occurring within twenty-four hours. However, those who have suffered a TIA are at high risk of experiencing a full stroke within the next five years.

Antihypertensive drugs most frequently associated with hypotension-induced TIAs include the thiazide diuretics and the sympathetic nervous system inhibitor, reserpine.

Another serious threat that accompanies hypotension, especially among the elderly, is the increased chance that dizziness or fainting may cause major injuries from falls.

As I discussed in depth in my previous book *Preventing Osteoporosis,* by the time they reach old age, one-third of all women and one-sixth of all men suffer a hip fracture. And hip fractures result in death in 12 to 20 percent of the cases.

One important defense against broken bones in the later years is to build up your bone mass through the programs I outlined in *Preventing Osteoporosis.* But another way is simply to avoid falling! And one important way for hypertensives on medications to avoid falls is to guard against the symptoms of hypotension.

Although studies are lacking on the link between dangerous hypotension and drugs other than diuretics, I recommend caution: no matter what drug a patient is using, he should be closely monitored for signs of hypotension as his blood pressure declines. If symptoms of low blood pressure appear, the dosage should be reduced or other adjustments made.

- *Reason 2.* Another possible danger in prescribing large doses of diuretics is the condition known as hypokalemia—an excessive loss of potassium from the blood.

Various studies have revealed that 10 to 40 percent of patients on diuretics may develop hypokalemia. This is because the increased urination that accompanies diuretic therapy tends to wash potassium as well as sodium out of the body. So, steps must be taken to replace the lost potassium through supplements or through adjustments to the diet (e.g., including more potassium-rich foods such as cantaloupe, tomatoes, cranberry juice, and bananas).

The mild form of hypokalemia can involve irregular heartbeats (arrhythmias), excessive urination (polyuria), and weakness of the muscles.

The most serious results of low potassium include damage to the heart, kidney, or muscles. Some patients, including those with existing heart conditions or abnormal ECGs (electrocardiograms), may experience such profound irregularities of the heartbeat that death results. Some deaths from heart attacks in the MRFIT project and similar studies may have resulted from such fatal arrhythmias.

In support of this reasoning, *The New England Journal of Medicine* published a report on May 4, 1989, p. 1177, which concluded "that short-term potassium depletion increases blood pressure in healthy, normotensive men and permits further increases in blood pressure after saline loading [an infusion of salt into the blood]."

Because of the potential threats from potassium loss with diuretics, the physician should check his patient's blood potassium level before beginning any drug therapy. Also, it's important for those on diuretics to have their potassium checked at regular intervals to be sure the levels of this element remain stable.

Note: Certain antihypertensive medications such as the ACE inhibitors and potassium-sparing diuretics may actually *raise* the level of potassium in a person's blood. Consequently, these may be desirable alternatives to other diuretics.

- *Reason 3.* Serious health problems or even death among those on diuretics may be due to disturbances in the blood lipid levels, including rises in total cholesterol and triglycerides.

In the six-year MRFIT study, those on diuretic therapy had total cholesterol levels averaging 4 mg/dl higher than did those not on diuretics. (*Note:* mg/dl refers to milligrams per deciliter—the usual way of measuring blood cholesterol.)

In addition, the patients on diuretics had "good" HDL cholesterol that averaged 0.8 mg/dl *less* than the levels of those not on such therapy. Finally, the diuretic-treated patients had triglycerides that were 35 mg/dl higher.

On the whole, then, the lipid picture for those on diuretics—and the level of cardiovascular risk, including heart attacks, related to those lipids—was worse than for those not on diuretic therapy.

- *Reason 4:* Thiazide diuretics may also damage glucose (blood sugar) tolerance and trigger diabetic problems. A 1984 study reported in the *British Medical Journal* by researcher C. Bengtsson and colleagues, along with other, similar investigations, confirmed the link between diuretics and diabetes: in the twelve-year Bengtsson study, an increased risk of diabetes was identified among patients on diuretics. This may be due to a decreased sensitivity to insulin.

- *Reason 5.* Diuretics tend to increase the level of uric acid in the blood (hyperuricemia), a process that may lead to an attack of gout. In most cases, however, the hyperuricemia associated with diuretics doesn't cause symptoms.

   (On the other hand, a *beneficial* effect of diuretics that's not commonly discussed is the effect they may have on the calcium level in the body. In patients with osteoporosis, diuretics may dramatically reduce calcium loss. But note: The diuretic effect of caffeine may have the *opposite* effect by causing calcium to be lost from the body. Specifically, two cups of coffee daily can result in a calcium loss of 100 mg per day.)

   In light of these and similar findings, my recommendations on diuretics and hypotension are as follows:

Recommendation 1. If diuretics are deemed necessary, it's best to keep patients on relatively low doses, if possible. The usual recommended minimum dosage for hydrocholorothiazide, for example, is 12.5 to 25 mg per day, with 50 mg the maximum.

Recommendation 2. When diuretic therapy seems appropriate, it's important to monitor blood potassium levels closely and in most cases to add potassium supplements or high-potassium foods to the diet. The diets included later in this book were designed with this high potassium requirement in mind.

Recommendation 3. Consider other drug options—especially ACE inhibitors, calcium blockers, and alpha blockers. These medications are especially appropriate in cases where potassium loss is a problem. Also, these drugs don't cause blood lipid problems, such as elevating total cholesterol, raising triglycerides, or lowering HDL cholesterol.

Note: The beta blockers (except for pindolol and acebutolol) may lower HDL cholesterol and may raise triglycerides. Still, a very recent study, reported in the April 14, 1989 issue of the *Journal of the American Medical Association,* concluded that beta blockers may prevent first heart attacks in patients with high blood pressure.

Recommendation 4. The patient should be monitored regularly for symptoms of hypotension, no matter which antihypertensive drug is being used. Special care should be taken to identify symptomatic hypotension among the elderly, who are at especially high risk for serious injury from falls or reduced blood flow to the brain and other organs.

Second Cause of Hypotension: Non-Drug-Related Postural Hypotension

You've already been introduced to the problem of postural hypotension—which occurs upon standing—in the preceding discussion of over-medication.

With or without antihypertensive drugs, however, the elderly are at increased risk for dizziness, fainting, and other postural hypotensive symptoms. By some estimates, as many as 10 percent of elderly hospital patients have hypotension. (Rossman, *Clinical Geriatrics,* 3d edition, p. 148.)

What factors other than drugs may promote postural hypotension?

- Eating a meal can result in a drop in blood pressure that might produce fainting and falls in some elderly patients, according to a study published in the February 1989 issue of *Archives of Internal Medicine.* This response presumably reflects an increase in blood flow to the digestive organs, which "steal" the blood away from the rest of the body.

  This study, performed by researchers Peitzman and Berger, involved 16 people, all over 75 years of age. They were active, healthy, and free of cardiovascular disease, and they were taking no blood pressure medications. Eight people younger than 50 years of age were used as controls.

The results: The elderly participants, but not the young ones, showed a significant drop in blood pressure after eating. Although no ill effects were noted in the elderly subjects, the researchers suggested that in less robust subjects, such a hypotensive response could be a factor in fainting and falls.

- A second nondrug factor behind postural hypotension has come to light in another series of studies showing that many of those with excessively low blood pressure may have below-normal blood sodium levels. This condition tends to decrease blood volume, with a resulting reduction of blood pressure and blood flow to the brain.

To overcome the symptoms of postural hypotension, one or more of a variety of treatments may be in order:

First, the physician should be certain that the patient is getting *enough salt*. Paradoxically, this approach is the exact opposite of the treatment for many hypertensives, which typically involves a *reduction* in salt intake. With more salt, the blood volume tends to rise, as does blood pressure.

In addition to increasing salt intake, the hypotensive patient might use some type of lower-body support, such as the elastic stockings mentioned earlier.

Finally, whenever postural hypotension continues to be a problem, it's important for the patient to develop new habits that will minimize the symptoms and dangers. Because one of the biggest threats to health is the tendency to fall upon standing or even sitting up too quickly, those with low blood pressure should be very careful about standing, getting out of bed, or otherwise moving about in such a way that the blood fails to get to the head fast enough.

One technique is simply to move from a sitting to a standing position very slowly. If feelings of dizziness or faintness occur, rise even *more* slowly, or sit back until the discomfort passes and then try again.

As for rising from bed, the patient should first sit up; then he should dangle his legs over the side of the bed; last, he should stand up *very* slowly, supporting himself with the side of the bed or some other sturdy structure.

Third Cause of Hypotension:
Other Cardiovascular or Organic Problems

Sometimes a drop of blood pressure—especially a *sudden* drop—may signal a major problem in the circulatory system. Examples include a hemorrhage in the stomach, a heart attack, or a problem with blood flow to the lungs (such as a pulmonary embolism, or blood clot in the lungs).

As far as heart attacks among older people are concerned, the signs are often different from the typical ones in younger people. Those under about age 60 to 65 frequently complain of chest pains or left-arm discomfort or numbness. Older people, in contrast, may faint or fall from hypotension as the initial symptom of a heart attack.

A similar reaction may result from an obstruction of the blood flow to the lungs due to a clot. Older patients may not notice any particular respiratory problems secondary to the clot; instead, hypotension resulting in a fall may be their initial symptom.

Also, patients with tumors that give off excessive epinephrine (adrenaline) may become dizzy when they stand up. Or they may experience extreme drops in blood pressure and even show signs of shock. Medications to offset this imbalance can be administered by physicians who accurately diagnose the problem.

* * *

Hypotension, then, is the other side of the coin of hypertension. To be sure, there are dangers—sometimes serious ones—that physicians and patients must be aware of when hypotension becomes symptomatic. At the same time, the outlook for treatment is often promising.

Fortunately, unlike hypertension, there *are* symptoms that accompany excessively low blood pressure. After being alerted by these physical signs, the physician can select from a number of proven methods, one of which will control the problem.

7

Sexuality and Hypertension

Many patients are happy to find that the impact of sexual intercourse on blood pressure is quite similar to that of aerobic exercise: Blood pressure goes up during the activity but then declines to near normal soon afterward. Also, the feelings of relaxation or well-being that follow intercourse are reminiscent of the cool-down phase after a workout.

A 1976 study reported by researcher E. D. Nemec and colleagues in the *American Heart Journal* revealed that, like aerobic exercise, sexual intercourse can lead to significant increases in blood pressure. Furthermore, it didn't make much difference what bodily position was used.

In this investigation, ten healthy young men were instructed to have intercourse from an on-top position. The results:

- Their blood pressure averaged 112/66 when they were at rest before the sexual activity, and their heart rate, 67 beats per minute.

- Upon insertion, their blood pressure rose to an average of 148/79, with a heart rate of 136.

- At orgasm, the blood pressure in these young men peaked at 163/81. At this stage, their heart rate was 189—about the expected maximum heart rate during aerobic exercise.

- Two minutes after orgasm, their blood pressure declined to 118/69, or almost normal, and their heart rate was down to 82.

When these men were engaging in sex on the bottom—a position that would seem to involve less isometric tensing of the muscles and hence lower blood pressure—there was practically no difference in their blood pressure:

- At rest before intercourse, their readings averaged 113/70, with a heart rate of 65.

- Upon initiating intercourse, their blood pressure rose to 143/74, while their heart rate accelerated to 136.

- With orgasm, their blood pressure increased to 161/77, and their heart rate reached a peak of 183 beats per minute.

- Finally, two minutes after orgasm, their average blood pressure dropped back to 121/71, and their heart rate was down to 77.

Overall, these blood pressure and heart rate responses are quite similar to those of the average young man before, during, and after aerobic exercise. In addition, the feelings of well-being and pleasant tiredness that often follow intercourse are much like the feelings experienced after aerobic activity.

However, there are some decided differences between sexual intercourse and aerobic exercise. First, from start to finish, the time involved in a sexual encounter is usually less than that in a typical aerobic workout. Heart rates during sexual intercourse usually rise to a high rate and then fall quickly after orgasm, while in aerobic exercise the heart rate stays at a relatively high level for a sustained period of time.

Studies on sudden death suggest that those who are involved in regular aerobic training (at about 70 percent of the maximum heart rate during workouts of 20 to 30 minutes each, three to four times a week) are more likely to develop overall fitness and protection against cardiovascular disease than are those who engage in shorter-term, higher-intensity exercise. Also, people who work out infrequently seem to be at higher cardiovascular risk.

Second, there are certain isometric maneuvers involved in sexual intercourse that usually don't accompany endurance sports such as running, cycling, or swimming. Isometrics, which involve tensing of the muscles (as in weight lifting), are probably responsible for those recorded cases where blood pressure has been driven up as high as 300/175 mm Hg.

When blood pressure rises in people who have hypertension, whether during sexual intercourse or exercise, I become concerned. Any extreme increase in blood pressure may aggravate an existing hypertensive condition and eventually lead to sustained elevation. In some cases, these sudden upward bursts of pressure may trigger serious hypertensive complications, such as a stroke or other target-organ damage.

Following are my basic guidelines for sexual activity in hypertensives:

Those on antihypertensive medication with blood pressure of 160/100 mm Hg or higher (either while on medications or while unmedicated) may be facing a potential hazard from sexual intercourse. I strongly urge that people in this category consult with their physicians before engaging in sex.

Those with uncontrolled hypertension, at a level of 175/110, probably should not engage in sex at all unless they can bring down these readings with medications.

Patients who *can* get their measurements below 160/100 with medications should not worry about having sex. The danger at these lower levels of hypertension are minimal, and fear of possible consequences shouldn't interfere with sexual enjoyment.

Note: As you'll see in chapter 8, I regard an average blood pressure reading of 175/110 mm Hg or higher to be an *absolute contraindication* to exercise. This means that those with such high blood pressure shouldn't exercise at all until they can bring down their measurements. If hypertension remains uncontrolled at these high ranges even on medications, the patient should continue to avoid exercise.

The Question of Impotence

An issue of great concern to many patients on antihypertensive medications is impotence, which may occur to some degree. The most important thing for you to know here is that you have many choices of treatment. Furthermore, one or more of these possibilities will likely enable you to lower your blood pressure *and* enjoy a full and rewarding sex life.

First, many people are able to keep down their blood pressure exclusively through non-drug treatments such as diet, exercise, or relaxation techniques. Far from hindering one's sexual performance, these approaches frequently enhance it!

Second, if a patient must take medications, using the nondrug approaches simultaneously will often lower his pressure on small dosages that don't interfere with sexual capacity.

Finally, if larger doses of drugs are necessary to control the hypertension, a medication such as an ACE inhibitor may be much better (in terms of continuing a normal sex life) than such drugs as diuretics or beta blockers. Physicians often have to experiment to find the best drug for the patient's needs. At the same time, it's incumbent on the patient to keep his doctor informed about both his sexual interests and the side effects he's experiencing.

One 51-year-old man, Robert, was physically and mentally vigorous, and sexually active in his relationship with his wife. An extremely confident man, he had risen near the top of his professional field, and he had experienced no serious health problems.

But then he was diagnosed as hypertensive, with an average blood pressure reading of 165/101. His physician placed him on a beta blocker, which brought his readings down to 140/80 within a few weeks.

Unfortunately, along with the drop in blood pressure, Robert noticed that it was almost impossible for him to have or to maintain an erection.

When he notified his physician, the doctor reduced Robert's daily dose of the beta blocker by about half. With this adjustment, Robert's blood pressure rose slightly, to 150/85, and he was able to have erections at least some of the time, though his ability to perform was considerably less than it had been before he had gone on the drug.

Finally, the doctor switched him to a relatively low dose of an ACE inhibitor and sent him home with this information: "I think this new drug will help a lot because it rarely if ever causes any of the side effects you're experiencing."

Sure enough, Robert's former sexual desire and ability to perform returned completely. Interestingly, though, his blood pressure level with the ACE inhibitor remained the same as it had been on the low dose of the beta blocker—about 150/85.

To understand Robert's case, we must first

consider that scientific studies have demonstrated that with practically *any* antihypertensive drug, sexual inadequacy may be a problem.

In the Medical Research Council Working Party Trial of 1981, scientists found that more than 13 percent of participants on the beta blocker propanolol and nearly 23 percent of those on the thiazide diuretic bendroflumethiazide were impotent after two years of therapy.

At the same time, however, more than 10 percent of those on a placebo (an inactive pill) in this trial also became impotent! The response to the placebo indicates that simply the *belief* that they were on a medication was enough to affect certain patients' sexual performance.

A variation of the placebo effect may have been influencing Robert's situation. First, he experienced impotence as a direct physiologic result of the beta-blocker dosage he initially received.

Then, mental factors may have begun to play a role. He apparently became convinced that *any* dosage of the first medication, the beta blocker, would make him impotent. But when the doctor gave him the ACE inhibitor with the assurance it would have no such side effects, Robert's impotence disappeared—even though his blood pressure stayed at the same level as at the lower dosage of beta blocker.

In many cases, then, sexual performance on

drugs or off may be influenced by mental factors. If a patient believes that a certain drug will
make him impotent, impotence is more likely to
occur. Furthermore, once one or more instances
of impotence occur, it is quite probable that a
kind of "performance anxiety" will begin: The
patient may lose confidence in his ability, and as
his confidence declines so does his ability to
perform.

However, there are some solid physiologic
reasons why impotence may occur with antihypertensive medications.

To return to Robert's case, you'll recall that
he became almost totally impotent with a dramatic drop of about 25 points in his systolic
pressure and 21 points in his diastolic pressure.
It's quite likely that this initial impact of the
medication on his sexual ability resulted from
physical rather than mental causes.

To have and sustain an erection, the blood
flow to the penis must increase by ten times the
normal flow. So, if one's blood pressure is
lowered by medications, it's likely that the
overall reduction will have a negative effect on a
man's ability to have an erection.

Conversely, raising the blood pressure by
reducing the medication may bring back the
patient's sexual ability—as long as psychologi-
cal factors haven't begun to enter the picture.

Some other possible influences of antihypertensive drugs that may lead to impotence or other reduction in sexual capacity include the following:

- The suppression of androgens (male hormones) by the potassium-sparing diuretic spironolactone

- Excessive calming or depression produced by the sympathetic nervous system inhibitors clonidine, reserpine, and methyldopa

- The blocking of impulses through the nerves of the sympathetic nervous system by various inhibiting drugs

- An inability to ejaculate produced by the sympathetic nervous system inhibitors guanethidine, guanadrel, and bethanidine

- The negative action of the alpha blocker prazosin on some of the alpha receptor mechanisms

(Horowitz and Goble, *Drugs*, p. 206.)

Due to the concerns about the impact of drugs, most alert physicians will question their patients closely before putting them on any antihypertensive medication to be certain that there's no preexisting problem with sexual function. In fact, it's been estimated that in as many as one-third of all cases, the impotence associated with high-blood-pressure drugs may already have been present before the administration of the medications.

Finally, a word about women: Up to now, the only solid studies on sexual dysfunction with hypertension or antihypertensive drugs have involved men, mainly because the erection of the penis is easier to observe and track than is female sexual arousal. So the connection between women's sexuality and hypertension is virtually unknown.

For that matter, much still needs to be investigated about the links between male sexuality and hypertension. For example, at present there are no valid studies comparing the impact of various antihypertensive drugs on impotence or related problems. Because of the intense interest in this subject, however, it's likely that in the near future, scientific investigations will produce additional, much-needed information on sexuality and hypertension.

8

Control
Through Exercise

Regular aerobic exercise—such as jogging, running, cycling, and swimming—is one of the most effective nondrug "medicines" for those at risk for hypertension.

But exactly what kind of aerobics program should you try—and, just as important, what kinds of exercise should you avoid?

Although an intelligently designed aerobics program will often help lower blood pressure, some types of physical activity may work *against* your attempt to control your hypertension.

For example, infrequent workouts usually have no beneficial impact on blood pressure. In addition, some muscle-tensing activities, such as weight lifting, may even be dangerous for those with hypertension.

Further, certain people with severe hypertension shouldn't do *any* strenuous exercise unless their blood pressure can be controlled with drugs. This is because athletic activity may trigger a serious health complication, like a stroke, for those whose blood pressure remains too high.

I've established a limit of 175/110 mm Hg for my patients. In other words, if a person's systolic or diastolic measurement doesn't drop below that level with medications, I don't permit vigorous exercise. Even at lower levels of hypertension, the decision regarding exercise should be made by a physician.

Another complexity in this picture is the question of exercise while taking beta-blocker medications. These drugs reduce the blood pressure by lowering the heart rate. But working out with a significantly lowered heart rate will affect performance, cause symptoms in some people, and definitely place a limit on the aerobic effect achievable by beta-blocker-treated patients.

To get the maximum benefit from exercise under such conditions, it's helpful to make use of a special formula for determining the target heart rate, which I'll discuss later.

Now, let's examine more closely what happens to blood pressure during different types of exercise.

What Happens to Blood Pressure During Aerobic Exercise

Either the systolic or the diastolic blood pressure, or both, go up during exercise. But the short-term *and* long-term responses of blood pressure can vary considerably, depending on the type of exercise in which the person engages and upon his or her overall health and physical fitness.

For example, a highly conditioned 21-year-old who was examined at the Aerobics Center was found to have a normal blood pressure of 114/72 mm Hg before he exercised on the treadmill.

As he began to walk and the work load increased, his systolic pressure rose steadily. During this first phase of the exercise, which lasted about twenty-five minutes, he was exercising aerobically. That is, he was consuming oxygen at about the same rate as he was expending it.

But by the thirtieth minute, he was exercising *an*aerobically—he was expending more oxygen than he was able to take in. At this point, he attained a maximum heart rate of 195 beats per minute, and a systolic blood pressure of 220 mm Hg. Finally, he was unable to continue because of exhaustion.

His diastolic pressure during the test dropped to a level lower than at the baseline (his initial, resting blood pressure measurement)—or about 60 mm Hg. This rise in the systolic but decline in the diastolic pressure during exercise is typical of a well-conditioned athlete of any age.

Also, note that both the systolic and diastolic pressures continued to decline during the ten-minute recovery. In fact, in the post-exercise resting phase, it's not uncommon for both the systolic and diastolic pressures to drop below their baseline levels in highly conditioned subjects.

Other clinical observations have revealed that these lower levels of blood pressure after exercise may persist for a half hour or longer. Then, the measurements creep back up to the original, baseline levels. A possible explanation for this phenomenon of lower blood pressure following aerobic exercise has been presented on pages 44–45 of chapter 2.

Normal Blood Pressure Response in a Highly Conditioned Man

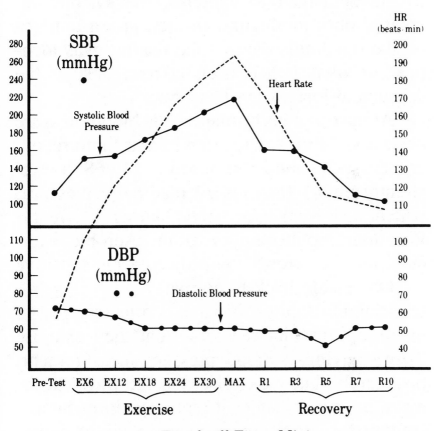

Treadmill Time (Min)

In my second example, the patient is a true "vascular reactor." In particular, he suffers from the "white-coat" or "doctor's office" syndrome. This man is highly conditioned, as indicated by his treadmill performance, which exceeded twenty-five minutes. But *prior* to stress testing, his systolic blood pressure was elevated at

170/74, and his heart rate was 80. In such a fit person, I would have expected a heart rate lower than 60, and also a lower systolic pressure.

As he began to exercise, the systolic increased only minimally. In fact, at ten minutes on the treadmill, the systolic reading was identical to what it had been at rest, despite the substantial increase in heart rate.

At maximal performance, his blood pressure peaked at 240/60. Then, ten minutes into recovery, the measurement dropped to 139/68, a level slightly higher than his average daily pressure, which had been ascertained during a twenty-four-hour monitoring program. Aerobic exercise, in other words, had lowered his sensitive blood pressure back to normal.

In light of cases like this, I often suggest to my true "vascular reactors" that they exercise *before* having a blood pressure measurement. Such preliminary exercise and the physical fatigue that accompanies it typically eliminate any "emotional" response associated with the white-coat phenomenon.

Another related point: In those with true hypertension, a post-exercise normal blood pressure, though temporary, *may* signal that exercise will be effective in treating hypertension—and that drugs may not be required.

A "Vascular Reactor" with "White-Coat" Syndrome (Systolic Pressure Only)

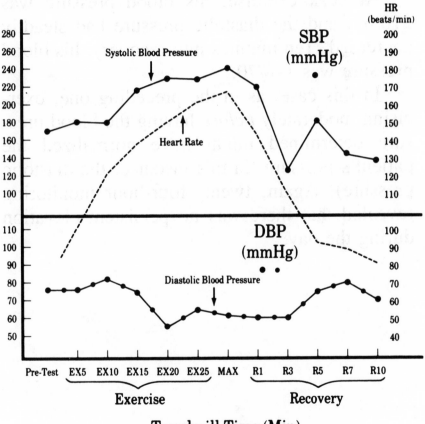

My next illustration involves another type of "vascular reactivity," but one limited to changes in the *diastolic* pressure. When this person was at rest immediately prior to stress testing, his pressure was elevated at 140/100. But the patient was in outstanding physical condition, as indicated by the time he was able to stay on the treadmill (more than twenty-five minutes).

At peak exercise, his blood pressure was 210/65, and the diastolic pressure had steadily decreased. Ten minutes into recovery, his blood pressure was 118/70.

In this case, as in the preceding one, exercising moderately *before* having the blood pressure determined might have normalized the patient's pressure (in this instance, the diastolic pressure). Again, twenty-four-hour monitoring revealed that there was no persistent elevation during the day.

A "Vascular Reactor" with "White-Coat" Syndrome (Diastolic Elevation Only)

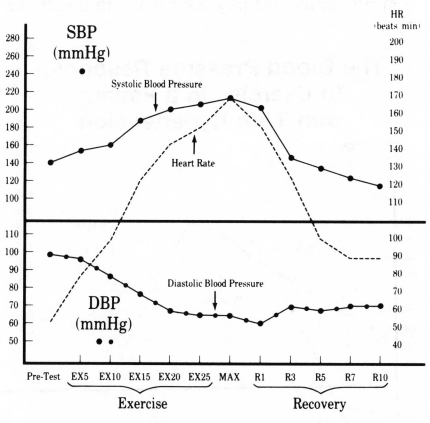

SBP (mmHg)

Systolic Blood Pressure

Heart Rate

HR (beats/min)

DBP (mmHg)

Diastolic Blood Pressure

Pre-Test EX5 EX10 EX15 EX20 EX25 MAX R1 R3 R5 R7 R10

Exercise   Recovery

Treadmill Time (Min)

In true hypertension, as reflected in the next graph, the blood pressure is elevated at rest (i.e., 140/102 mm Hg). With exercise in this case, the systolic pressure increases substantially, to levels of 260 mm Hg or higher. Then, during recovery, it drops only to the preexercise level.

The diastolic pressure in this third example doesn't change substantially.

Note: The maximum blood pressure usually considered acceptable during exercise is 240/120 mm Hg. Unless the physician is familiar with the

The Blood Pressure Response to Exercise in a Patient with True Hypertension

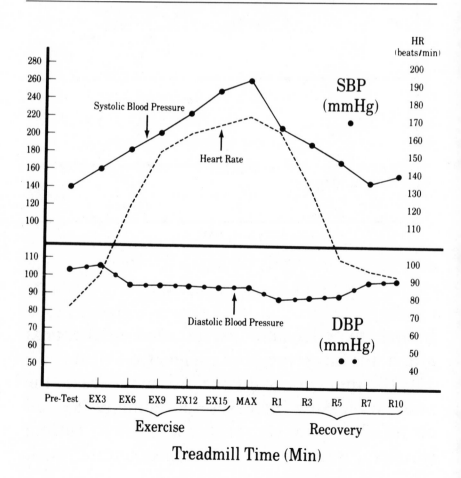

patient (as was the situation here), I recommend termination of an exercise test or of a workout if either the systolic or diastolic levels exceed those values.

My view may seem extremely conservative, since systolic pressure frequently exceeds 240 mm Hg during weight lifting. But in general, I believe it's best to be as cautious and safe as possible in dealing with any above-normal elevation in pressures during exercise.

Among people who are in poor physical condition, the blood pressure response following maximal performance may involve symptoms of hypotension or near-fainting. In the following graph, you can see that the preexercise blood pressure in one such case was low normal, at 90/70 mm Hg. In response to exercise, the systolic pressure steadily increased, but peaked at only 158 mm Hg, whereas the diastolic pressure steadily declined.

During recovery, the systolic pressure dropped immediately to below 80 mm Hg. As a result, the walking cool-down had to be stopped to prevent the patient from fainting. He was then placed in the supine position, at which point his pressure began to rise.

By ten minutes into the recovery phase, his pressure was normal at 100/50 mm Hg. He had no further problems but was advised to enter a slowly progressive conditioning program. Also, he was told not to exercise vigorously unless he could do so under medical supervision.

This post-exercise, hypotensive, near-fainting response is most commonly seen in deconditioned or unfit people. But it can appear in anyone, man or woman, fit or unfit, if the person is pushed to total exhaustion—or to what I call the "supermax" level of exercise.

For instance, look at the number of people who are "walking zombies," or nearly unconscious on their feet, after a marathon. In this condition, I usually recommend that the individual keep moving, with support if necessary, to help the return of blood from the legs into the general circulation.

If people in this situation can keep moving, their recovery time usually will be accelerated. When they must lie down, however, it may take two to three times as long for their bodies to readjust. Should walking be impossible, even in a stooped-over position, I recommend that the person assume the supine position, with feet elevated, until the blood pressure response is normal or the symptoms disappear.

The Hypotensive or Near-Fainting Response with Exercise

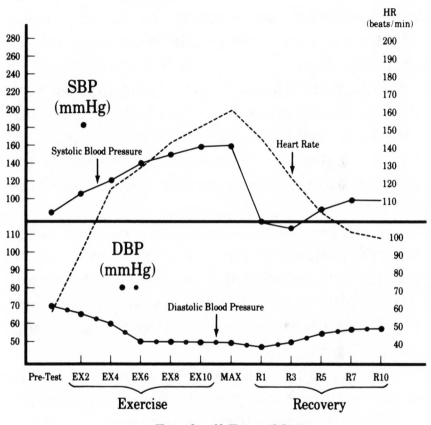

Treadmill Time (Min)

A rare but potentially dangerous blood pressure response sometimes occurs while taking a stress test. Called "cardiac or heart decompensation with exercise," this condition is characterized by decreasing heart rate and systolic blood pressure, even in the presence of an increasing work load. (See the graph on page 297.)

Notice that the patient whose case is presented there walked twelve minutes on the treadmill, but that he reached the peak systolic pressure at five minutes and peak heart rate at eight minutes.

Unless the physician is very familiar with the patient, I advise that the stress test be discontinued whenever the heart rate or systolic pressure begins to drop with demanding exercise. If the exercise isn't stopped, cardiac failure can occur abruptly.

The physical condition of this patient, which *was* well known to the physician, didn't lead to any problems during this particular test or later. You'll also notice that the blood pressure and heart rate responses during recovery were normal.

In teaching physicians proper treadmill stress-testing techniques, I always use this patient's response as an example of an "abnormal" test, even though the electrocardiogram may be completely normal. The majority of such patients have underlying, moderate to severe heart disease, and their exercise programs must be limited to participation in cardiac rehabilitation classes.

Cardiac Decompensation Occurring with Exercise

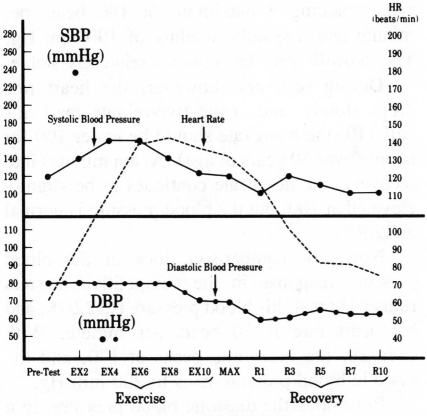

In my final examples, I want to document the heart rate and blood pressure responses in two men, 50 years of age, one in average physical condition, the other a highly competitive masters runner.

In the first example—the man in average shape—the blood pressure at rest is normal (120/80 mm Hg), and the heart rate is 68 beats per minute. Both the heart rate and blood pressure in this patient increase steadily with exercise, reaching a maximum of 180 beats per minute and a systolic reading of 190 mm Hg. The diastolic pressure remains relatively stable.

During recovery, however, the heart rate drops slowly, and at the five-minute mark it's still 110 (the heart rate should be under 100 for people over 50 years of age). At ten minutes into recovery, the heart rate continues to be slightly elevated at 100, but the blood pressure is normal at 120/70.

Now, for comparison, look at the blood pressure response in the competitive masters runner. At rest, his blood pressure is 122/78, and his heart rate is 50 beats per minute. With exercise, the heart rate peaks at 170, and the systolic blood pressure rises to 200 mm Hg.

But notice the diastolic blood pressure: In a manner characteristic of a highly conditioned person, it actually *drops* during the increasing work load. In the initial minutes of recovery, the heart rate decreases rapidly, and by the fifth minute it's only 85.

This type of accelerated drop in heart rate during recovery is seen in well-trained endurance athletes and in people with near-"syncopal" (fainting) responses. In this particular case, the readings were indicative only of an exceptional level of fitness.

By ten minutes into the recovery phase, the conditioned man's blood pressure was again normal, at 120/68 mm Hg, and his heart rate had stabilized at 85 beats per minute.

Because of the need to "repay" the oxygen debt incurred with exhaustive exercise, you can't expect the recovery heart rate to return to the preexercise levels until one and a half or two hours have elapsed. (But note: There's a continuing benefit with the higher heart rate. Your body continues to burn calories during the recovery that follows exhaustive and demanding exercise!)

Blood Pressure and Heart Rate Response (A 50-Year-Old Man in Average Condition)

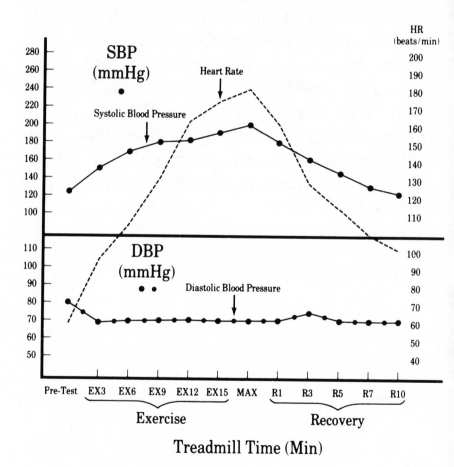

Blood Pressure and Heart Rate Response (A Highly Conditioned 50-Year-Old Man)

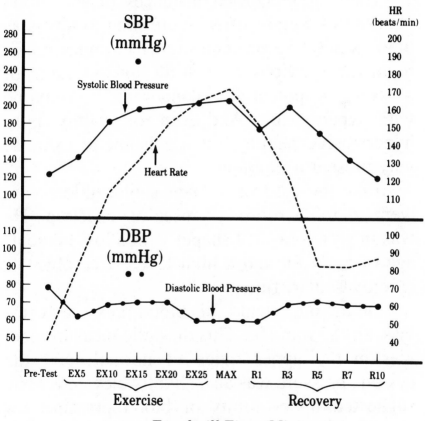

Treadmill Time (Min)

The dangers of isometric exercise. Any exercise that involves relatively static tensing of the muscles over a period of several seconds is known as isometric exercise. The most common examples of this type of activity include weight training, or the lifting of any heavy object. In fact, calisthenics, such as push-ups or supine straight leg lifts, may have an isometric component and should be avoided by those with uncontrolled hypertension.

There are recorded instances of the blood pressure of weight lifters increasing to levels as high as 300/150 or even higher during a maximum lift. Obviously, such an upward surge of pressure is potentially dangerous for anyone with hypertension. And even for healthy, non-hypertensive people, intense isometic exercise may present a problem.

Take the case of a 17-year-old athlete who went in for a routine, preseason checkup. He was in great physical shape, with a low percentage of body fat and a high level of aerobic, or cardiovascular, fitness.

On the other hand, his blood pressure at rest was 150/85 mm Hg. This diastolic measurement was in the upper range of normal, and the systolic pressure was also slightly elevated. (The suggested upper limits of blood pressure for children 14 to 18 years of age are 135/90 mm Hg.)

This young patient's systolic pressure—according to the 1988 Joint National Committee's guidelines for hypertension among young people—placed him in the 99th percentile for systolic pressure among all 16-to-18-year-olds. Such a measurement qualified this adolescent as potentially at risk for significant systolic hypertension.

Later exams during the next one to two months confirmed that the boy did indeed have a high systolic blood pressure. In addition, the readings were not the result of the "white-coat" phenomenon: during the preceding two annual exams, his pressure had been normal.

Upon further questioning, the doctor learned that the boy had engaged in heavy weight training during the past two years, and even more vigorously throughout the preceding summer.

The physician determined that this weight training was the *only* unusual risk factor that might account for his hypertension. Consequently, he requested that the boy discontinue his weight training entirely and concentrate on aerobic activities such as running.

This recommendation met with some resistance because the youngster wanted to be as big and strong as possible for football. But he finally complied with his doctor's advice.

When the boy's blood pressure was reevaluated a month later, both the systolic and diastolic readings had begun to decline. They continued to drop even more during the succeeding months as the boy minimized his weight training.

Note: This example *doesn't* mean that all weight training causes hypertension. But frequent blood pressure monitoring should be done for those who engage in heavy weight lifting.

The higher blood pressure produced by isometric exercise has been confirmed in a number of studies, including one reported in the *Archives of Internal Medicine* in 1984. There, researcher M. H. Maxwell and several other investigators compared the differences in blood pressure responses among normotensive patients who engaged first in aerobic exercise, then in isometric exercise.

The scientists discovered that when the participants did isometric exercises, systolic pressure increased from an average of 120 to more than 220 mm Hg. The diastolic pressure increased from slightly above 80 to an average to 140 mm Hg.

In contrast, when the participants engaged in aerobic activity, the systolic pressure increased from 120 to 180 mm Hg. The difference in diastolic readings was even more dramatic: the diastolic pressures of the aerobic exercisers actually *declined* from an average of 80 to well below 60 mm Hg! (You'll note that this finding is consistent with our report from the Aerobics Center, illustrated on page 287 earlier in this chapter.)

My conclusion: Since there is an exaggerated

increase in both the systolic and diastolic blood pressures during heavy weight lifting, such activity should be avoided both by hypertensives *and* by those with normal blood pressure.

On the other hand, aerobic (endurance-type) exercise has been shown to have the opposite effect, as we'll see in the following section.

Endurance Exercise Can Lower Blood Pressure

Many studies have demonstrated the benefits of aerobic exercise in lowering blood pressure.

Recognizing these findings, an article published in "Hypertension," the 1988 Consensus Conference on Exercise, Fitness and Health reported: "Individuals with essential hypertension can decrease their resting systolic and diastolic blood pressure by approximately 10 mm Hg with endurance exercise training."

Here's an example of how this principle can work:

A 40-year-old man weighed 169 pounds and had a blood pressure reading of 118/91 mm Hg—i.e., a mildly elevated diastolic pressure. Subsequently, he embarked on an exercise program designed by Dr. Salah el-Dean and colleagues at the School of Pharmacy at the University of Mississippi. The program required the participant to begin exercising on a rowing machine for fifteen minutes three times a week, with a gradual increase in rowing time to forty-five minutes per session.

After seven months, this man experienced an 8 percent decline in weight. Also, his blood pressure dropped to 111/81, or well within the normal range.

Although this is a single case history, similar results have been reported frequently, both in ordinary clinical situations and in larger studies. For example:

- The 1988 U.S. Railroad Study found that over a twenty-year period, middle-aged men with lower levels of physical fitness—as revealed by their higher heart rates during submaximal exercise—are at greater risk of dying from coronary heart disease, cardiovascular disease, and other causes. Most important for our purposes, these researchers noted that the higher death risk for these men is *"largely due to higher blood pressure levels."* (Emphasis by Dr. Cooper.)

- During a sixteen-week aerobic exercise program conducted at the Aerobics Center in Dallas, endurance exercise significantly lowered the blood pressure of mildly hypertensive patients.

    Investigator John Duncan and several

colleagues, reporting in the *Journal of the American Medical Association,* found that the systolic pressures dropped from an average of 146.3 to 133.9 mm Hg, and the diastolic readings from 94.3 to 87.2 mm Hg.

The exercise program utilized in this study consisted of three one-hour sessions per week and included the following activities: (1) a 10 to 15 minute warm-up; (2) a walking and jogging phase of about 40 minutes, at 70 to 80 percent of maximal heart rate; and (3) a 10-minute cool-down period. As the program progressed and the participants achieved higher levels of fitness, the jogging was increased and the walking was decreased.

- Twelve hypertensive Japanese patients were placed on a mild aerobic exercise program for ten to twenty weeks, according to researcher Akira Kiyonaga's report in the journal *Hypertension.*

  The results: There was a significant reduction in plasma catecholamine levels. Also, after ten weeks, the researchers noted a reduction in average systolic/diastolic pressures of more than 20/10 mm Hg in 50 percent of the patients. After the full twenty-week program, 78 percent of the participants experienced a similar reduction in blood pressure.

Clearly, then, the cardiovascular fitness produced by aerobic exercise can have a beneficial effect on lowering blood pressure. However, patients on antihypertensive medications such as beta blockers, which limit heart rate, have sometimes found it difficult to achieve higher levels of cardiovascular fitness. What can be done for them?

The Answer for Those on Beta Blockers

Those on beta blockers often find that they can't reach the heart rates during exercise necessary to achieve an aerobic training effect—i.e., the target heart rate zone. The reason: Their hearts simply won't pump fast enough. The drug in effect places a "governor" on their maximum heart rate response, and they become fatigued at a much lower level.

But those on antihypertensive medications need not despair about improving their cardiovascular conditioning—because, first of all, there are alternatives to beta blockers. Our researchers at the Institute for Aerobics Research in Dallas determined in a 1989 investigation that a beta blocker (in this case propranolol) does indeed limit the training effect of endurance exercise, but an ACE inhibitor (fosinopril) has relatively little impact.

In this study, hypertensive men taking the ACE inhibitor increased their treadmill performance time by an average of 3.4 minutes after a 12-week exercise program. Those on the beta blocker, however, increased their time by only 1.1 minutes. The men on a placebo only did slightly better than those on the ACE inhibitor: They improved their time by 3.7 minutes.

Sometimes, a physician may feel that a beta blocker is still the best medication, despite the negative effect on endurance conditioning. But even when beta blockers must be used, there is evidence that exercise is worthwhile, as the following experience suggests.

Tom, a reasonably well-conditioned 40-year-old, had a maximum heart rate of 185 beats per minute. This means that when he exercised to exhaustion, his heart rate peaked at that rate.

If he tried to push himself beyond that point, he became exhausted and had either to stop exercising or to cut back sharply on his activity until he "caught his breath."

When a *normotensive* person embarks on a standard aerobic exercise program, he is usually advised to exercise at an intensity that requires him to work out at 70 to 80 percent of his maximum heart rate for twenty to thirty minute periods, three to four times a week. The exercises in which such a person might engage include walking, jogging, swimming, cycling, or any other endurance activity that will elevate his rate to the "target heart zone" known to produce an aerobic training effect.

But a physical exam revealed that Tom was hypertensive, with a blood pressure averaging 155/98. Subsequent checkups confirmed this finding. As a result, he was placed on a beta blocker, which dropped his blood pressure to normal. Unfortunately, the drug also reduced his maximum heart rate from 185 to 153 beats per minute.

The questions that Tom confronted were: "Is there any point in my continuing to exercise?" And if so, "What should my target heart rate be?"

In answering these questions, our Aerobics Center staff, led by researcher John Duncan, has concluded that those on beta blockers should indeed continue to exercise. To assist these patients, we've devised the following formula so that those on this medication can quickly and accurately find their target heart rates. *Important:* Our research up to now has only confirmed a formula that applies to men on "noncardioselective" beta blockers, including Corgard (nadolol) and Inderal (propranolol). Also, the formula applies only to dosages of these drugs ranging from 10 to 160* mg. Further research will undoubtedly give us other formulas that can be used by all those on beta blockers.

First, the formula used to determine the patient's maximum heart rate is 195, minus 80 percent of his age, minus 20 percent of the dose of the drug.

Taking Tom's case as an example, assume that he began to take 50 mg per day of a beta blocker. Also, we know that he's 40 years old. So, we have 195 minus 80 percent of 40 years (= 32), minus 20 percent of 50 mg (= 10), equals 153 beats per minute for the maximal heart rate.

Then, to get the target heart rate at which endurance exercise should be conducted, the patient should use this standard formula:

Take 80 percent of the maximum heart rate (in this case, 153 x .80 = 122.4), and the result is the heart rate necessary to obtain a training effect.

At the Institute for Aerobics Research, we've conducted extensive research on the effect of beta blockers on exercise training. Here are some of our major conclusions, which should be helpful for you to keep in mind as guidelines if you're on beta blockers:

*Total dosage of medication each day.

1. Those on beta blockers can expect to improve their aerobic fitness with endurance exercise.

2. The "selective blockers" like Tenormin (atenolol) are preferable to "nonselective blockers" such as Inderal (propranolol).

3. Even selective blockers may impair exercise ability in some hypertensive patients; so physicians should watch for this problem and be ready to prescribe other medications. One possibility: Recent research has suggested that the alpha blocker Minipress is preferred by hypertensive joggers to the selective beta blocker atenolol. The reason: Atenonol lowers the output of the heart during exercise.

4. Any exercise program for a person on beta blockers should be based on the results of a testing of individual exercise performance while the person is on the medication.

5. Exercise training during beta-blocker therapy may offset the lowering of HDL ("good") cholesterol by the drug.

6. Nonselective beta blockers like propranolol may make a patient more susceptible to overheating during exercise. As a result, those on beta blockers should observe strict guidelines for the prevention of heat injury.

Obviously, the training effect while exercising on beta blockers will be less than while exercising without such medication. Still, I strongly recommend exercise for those on beta blockers, provided that their physicians concur. Aerobic exercise can be an extremely important and powerful tool in lowering blood pressure and should be employed whenever possible, even in conjunction with beta-blocker therapy.

Now, with this background about the benefits of exercise, let's move on to some special therapy programs designed specifically for those with high blood pressure.

Exercise Programs as Therapy for Hypertension

The following exercises are recommended especially for those who have been diagnosed with hypertension or who have a tendency to develop it.

I've purposely excluded exercises that require tensing or straining, such as heavy weight training or highly resistant calisthenics (such as push-ups). These are known to raise blood pressure levels. Yet, if your hypertension is only mild, your physician may allow or even recommend light muscle-building activities.

For example, you may be at risk for osteoporosis. Therefore, your doctor may feel that even though you are mildly hypertensive, you should engage in additional weight-bearing exercises to increase your bone density. I've included a number of such exercises in my book *Preventing Osteoporosis*.

However, any decision to add weight-bearing exercises to the suggested programs should be made *only* in consultation with your physician.

Following are four other guidelines you should follow with these exercise programs:

1. Remember—blood pressure measurements greater than 175/110 mm Hg, with or without medication, are a *contraindication* to *any* vigorous exercise program. Only when *both* the systolic and diastolic readings can be controlled with medication is vigorous exercise permitted. **Important:** This limitation includes the exercise programs found in this book as well as those from other sources.

2. Be sure to have a thorough physical exam before embarking on this program. If hypertension is diagnosed, proceed only with the full knowledge and supervision of your physician.

3. If your blood pressure is 160/105 or higher, begin an exercise program *only* after your doctor has started you on appropriate drug

therapy. Your response to such therapy will determine the point at which you can embark on an exercise program.

4. If you are on drugs for hypertension when you begin this program, reduce the dosages of those drugs *only* with the permission of your physician.

The Exercise Program for Hypertension

Walking

	Distance	Time Goals (min)				
			Age (years)			
Week	(miles)	<30	30–49	50–59	60+	Freq/wk
1	1.0	16:00	17:00	19:00	22:00	4–5x
2	1.0	14:00	15:00	17:00	20:00	4–5x
3	1.5	22:00	24:00	26:00	30:00	4–5x
4	1.5	21:00	23:00	25:00	29:00	4–5x
5	2.0	29:00	32:00	34:00	39:00	4–5x
6	2.0	28:00	31:00	33:00	38:00	4–5x
7	2.5	36:00	40:00	42:00	48:00	4–5x
8	2.5	35:00	39:00	41:00	47:00	4–5x
9	3.0	43:00	48:00	50:00	57:00	4–5x
10	3.0	42:30	47:00	49:00	55:00	4–5x
11	3.0	42:00	46:00	48:00	53:00	4–5x
12	3.0	<42:00	<45:00	<47:00	<51:00	3–4x

By week 12, an adequate aerobic fitness level has been reached and should be maintained by walking the prescribed distance in the allotted time. Exercising four to five times per week is recommended, but even three times per week is enough to assure a satisfactory level of fitness.

<Means "less than."

Swimming

	Distance	Time Goals (min)				
			Age (years)			
Week	(yards)	<30	30–49	50–59	60+	Freq/wk
1	200	6:00	7:00	8:00	8:00	4–5x
2	300	9:00	9:30	10:00	11:00	4–5x
3	400	12:00	12:00	13:00	14:00	4–5x
4	450	13:00	13:00	14:00	15:00	4–5x
5	500	14:00	14:00	15:00	16:00	4–5x
6	600	16:00	17:00	18:00	19:00	4–5x
7	600	skip	skip	17:00	18:00	4–5x
8	700	18:00	19:00	20:00	21:00	4–5x
9	700	skip	skip	19:30	20:00	4–5x
10	800	20:00	21:00	22:00	23:00	3–4x
11	900	22:30	24:00	25:00	26:00	3–4x
12	1000	<25:00	<26:30	<28:00	<30:00	3–4x

Use the stroke that enables you to swim the required distance in the allotted time. During the initial weeks, rest when necessary (this is taken into consideration in the time goals). The programs for the under 30 and 30 to 39 age groups are only 10 weeks in duration, so skip the weeks indicated. Try to reach the time goals by the end of the week and if the goal cannot be reached, repeat the week.

The three stretching exercises used in conjunction with the Aqua-Aerobics Program (see pages 323–325) should be used prior to beginning to swim.

<Means "less than."

Stationary Cycling

| | | Time Goals (min) | | | | |
| | | Age (years) | | | | |
Week	Speed (mph/rpm)	<30	30–49	50–59	60+	Freq/wk
1	15/55	8:00	6:00	5:00	4:00	4–5x
2	15/55	10:00	8:00	7:00	6:00	4–5x
3	15/55	12:00	10:00	9:00	8:00	4–5x
4	17.5/65	14:00	12:00	11:00	10:00	4–5x
5	17.5/65	16:00	14:00	13:00	12:00	4–5x
6	17.5/65	18:00	16:00	15:00	14:00	4–5x
7	17.5/65	20:00	18:00	17:00	16:00	4–5x
8	17.5/65	22:00	20:00	19:00	18:00	4–5x
9	20/75	24:00	22:00	21:00	20:00	4–5x
10	20/75	26:00	24:00	23:00	22:00	4–5x
11	25/90	28:00	26:00	25:00	24:00	4–5x
12	25/90	30:00	28:00	27:00	25:00	4–5x

During the first 6 weeks, warm up by cycling slowly for 3 minutes, at 18 to 20 mph, with no resistance, before beginning the actual workout. At the conclusion of the exercise, cool down by cycling for 3 minutes without resistance.

Add enough resistance or cycle fast enough that the pulse rate counted for 10 seconds immediately after exercise and multiplied by 6 equals these heart rates:

Patients Not on Beta Blockers

Less than 30 years of age	140–160
30–49 years of age	135–155
50–59 years of age	130–150
60+ years of age	110–130

Patients on Beta Blockers

Those on beta blockers should adjust their heart rates accordingly. If the pulse rate is higher, lower the resistance before exercising again; if it is lower, increase the resistance.

Treadmill Walking

			Time Goals (min)				
	Speed			*Age (years)*			
Week	*(mph)*	*Incline (%)*	*<30*	*30–49*	*50–59*	*60+*	*Freq/wk*
1	3.0	0%	20:00	18:00	15:00	10:00	4–5x
2	3.0	0%	20:00	18:00	16:00	12:00	4–5x
3	3.25	0%	20:00	18:00	16:00	12:00	4–5x
4	3.25	0%	22:00	20:00	18:00	14:00	4–5x
5	3.5	0%	22:00	20:00	18:00	15:00	4–5x
6	3.5	5%	24:00	22:00*	20:00*	16:00*	4–5x
7	4.0	5%	24:00	22:00	20:00	16:00	4–5x

	Speed			Time Goals (min)			
				Age (years)			
Week	(mph)	Incline (%)	<30	30–49	50–59	60+	Freq/wk
8	4.0	7½%	26:00	24:00	22:00	18:00	4–5x
9	4.0	7½%	28:00	26:00	24:00	20:00	4–5x
10	4.0	10%	30:00	28:00	25:00	22:00	4–5x

*Beginning with week 6, the following inclines can be used to increase the work load and aerobic benefit:

Age (years)

Week	30–49	50–59	60+
6	5%	2½%	0%
7	5%	2½%	0%
8	7½%	5%	2½%
9	7½%	5%	2½%
10	10%	7½%	5%

Always warm up for 3 to 5 minutes at 2 mph, no incline, and cool down for 5 minutes at 2 mph, no incline.

These programs assume that the treadmill is motor driven, not self-propelled.

Exercising four to five times per week is recommended, but even three times per week is enough to assure a satisfactory level of fitness.

Cycling (outdoors)

		Time Goals (min)				
	Distance		*Age (years)*			
Week	*(miles)*	*<30*	*30–49*	*50–59*	*60 + * *	*Freq/wk*
1	4.0	24:00	25:00	27:00	30:00	4–5x
2	4.0	22:00	23:00	25:00	28:00	4–5x
3	4.0	20:00	22:00	24:00	27:00	4–5x
4	5.0	28:00	30:00	32:00	36:00	4–5x
5	5.0	26:00	29:00	31:00	35:00	4–5x
6	5.0	24:00	27:00	29:00	34:00	4–5x
7	6.0	32:00	36:00	38:00	44:00	4–5x
8	6.0	30:00	34:00	36:00	42:00	4–5x
9	6.0	28:00	33:00	35:00	40:00	4–5x
10	7.0	37:00	41:00	44:00	49:00	4–5x
11	7.0	35:00	38:00	41:00	47:00	4–5x
12	7.0	<33:00	<35:00	<38:00	<45:00	4–5x

By week 12, an adequate level of aerobic fitness has been reached and should be maintained by cycling the prescribed distance in the allotted time. Exercising four to five times per week is recommended. But even three times per week is enough to assure a satisfactory level of fitness.

*Cycling outdoors is not usually recommended for the totally inactive person past 60 years of age. But when a regular cyclist reaches 60, it is recommended that the cycling be continued without restrictions. To avoid problems including falls and fractures, three-wheeled cycling is encouraged, and this progressive program is designed for that type of bicycle.

< Means "less than."

Introduction to Aqua-Aerobics

Aqua-aerobics are exercises that you do while standing in a swimming pool or holding on to the sides of the pool. The main work occurs as a result of your pushing your limbs and trunk through the resistance of the water (see pages 339–340, "A Note on the Physics of Water Exercise").

These exercises can produce strength and aerobic conditioning. They are ideal for those with bone, joint, or muscle problems that are aggravated by activities done on land, against the force of gravity.

The first step is to warm up with some stretching exercises. Then, move on to the main aqua-aerobics workout. A graduated system of age-adjusted repetitions has also been included.

(*Note:* The source for all the following aqua-aerobics exercises and the accompanying illustrations is the *Aerobics* newsletter, copyright 1981, Institute for Aerobics Research.)

The Aqua-Aerobics Exercises

Stretching Exercise 1

1. Place your right foot flat against the pool wall.

2. Stretch forward, moving your upper body toward the knee. Keep the back straight and the chin up or bent slightly forward.

3. Hold for 10 to 20 seconds, then repeat for left leg.

This movement stretches the hamstrings, the calf muscles, and the lower back.

Stretching Exercise 2

1. Place both feet against the pool wall and hold on to the edge with both hands. Knees and elbows are bent. Hold for 10 to 20 seconds.

2. Slowly stretch out your legs while straightening your elbows and knees. Your feet should be flat against the wall. Hold for 10 to 20 seconds.

This exercise also stretches the hamstrings, the calf muscles, and the lower back.

Stretching Exercise 3

1. Place your left foot 12 to 18 inches behind your right foot. Both hands should be flat against the pool wall, with toes pointing straight ahead.

2. Lean toward the pool wall, keeping your left knee straight and your left foot flat on the pool bottom.

3. Hold this position for 10 to 20 seconds, then repeat the movement for the right leg.

This exercise stretches the calf muscles and the Achilles tendon.

Arm Exercise 1

1. Place one foot in front of the other and bend your knees so that your shoulders are under water. Your arms should be held straight out to the sides, palms facing down.

2. With both arms working, inscribe figure 8s with your hands in the water. Keep your fingers together and your elbows and arms straight.

3. Begin with 10 repetitions, then follow the age-adjusted recommendations in the chart on page 334.

Arm Exercise 2

1. Place one foot in front of the other and bend your knees so that your shoulders are under water. Your arms should be held straight out in front of you, with palms facing down.

2. Swing your arms down by your sides and behind you, keeping your fingers together and your arms straight.

3. Rotate your arms so that the palms face forward and swing them back up. Throughout these motions, keep your arms completely under water.

4. Begin with 10 repetitions and then follow the age-adjusted recommendations in the chart on page 334.

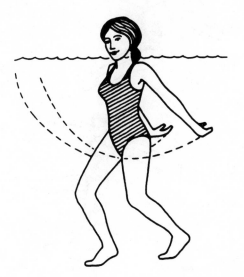

Thigh Exercise 1

1. Place your back against the pool wall and drape your arms along the pool edge to support your body. Your legs should be held straight out in front of your body, parallel to the bottom of the pool. Ankles should be flexed.

2. Pull your legs wide apart and then pull them back together.

3. Begin with 5 repetitions and then follow the age-adjusted recommendations in the chart on page 334.

Note: Keep your stomach tucked in and press your lower back against the wall.

Thigh Exercise 2

1. Place your back against the pool wall in waist-deep water. Use both arms for support on the side of the pool. Stand on your left leg, with your right leg lifted straight up to the side. Your right ankle should be flexed.

2. Swing your right leg in front of your body and cross it over to your left side.

3. Swing your right leg back across your body and assume a standing position, with both feet on the bottom of the pool.

4. Repeat with left leg.

5. Begin with 5 repetitions, then follow the age-adjusted recommendations in the chart on page 335.

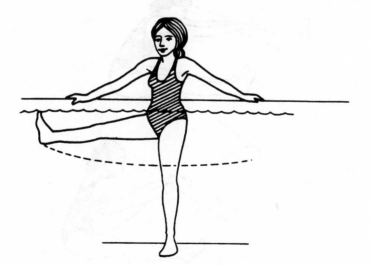

Thigh Exercise 3

1. Place your feet against the pool wall and hold on to the edge of the pool with both hands. Your knees and elbows should remain straight.

2. Push off with your feet and pull your legs apart into a straddle position. Your elbows will bend naturally as your body moves into the wall.

3. Push off with your feet again. Holding your legs straight, pull them together so that you return to the original position.

4. Begin with 5 repetitions and then follow the age-adjusted recommendations in the chart on page 335.

Note: Remember to use your stomach muscles in executing these movements.

Waist and Stomach Exercise 1

1. Place your back against the pool wall and support your body by extending your arms along the edge of the pool. Your legs should be straight out in front of you, parallel to the bottom of the pool.

2. Keeping your back to the wall, swing both legs to the left side of the wall.

3. Contract your abdominal muscles and swing both legs across your body, toward the right side of the pool.

4. Begin with 8 repetitions (4 to the right and 4 to the left), then follow the age-adjusted recommendations in the chart on page 335.

Waist and Stomach Exercise 2

1. Place your back toward the pool wall. Suspend your body from the edge by supporting yourself with both arms along the side of the pool. Allow your back to drift away from the wall.

2. Simultaneously pedal your legs as if you were riding a bike. Also, twist at the hips as you execute this movement. Alternate the twisting motion from the right side to the left. (i.e., as your right knee comes up toward your chest, rotate your hips to the left. Then, as the left leg comes up, rotate your hips to the right.)

Note: The bent knee is always on the top, and the legs are always under the water.

3. Begin with 20 pedaling motions (10 to the right and 10 to the left), then follow the age-adjusted recommendations in the chart on page 336.

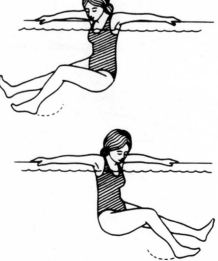

Waist and Stomach Exercise 3

1. Crouch so that your shoulders are under the water, with your knees bent and your weight on the balls of your feet.

2. Quickly rotate your hips back and forth, from right to left. Your arms will go in the opposite direction from your hips. During the twisting movement, your foot should leave the bottom of the pool.

3. Begin with 20 rotations (10 to the right and 10 to the left), and then follow the age-adjusted recommendations in the chart on page 336.

Note: Hold your stomach in tightly throughout the exercise.

Aqua-Aerobics Stretching Exercises

| | | Repetitions | | | |
| | | Age (years) | | | |
Week	<30	30–49	50–59	60+	Freq/wk
			Arms 1		
1	10	10	10	10	3–4x
2	20	18	16	15	3–4x
3	30	25	22	20	3–4x
4	40	32	30	20	3–4x
5	45	40	35	25	3–4x
6	50	45	40	30	3–4x
			Arms 2		
1	10	10	10	10	3–4x
2	20	18	16	15	3–4x
3	30	25	22	20	3–4x
4	40	32	30	20	3–4x
5	45	40	35	25	3–4x
6	50	45	40	30	3–4x
			Thighs 1		
1	5	5	5	5	3–4x
2	10	9	8	7	3–4x
3	15	13	11	9	3–4x
4	20	17	14	11	3–4x
5	20	18	15	13	3–4x
6	25	22	18	15	3–4x

	Repetitions			
	Age (years)			
Week	<30	30–49	50–59	60+	Freq/wk

Thighs 2

Week	<30	30–49	50–59	60+	Freq/wk
1	15	5	5	5	3–4x
2	10	9	8	7	3–4x
3	15	13	11	9	3–4x
4	20	17	14	11	3–4x
5	20	18	15	13	3–4x
6	25	22	18	15	3–4x

Thighs 3

Week	<30	30–49	50–59	60+	Freq/wk
1	5	5	5	5	3–4x
2	10	9	8	7	3–4x
3	15	13	11	9	3–4x
4	20	17	14	11	3–4x
5	20	18	15	13	3–4x
6	25	22	18	15	3–4x

Waist & Stomach 1

Week	<30	30–49	50–59	60+	Freq/wk
1	8	8	8	8	3–4x
2	10	10	8	8	3–4x
3	12	12	10	10	3–4x
4	16	14	12	12	3–4x
5	20	18	16	14	3–4x
6	24	20	18	16	3–4x

	Repetitions				
	Age (years)				
Week	*<30*	*30–49*	*50–59*	*60+*	*Freq/wk*
Waist & Stomach 2					
1	20	20	20	20	3–4x
2	30	28	26	24	3–4x
3	40	36	32	28	3–4x
4	50	44	38	32	3–4x
5	60	52	44	36	3–4x
6	70	60	50	40	3–4x
Waist & Stomach 3					
1	20	20	20	20	3–4x
2	30	28	26	24	3–4x
3	40	36	32	28	3–4x
4	50	44	38	32	3–4x
5	60	52	44	36	3–4x
6	70	60	50	40	3–4x

< Means "less than."

Source: *Aerobics Newsletter* © 1981, Institute for Aerobics Research

Water Running and Walking

Water running and walking are not only good aerobic exercises but they are the only known ways to recover from a sports injury while improving performance. Exercise in water that is waist-deep and bring your knees up so that your feet are at least 6 to 8 inches off the bottom of the pool. Adjust the steps per minute to a pace that you can keep for the required time, age-adjusted. Exercise either in place or move around the pool. Remember: This type of exercise is a replacement for aqua-aerobics and is not expected to be done in conjunction with that type of exercise. However, 2 minutes of water running or walking is a good way to finish up an aqua-aerobics exercise class.

Water Running

	Minutes				
		Age (years)			
Week	30	30–49	50–59	60+	Freq/wk
1	2	2	2	1	3–4x
2	4	3	2	2	3–4x
3	6	5	4	3	3–4x
4	8	7	6	4	3–4x
5	10	9	8	6	3–4x
6	12	11	10	8	3–4x
7	14	13	12	10	3–4x
8	16	15	14	12	3–4x
9	18	17	16	14	3–4x
10	20	20	18	15	3–4x

Water Walking

| Week | Minutes Age (years) | | | | Freq/wk |
	30	30–49	50–59	60+	
1	5	5	5	5	3–4x
2	8	8	7	6	3–4x
3	10	9	8	7	3–4x
4	12	10	9	8	3–4x
5	15	14	12	10	3–4x
6	18	16	14	12	3–4x
7	20	18	16	14	3–4x
8	22	20	18	16	3–4x
9	24	22	20	18	3–4x
10	25	24	22	20	3–4x

A Note on the Physics of Water Exercise

The cardiovascular effects of exercise, whether on land or in the water, are fundamentally the same. But the *physics* underlying land and water exercises are quite different.

During water exercises such as swimming, the water supports from 93 to 100 percent of a swimmer's weight. As a result, an extremely obese person will expend little or no energy to stay afloat because fat floats in water. An extremely lean person, on the other hand, will expend considerably more energy to stay afloat. The reason: He can't float as easily because lean muscle tissue sinks in water, so he must tread water to stay afloat.

Another way to think of this is in terms of a person's loss of weight in water: An athletic, lean male, after completely exhaling, will usually weigh approximately 7 to 10 pounds when submerged in water. But an obese person under the same circumstances will be buoyant—that is, he will have *no* weight and will float.

With water exercises in which the participant is only partially submerged (e.g., water volleyball in a shallow pool), the water supports about half of the participant's body weight. A simple rule of thumb: Water roughly supports the percentage of the body submerged in it. So, a 150-pound male standing in water up to his navel would weigh about 75 pounds if he stood on a scale located at the bottom of the pool.

One difference between land exercises (e.g., running or walking) and water exercises (e.g., swimming or scuba diving) is that land activities generally test the body's ability to overcome gravity by forcing the individual to accelerate his mass against gravity. The role of air resistance (except on windy days) is usually negligible.

Water exercises, in contrast, primarily test the body's ability to move itself through a viscous resistance—i.e., water. Even though great effort may be required to move through the water, the work necessary to overcome gravity is generally negligible.

Half-submerged exercises seem to incorporate the best of the two worlds. The participant is forced to support some of his mass against gravity, though not as much as he would on land. He must also move half of his body through water, which is much more viscous than air.

In deeper water, the participant will face greater viscous water resistance and proportionately less impact to the skeletal system and joints. In shallow water, less viscous resistance is encountered, but there will be greater impact shocks to the body because of the greater influence of gravity.

The implications of water exercises for those with joint, skeletal, or muscle problems that are aggravated by gravity are obvious: Cardiovascular fitness is possible without the high risk of injury or discomfort that may accompany land exercises such as running or jogging.

9

Control
Through Diet

What should be the role of diet in controlling hypertension?

Lawrence Beilin, in his "State of the Art Lecture" published in the Australian *Journal of Hypertension*, sums up the current understanding:

"There is now substantial evidence to suggest that diet, physical inactivity and alcohol consumption are the three major environmental influences on blood pressure levels. . . ."

Many hypertensives, especially those with mild forms of the disease, have gained *complete* control over their blood pressure through dietary means. But even if diet alone won't do the job for you, a wise food plan, combined with other pressure-lowering treatments such as exercise and/or medications, is an essential ingredient in *any* treatment strategy.

An effective meal plan will meet the challenge of high blood pressure—and the risk factors associated with hypertension—in a number of ways:

Principle 1. Stay at your ideal weight. The plan should reduce excess weight, or promote the maintenance of one's ideal weight. A major objective is to eliminate upper-body fat (at the waist and above), which is an important risk factor for hypertension.

Because there are no known techniques for spot reducing, the goal should be to get rid of excess weight *throughout* the body. This approach will automatically cut down on upper-body fat.

Principle 2. Take in plenty of potassium. The menus should be high in potassium, especially for those on a diuretic medication that causes the loss of potassium through excessive urination.

Your diet should contain an extra 1,000 to 2,000 mg of potassium over and above the normal requirement, or a total of approximately 4,000 to 5,000 mg daily.

Usually, six to eight high-potassium foods will meet this goal.

The following charts may be used as a guide to ensure that your diet provides adequate potassium to replace any urinary losses. *Note:* Many of these foods have been included in the Menu and Recipe sections of the Antihypertensive Meal Plan presented later in this chapter.

High-Potassium Foods

The following list of foods high in potassium may be used as a guide to ensure that your diet contains adequate potassium to replace urinary losses. Plan your diet to contain an extra 1,000 to 2,000 mg of potassium daily (for a total of 4–5,000 mg daily) if you have a potassium deficiency or are undergoing chronic therapy with diuretics. Usually, six to eight high-potassium foods will meet this goal.

Fruits	*Serving Size*	*Approximate Potassium Content (mg)*
Apricots	3 medium	280
Avocado	½	680
Banana	1 medium	440

Fruits	*Serving Size*	*Approximate Potassium Content (mg)*
Cantaloupe	½ melon	800
Dates	10 pieces	520
Grapefruit	1 cup, or 1 large	260
Honeydew melon	⅛ melon	210
Orange	1 medium	270
Prunes, dried	5 pieces	350
Raisins	2 tablespoons	140
Strawberries, fresh	1 cup	250
Watermelon	1 cup	160

Juices and Milk		
Grapefruit juice	1 cup	400
Milk	1 cup	370
Orange juice	1 cup	500
Pineapple juice	1 cup	380
Prune juice	1 cup	600
Tomato juice	1 cup	540

Vegetables		
Artichoke	1 medium	360
Broccoli, cooked	½ cup	200

Vegetables	Serving Size	Approximate Potassium Content (mg)
Brussels sprouts, cooked	½ cup	230
Carrots, cooked	½ cup	160
Dried beans	½ cup	420
Greens, cooked	½ cup	160
Lima beans, cooked	½ cup	360
Potato, baked	2½-inch	450
Spinach, cooked	½ cup	300
Squash, winter	½ cup	470
Sweet potato, baked	1 small	340
Tomato, raw	1 medium	300

Meats and Nuts		
Beef	3 ounces	200–300
Fish	3 ounces	350–500
Hamburger	3 ounces	200–250
Turkey & chicken	3 ounces	200–350
Peanuts	3½ ounces	630

Miscellaneous

Bran cereal, wheat germ, whole-grain breads and cereals, peanut butter, chocolate, catsup, dried parsley, instant tea or coffee or Postum, salt substitute (with physician's consent).

Principle 3. Limit sodium. A diet to control hypertension should limit sodium intake significantly—preferably keeping the consumption at a level of about 2 grams (2,000 mg) per day. The following suggestions should give you some ideas about how to achieve this goal.

More on Sodium Management

The average person should be eating about 1,100 to 3,300 mg of sodium per day, according to the Food and Nutrition Board of the National Academy of Sciences. For hypertensives or those at risk for high blood pressure, I recommend 2,000 mg or less daily.

Despite these recommendations, however, the typical American *actually* averages about 3,000 to 5,850 mg of sodium per day! Remember: Salt is composed of approximately 40 percent sodium and 60 percent chloride. So if a person is consuming 4,000 mg of sodium daily, he's taking in 10,000 mg of salt!

Where does all this sodium come from? The following chart, printed in *Environmental Nutrition* (March 1988) and adapted from the National Dairy Council's *Contemporary Topics in Nutrition*, should give you an idea:

Sources of Dietary Sodium

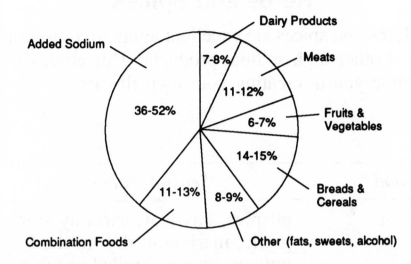

Note: According to other authoritative reports, the "added sodium" category comprises less than one-third of the total, and greater amounts come from various processed foods. (See Fregly, "Estimates of Sodium and Potassium Intake.")

Salt seems to confront us at every turn as we attempt to plan a restrictive diet. However, plenty of low-sodium strategies are available. Following are some practical suggestions about how to limit your daily sodium intake:

Sodium suggestion 1. First, reduce the salt in your cooking to half the amount you would normally use. Then, gradually cut salt completely, and add more herbs and spices. The following chart can help you create your own herb-and-spice flavors.

How to Cook with Herbs and Spices

Herbs and spices are excellent alternatives to salt and other high-sodium products. This chart can guide you in creating your own flavors.

Food	*Season with—*
Beef	allspice, bay leaf, caraway seed, garlic, marjoram, dry mustard, nutmeg, onion, broiled peaches, pepper, green pepper, thyme
Fish	bay leaf, curry, marjoram, dry mustard, lemon, parsley, margarine, lemon juice, green pepper, tomatoes
Lamb	basil, curry, garlic powder, mint, rosemary, thyme
Poultry	cranberries, parsley, paprika, rosemary, sage, thyme
Veal	bay leaf, curry, ginger, marjoram, oregano, rosemary, thyme
Eggs	curry, dry mustard, onion, paprika, parsley, thyme, green pepper, tomatoes

Food	Season with—
Asparagus	caraway seed, lemon juice, mustard seed, sesame seed, tarragon
Beans	basil, dill seed, unsalted French dressing, lemon juice, marjoram, mint, mustard seed, nutmeg, oregano, sage, savory, tarragon, thyme
Beets	allspice, bay leaves, caraway seed, cloves, dill seed, mustard seed, tarragon
Broccoli	caraway seed, dill seed, mustard seed, oregano, tarragon
Cabbage	caraway seed, dill seed, mint, mustard seed, dry mustard, nutmeg, poppy seed, savory, thyme, vinegar
Cauliflower	caraway seed, chives, dill seed, lemon juice, mace, nutmeg, parsley, rosemary, tarragon
Corn	curry, green pepper
Cucumbers	basil, dill seed, lemon juice, mint, tarragon, nutmeg

Food	Season with—
Eggplant	chives, grated onion or garlic, marjoram, oregano, chopped parsley, tarragon
Lettuce salad	basil, caraway seed, chives, dill, garlic, lemon, onion, tarragon, thyme, vinegar
Onions	caraway seed, mustard seed, nutmeg, oregano, pepper, sage, thyme
Peas	basil, dill, marjoram, mint, oregano, lemon, parsley, green pepper, poppy seed, rosemary, sage, savory, thyme
Potatoes	basil, bay leaves, caraway seed, chives, dill seed, mace, mustard seed, onion, oregano, paprika, parsley, green pepper, poppy seed, rosemary, thyme
Spinach	basil, mace, marjoram, nutmeg, oregano
Squash	allspice, basil, cinnamon, chives, cloves, fennel, ginger, mace, mustard seed, nutmeg, onion, rosemary
Sweet potatoes	allspice, cardamon, cinnamon, cloves, nutmeg

Food	*Season with—*
Tomatoes	allspice, basil, bay leaf, curry, marjoram, onion, sage, thyme

- When experimenting with herbs and spices, add small amounts at a time, ¼ teaspoon of dried herbs for every 4 servings of food.
- Fresh herbs can be substituted for dried herbs:
  ⅓ teaspoon ground herbs = 1 teaspoon dried herbs = 1 tablespoon fresh herbs.
- One average-size fresh garlic clove = ⅛ teaspoon dehydrated powder, minced, or chopped garlic.
- Leaf herbs should be crushed before adding to recipes to release more flavor.
- Use pure herbs and spices instead of seasoned salt (onion and garlic powder—*not* onion and garlic salt).
- Whole spices such as stick cinnamon and cloves can enhance the flavor of beverages. Ground spices can "cloud" the liquid.
- Whole spices should be added at the beginning of the cooking process. Ground

spices should be added toward the end, since their flavors are quickly released in hot foods.

• Herbs and spices should be stored in a cool, dry, dark place (not over the kitchen stove). They have a six-month shelf life; they can be frozen in plastic bags.

• Prepare your own salt-free blends to use in cooking and in the salt shaker at your table.

1. Season-All (mix for meats and vegetables)

1 teaspoon basil	1 teaspoon mace
1 teaspoon marjoram	1 teaspoon ground cloves
1 teaspoon thyme	¼ teaspoon nutmeg
1 teaspoon oregano	1 teaspoon black pepper
1 teaspoon parsley	¼ teaspoon cayenne
1 teaspoon savory	

2. All-Purpose Spice Blend

5 teaspoons onion powder	2½ teaspoons garlic powder
2½ teaspoons paprika	2½ teaspoons mustard powder
1¼ teaspoons thyme	½ teaspoon ground white pepper
¼ teaspoon celery seed	

3. Herbed Seasoning Blend

2 tablespoons dill weed or basil

1 teaspoon oregano leaves, crushed

2 tablespoons onion powder

¼ teaspoon grated lemon peel (dried)

1 teaspoon celery seed

1/16 teaspoon black pepper

4. Spicy Flavor Blend

2 tablespoons savory, crushed

2½ teaspoons onion powder

1⅜ teaspoons curry powder

1¼ teaspoons cumin

1 tablespoon powdered mustard

1¼ teaspoons ground white pepper

½ teaspoon garlic powder

Sodium suggestion 2. Avoid adding salt to your foods after cooking has been completed, or at the dinner table.

Sodium suggestion 3. Use oil and vinegar in place of commercial salad dressings, which are high in sodium. Or, reduce the sodium in bottled dressing by diluting it with an equal amount of water and vinegar.

Sodium suggestion 4. Substitute one tablespoon of vinegar (no sodium) mixed with one cup of skim milk (125 mg sodium) for one cup of buttermilk (318 mg sodium).

Sodium suggestion 5. Substitute the following recipes for canned tomato products:

- One can of salt-free tomato paste *plus* 1 can of cold water *equals* salt-free tomato puree.

- One can of salt-free tomato paste *plus* 2 cans of cold water *equals* salt-free tomato sauce.

- One can of salt-free tomato paste *plus* 3 cans of cold water *plus* lemon juice *plus* tabasco sauce *equals* salt-free tomato juice.

- One can of salt-free tomato paste *plus* 2 cans of cold water *plus* 2 tablespoons of apple cider *plus* 1½ tablespoons of frozen pineapple-juice concentrate *equals* salt-free catsup.

Sodium suggestion 6. Substitute low-sodium ("lite") soy sauce for regular soy sauce, or dilute regular soy sauce with an equal part of water.

Sodium suggestion 7. Make your own low-sodium bouillon cubes: Freeze low-sodium chicken broth in a miniature ice tray. Then, pop cubes out and store them in the freezer for later use.

Sodium suggestion 8. Read food labels closely. Many reduced-sodium products are available. The Food and Drug Administration has established these label criteria:

- "No sodium" or "sodium-free": less than 5 mg of sodium per serving

- "Very low-sodium": 35 mg of sodium or less per serving

- "Low-sodium": 140 mg of sodium or less per serving

- "Reduced sodium": sodium content reduced by 75 percent as compared with similar products prepared with salt

- "Unsalted": food product that is normally salted has been processed without salt.

Sodium suggestion 9. Prepare your own marinade recipes as follows:

- *For fish:*
  1 teaspoon tarragon
  1 tablespoon lemon juice
  1 teaspoon low-sodium soy sauce
  freshly ground pepper to taste

- *For poultry:*
  1 small minced onion
  1 minced garlic clove
  ¼ cup low-sodium catsup
  ¼ cup low-sodium soy sauce
  1 cup white wine

1½ tablespoons brown sugar
freshly ground pepper to taste

- *For turkey:*
½ cup Kitchen Bouquet (a liquid seasoning blend) generously rubbed over turkey
1 small chopped onion
4 sliced celery stalks
6 tablespoons garlic powder
6 tablespoons onion powder
2 to 3 tablespoons freshly ground pepper

Sodium suggestion 10. Limit or eliminate such high-sodium foods as these:

Salty or smoked meats—ham, bacon, luncheon meats, hot dogs, sausage, chipped or corned beef, salt pork.

Salty or smoked fish—anchovies, caviar, herring, sardines. *Note:* choose tuna packed in water or "reduced sodium" brands.

Processed cheeses or cheese products. Look for "natural" cheese on the label.

Consommé, canned soups (unless low-sodium), dried soup mixes.

Canned vegetables or vegetable juice (unless low-sodium), sauerkraut, pork and beans.

Snack foods—potato chips, pretzels, salted nuts, salted popcorn, snack crackers, party dips and spreads, crackers with salted toppings.

Olives, pickles, relishes, bottled salad dressings (unless low-sodium).

Meat extracts and tenderizers.

Prepared sauces—barbecue, chili, steak, soy, tomato, tartar, worcestershire, mustard, catsup.

Condiments—spices containing salt or MSG (monosodium glutamate), lemon pepper.

Other foods—frozen dinners, instant cereals, instant pudding mixes, pizza, fast foods, pot pies.

Breakfast cereals, except for those *lowest* in sodium. (The lowest-sodium cereals include shredded wheat, puffed wheat, puffed rice, low-sodium corn flakes, low-sodium Rice Krispies.)

Sodium suggestion 11. Check your medicines. They often contain salt (e.g., Alka-Seltzer, various antacids such as Rolaids, Metamucil instant mix, Vick's cough medicines, laxatives, pain relievers, and sedatives).

Sodium suggestion 12. Use available unsalted or low-sodium commercial products. (See the following list.)

Some Currently Available Unsalted or Low-Sodium Products

Condiments

Unsalted margarine
Unsalted diet
  margarine
Unsalted
  mayonnaise
Unsalted salad
  dressings
Unsalted catsup
Lite soy sauce

Salt-free seasonings
  (see "How to
  Cook with Herbs
  and Spices,"
  pages 348–351)
Low-sodium canned
  broth
Low-sodium
  bouillon cubes

Protein

Low-sodium tuna,
  packed in water
Low-sodium peanut
  butter

Low-sodium cheeses
Low-sodium cottage
  cheese

Snacks

Unsalted rice cakes
Unsalted popcorn
Unsalted melba toast
Crackers with unsalted
  tops

Low-sodium crackers
Unsalted nuts
Unsalted pretzels
Unsalted chips

Vegetables

Low-sodium canned soups	Low-sodium spaghetti sauce
Low-sodium canned vegetables	Low-sodium tomato juice
Low-sodium tomato sauce	Low-sodium V-8 juice
	Low-sodium pickles

Sodium suggestion 13. Use commercial seasoning alternatives to sodium. (See the following list.)

Low-Sodium Commercial Seasoning Products

- *Salt substitutes* taste like salt but contain little or no sodium. These products usually contain potassium chloride (KCl) and should be used as directed by a physician or dietitian and are unadvisable for kidney patients:

Salt substitutes containing potassium chloride:
  Morton Salt Substitute
  Estee Salt-It Salt Substitute
  Estee Salt-It Seasoning
  Kroger Seasoned Salt Substitute

- *Commercial Low-Sodium Seasonings:*
  Lawry's Seasoned Pepper
  Salt-Free 17 Seasoning
  Natural Choice
  Seasoned Salt-Free

Adolph's Unsalted 100% Natural Tenderizer

McCormick Chinese Five Spice
Italian Seasoning
Salt-Free Parsley Patch Lemon
Pepper
Salt-Free Parsley Patch
All-Purpose Seasoning
Salt-Free Parsley Patch Popcorn
Blend
Salt-Free Parsley Patch Sesame
All-Purpose Seasoning
Salt-Free Parsley Patch Garlic
Salt-less
Salt-Free Parsley Patch It's
A Dilly

Norcliff Thayer, Inc. Seasoned No Salt

Mrs. Dash Lemon and Herb Salt-Free
Extra Spice
Original Blend
Low Pepper No Garlic

Kroger Italian Seasoning

Future Foods, Inc. Salt-Free Enhance—
All-Purpose Seasoning

Jane's Krazy Mixed-Up Pepper

Estee Salt-Free Seasoning Sense All-Purpose
   Spice Blend
   Salt-Free Seasoning Sense Mexican
   Spice Blend
   Salt-Free Seasoning Sense Oriental
   Spice Blend

Voyager Captain's Table All-Purpose
   Seasoning

Spice Islands No-Salt All-Purpose Seasoning

- *Commercial Low-Sodium Liquid Seasonings:*
  Kikkoman Low-Sodium Soy Sauce
  Angostura Aromatic Bitters
  Kitchen Bouquet
  Wyler's Low-Sodium Bouillon Cubes
  Featherweight Low-Sodium Bouillon
     Granules
  Tabasco Sauce
  Hot Pepper Sauce
  Low-Sodium V-8 Juice

- *Other Seasoning Suggestions:*
  Horseradish
  Orange or lemon zest—shredded colored part
  of the peel (with discarded white bitter layer)

Sodium suggestion 14. Choose "natural" or
unprocessed foods over processed foods whenever possible. As a general rule, the sodium

content of food increases as food processing increases.

To learn more about the sodium content of various seasonings and foods, consider the following chart:

Sodium Comparisons

Note: Sodium content increases as food processing increases.

Food	Amount	Sodium (mg)
Apple	1 medium	1
Applesauce	1 cup	6
Apple pie	⅛ pie, frozen	482
Bread	1 slice	130
Homemade biscuit	1 biscuit	175
Canned biscuit	1 biscuit	270
Butter	1 tablespoon, unsalted	2
Butter	1 tablespoon, salted	120
Margarine	1 tablespoon	150
Cabbage	1 cup	22
Cole slaw	1 cup	150
Sauerkraut	1 cup, canned	1,760
Chicken	3 ounces, baked	86

Food	Amount	Sodium (mg)
Fast-food chicken	3 ounces, fried	500
Chicken pie	1 pie, frozen	863
Corn	1 ear	1
Corn flakes	1 cup	325
Canned kernels	1 cup	400
Lemon	1 lemon	3
Soy sauce	1 tablespoon	1,330
Salt	1 teaspoon	2,130
Peanuts without salt	1 ounce (30 nuts)	1
Peanut butter	1 tablespoon	95
Peanuts with salt	1 ounce (30 nuts)	120
Cheese, cheddar	1 ounce	175
Cheese spread	1 ounce	380
Cheese soup	1 cup, canned	1,020
Pork chop	3 ounces, baked	54
Bacon	3 pieces	303
Sausage	1 patty	418
Baked potato	1 medium	5
French fries	½ cup (18 fries)	120
Potato chips	½ cup (10 chips)	200
Tomato	1 medium	4
Tomato juice	1 cup	500
Tomato sauce	1 cup (Del Monte)	1,300

Food	Amount	Sodium (mg)
Tomato paste	1 cup (Del Monte)	60
Tomato soup	1 cup, canned	970
Spaghetti sauce	1 cup	2,000
Tuna in water	3 ounces	372
Tuna in oil	3 ounces	442
Tuna noodle casserole	1 cup	715
Water	12 ounces, tap	4
Soft drink	12 ounces	30–60
Club soda	12 ounces	90

Printed with permission from *The Balancing Act* by G. Kostas and K. Rojohn, © 1989.

Low-Sodium Strategies for Eating Out

As conscientious and disciplined as a person may be in preparing and eating low-sodium dishes, the best of intentions may fall by the wayside at a restaurant. As a result, it's *essential* for those on a low-sodium diet to devise and strictly adhere to eating strategies that will keep their consumption of sodium as low as possible. Following are a few general guidelines:

- When you order in a restaurant, choose simply prepared dishes, such as grilled meat, a baked potato, or a tossed salad with oil and vinegar dressing. Avoid casseroles and combination dishes of unknown (and probably sodium-rich) ingredients.

- Request that dishes be prepared without added salt, monosodium glutamate (MSG), or sauces.

- Request that dishes be prepared with lemon juice instead of salt.

- When you travel by air, request low-sodium meals or fresh fruit plates at least twenty-four hours in advance of your departure (or earlier if the airline requires more notice).

In addition, it's important for those committed to a low-sodium diet to know what to do about fast food meals. To this end, consult the "Tips on Ordering at a Fast Food Restaurant" (below) and the "Nutritional Values of Certain Lower Sodium Fast Food Meals" (pages 368–370). A more complete listing of the nutritional values of fast foods is in appendix III.

Tips on Ordering at
a Fast Food Restaurant

1. Dine defensively: Choose items that aren't excessive in fat, sodium, or calories. Bal-

ance your fast food meal with a nutritious breakfast and dinner that include fewer fat calories, more fruit, more vegetables, and lower-fat dairy products than you normally eat.

2. Choose roast beef sandwiches instead of burgers.

3. Choose a small, plain burger instead of a larger, deluxe hamburger, or split a sandwich with a friend.

4. Omit mayonnaise (1 tablespoon = 100 calories) and cheese (1 ounce = 100 calories) from your sandwich. Instead, order lettuce, tomato, and onion (1 slice = 20 calories).

5. In place of a traditional burger, choose a baked potato and salad. Dressing suggestions: low-calorie dressings, lemon juice, picante sauce, or a small amount of cottage cheese.

6. Limit fried foods. Calories are almost triple in deep-fried items. Fat can be reduced significantly by removing the crust before eating (i.e., on fried chicken). Also, choose "regular" fried instead of "extra crispy."

7. Skip French fries, or split an order, or choose a baked potato instead.

8. Limit desserts, sweets, milkshakes, pies, and ice cream, or carry a piece of fruit from home to add to your meal.

9. Salad bars: eat carrots, tomatoes, cucumbers, mushrooms, green peppers, lettuce, and dark green vegetables, as desired. Limit dressings, croutons, pasta, potato-type salads, cheeses, nuts, and seeds. For dressings, use oil and vinegar, flavored vinegar, fresh squeezed lemon, or low-calorie varieties. Some packets of regular salad dressing contain more than 300 calories and in excess of 300 mg of sodium. Also, they may have more fat than a large burger!

10. Pizza: Order cheese pizza with green peppers, onions, and mushrooms. Limit servings to 1 to 2 pieces, and order a dinner salad. *Note:* This meal contains about 1,000 mg of sodium—half a day's allowance for those on a low-sodium diet!

11. Omit pickles, mustard, catsup, special sauces, cheese, processed meats (such as bacon, ham, sausage, hot dogs, pepperoni, and salami), anchovies, and olives.

Nutritional Values of Lower Sodium Fast Food Meals

	Calories	Fat (g)	Cholesterol (mg)	Sodium (mg)
McDonald's				
Chicken Salad Oriental	146	4	92	270
Lite vinaigrette dressing (½ packet)	25	1	1	150
2% Milk (8 ounces)	121	5	5	145
Fresh fruit (from home)	80	0	0	0
Total	372	10	98	565
Burger King				
Hamburger	275	12	37	509
Side salad	20	0	0	10
Reduced-calorie Italian dressing (½ packet)	7	0	0	213
2% Milk (8 ounces)	121	5	5	145
Total	423	17	42	877

	Calories	Fat (g)	Cholesterol (mg)	Sodium (mg)
Arby's				
Regular Roast Beef Sandwich	353	15	39	588
Fresh fruit (from home)	80	0	0	0
Total	433	15	39	588
Jack-in-the-Box				
Chicken Fajita Pita	292	8	34	703
Side salad	51	3	0	84
Reduced-calorie French dressing (½ packet)	40	2	0	150
Total	383	13	34	937
Wendy's				
Chicken Sandwich/no mayonnaise	340	12	60	565
½ Baked potato	125	1	0	30
Total	465	13	60	595
Or: Baked potato with ¼ cup cottage cheese	250	2	0	60
	55	2	10	213

	Calories	Fat (g)	Cholesterol (mg)	Sodium (mg)
Wendy's (continued)				
or 2 tablespoons grated imitation cheddar cheese	40	3	N/A	155
or 2 tablespoons grated Parmesan cheese	50	5	0	255
or taco sauce (1 packet)	10	0	0	105
or chives, mushooms, green onions (use as desired)	0	0	0	0
Total	250–315	2–7	0–10	60–315

With these principles in mind, let's move on to the meal plans designed to prevent or treat hypertension. The first step in using the menus requires an understanding of the food exchange system, which will give you greater flexibility in departing from the listed menus and meals and in building your own personal diet program.

Understanding the Food Exchange System

Some people prefer to follow our menus exactly as they are presented. But many may want to experiment with different foods, substituting here and eliminating there, and thus injecting more variety into the plan.

To this end, our menus have been set up according to the food exchange system. This concept is based on the principle that certain foods are interchangeable with others so that dieters can choose what they want to eat on a given day.

For an exchange system to work properly, similar foods must be grouped together according to their content of carbohydrate, protein, and fat. All the choices on each exchange list are roughly equal in calories. With these comparable groupings, any food on a list can be exchanged for any other food on the same list.

For example, as you examine the menus, you'll see that the food exchange category is listed after each food item. So (Milk) refers to milk products, and (Meat) refers to various types of protein-rich foods, such as fish, poultry, and beans.

More specifically, the exchange groups include the following categories:

1. Milk and milk products—protein sources

2. Meat and substitutes—protein sources

3. Bread/starches—complex carbohydrate sources

4. Vegetables—complex carbohydrate sources

5. Fruits—complex carbohydrate sources

6. Fats—fat sources

Note: When I use the term *complex carbohydrates*, I'm referring to foods that don't just contain simple sugars but instead provide a relatively wide range of nutrients, in addition to their sugar content.

With this information at your fingertips, feel free to substitute (i.e, "exchange") one type of milk product for another, or one type of meat for another, *provided* that the portions are the same, as indicated in the exchange tables.

Caution: If the portion size varies, so will the calories and nutrients. On the other hand, if the food types and portion sizes stay constant, you can vary the menus, while keeping comparable calorie and nutrient levels.

Finally, a word about the way the diets are balanced: Any well-constructed diet must include the basic nutrients of carbohydrate, protein, and fat. In our menus, these nutrients are available in the following percentages each day:

- Carbohydrates—50 to 70 percent of total calories

- Protein—10 to 20 percent of total calories

- Fat—20 to 30 percent of total calories

Using the exchange system will provide you with a variety of food choices and ensure a good balance of carbohydrate, protein, and fat throughout the day. In addition, you'll get an excellent mix of vitamins and minerals.

Following is a detailed listing of the food exchanges in each of the main categories. I've also included some tips on preparing meats, and on identifying specific portions of foods for purposes of the exchange system.

Protein

Milk & Milk Products
One serving contains 80 calories
(8 grams protein, 12 grams carbohydrate)

Eat	
Milk (nonfat, skim, ½%, 1%)	1 cup
evaporated	½ cup
powdered	¼ cup
Low-fat 2% milk	¼ cup
Buttermilk (made from nonfat milk)[4]	1 cup

Yogurt
  from skim milk, plain,
    unflavored   1 cup
  from low-fat milk, plain,
    unflavored   ½ cup
Low-calorie hot cocoa or
  milkshake
    (i.e., Alba, Swiss Miss,
    Carnation, etc.)   1 cup

Avoid

Whole milk products:	Instant breakfast
chocolate	drinks[4]
condensed	Flavored yogurts
dried	Eggnog
evaporated	Ice cream
Buttermilk (made from	Custard
whole milk)[4]	Pudding
Flavored milk drink	
mixes[4]	

[4]high in salt (sodium)

Protein

Meat/Substitutes
One serving (1 ounce) contains 70 calories
(8 grams protein, 3–5 grams fat)
Eat 4–8 ounces meat or substitutes daily

Eat

Choose 10 + meals per week:

Poultry (without skin)	
chicken, turkey, cornish	
hen, squab	1 ounce
Fish—any kind (fresh or frozen)	1 ounce
water-packed tuna or	
salmon, crab or lobster[4]	¼ cup
clams, oysters, scallops,	
shrimp	5 or 1 ounce
sardines, drained[4]	3
Veal—any lean cut	1 ounce
Peanut butter,[4] not	
hydrogenated (read labels)	1 tablespoon
Dried beans, peas (count	
as 1 meat + 1 bread)	½ cup
Chicken or turkey cold cuts[4]	
turkey ham, turkey bologna	1 ounce

[4]high in salt (sodium)

Limit to 4 meals per week:

Lean beef cuts

    tenderloin (sirloin, filet,

        T-bone, porterhouse),

        round, cube, flank   1 ounce

    roasts, stews—sirloin tip,

        round rump, chuck, arm   1 ounce

    other—ground round

        (chuck 15% fat ground

        beef), chipped beef,

        venison   1 ounce

Lean lamb cuts—leg, chops,

    loin, shoulder   1 ounce

Lean pork and ham[4]

    center cut steaks, loin

        chops, smoked ham[4]   1 ounce

Limit to 3 to 5 ounces per week:

Cholesterol-free cheese[4]

    Cheezola, Countdown,

        Kraft "Golden Image," etc.   1 ounce

Low-fat cheese[4]

    low-fat cottage cheese,

        Laughing Cow, farmer's,   1 ounce or

        skim ricotta   ¼ cup

Medium-fat cheese[4]

    Bonbel, mozzarella,   1 ounce or

        Parmesan, neufchatel   ¼ cup

[4]high in salt (sodium)

Limit to 1 to 3 egg yolks per week:

Whole egg   1
Egg substitutes[4]
   (cholesterol-free)   ¼ cup
Egg whites   as desired

Limit to one 3-ounce serving per month:

Organ meats—liver, heart,
   brains, kidney

Avoid

Poultry—duck, goose, poultry skin
Fish—fish roe (caviar); limit shrimp
Meats—fried, with gravies, sauces, breading,
         casseroles
      high fat meats:
      beef—brisket, corned beef, ground
            hamburger, club or rib steaks, rib
            roasts, spare ribs
      pork—bacon,[4] deviled ham,[4] loin,
            spare ribs, sausage,[4] cold cuts[4]
      pork—hot dogs,[4] luncheon meats[4]
Cheese[4]—all except skim milk or cholesterol-
         free cheese (see list page 376)
Convenience foods—canned[4] or frozen meats,
cream cheese, cheese spreads,[4] dips,[4] packaged
dinners,[4] pork and beans,[4] pizza,[4] fast foods,[4]
cold cuts.[4]

[4]high in salt (sodium)

Carbohydrate

Starches
One serving contains 70 calories
(2 grams of protein, 15 grams of carbohydrate)

Eat

Bread and substitutes:

Bread, any type	1 slice
Bread, "extra thin" (30 calories/slice)	2 slices
Bread crumbs	3 tablespoons
Bagel, small	½
Biscuit (2″ across, made with proper fat)	1
Cornbread, 1½″ cube	1
English muffin	½
Hamburger or hot dog bun	½
Pita or pocket bread	½
Rice cakes	2
Roll, plain soft	1
Tortilla (6″ diameter, made without lard)	1

Cereal and cereal products:

Bran cereals	½ cup
Dry cereal (flaked)	¼ cup
Dry cereal (puffed)	1 cup
Grapenuts	¼ cup
Cooked cereal (oatmeal, etc.)	½ cup

Cooked grits, noodles, rice, spaghetti	½ cup
Popcorn (popped, no fat added)	3 cups
Wheat germ or bran	¼ cup

Starchy Vegetables:

Corn	½ cup
Corn-on-the-cob (3″ long)	1 small
Mixed vegetables	½ cup
Lima Beans	½ cup
Parsnips	½ cup
Peas, green[4] (canned or frozen)	½ cup
Potato, white	1 small
Potato, mashed	½ cup
Pumpkin[2]	¼ cup
Winter squash (acorn or butternut)[2]	½ cup
Yam or sweet potato[2]	¼ cup

Crackers:

Animal	10
Arrowroot	3
Bread sticks (4″ x ¼″)	2
Graham, 2½″ square	2
Holland rusks	1½
Matzoth, 4″ x 6″	½
Melba Toast	4

[2]high in Vitamin A

[4]high in salt (sodium)

Oyster (½ cup)[4]	20
Pretzels, 3⅛″ x ⅛″[4]	25
Pretzels (unsalted small circles)	10
Rye Wafers, 2″ x 3½″	3
Rye Krisp[4]	3
Saltines, 2″ square[4]	6
Soda, 2½″ square[4]	4

Dried beans and Lentils:

Beans, Peas, Lentils dried and cooked	½ cup
(½ cup = 1 meat + 1 starch)	
Baked beans, no pork (if canned)[4]	¼ cup
Chickpeas, garbanzo beans	¼ cup

Miscellaneous:

Catsup, chili sauce or BBQ sauce[4]	¼ cup
Tomato sauce[4]	½ cup
Cornmeal, cornstarch, flour	2 tablespoons
Cornflake crumbs	3 tablespoons

Soups: 1 cup

Broth or tomato-based
(i.e., vegetable, chicken noodle)[4]
Homemade, with allowed ingredients
Canned soup[4]—refrigerate and remove
hardened fat
Fat-free broth or consommé—eat as desired

---

[4]high in salt (sodium)

Avoid

Butter rolls
Cereals, sugar-coated
Coffee cake[4]
Commercial baked
  goods
Commercial popcorn[4]
Cornbread, biscuit,
  bread, cake mixes[4]
Crackers, flavored[4]
Cream soup[4]

Croissants
Doughnuts[4]
Egg & cheese bread
Fried foods
Granola cereals
  unless homemade
Pancakes, waffles[4]
Pastries[4]
Potato chips[4]
Sweet rolls[4]

Note: Read food labels carefully to avoid foods with undesirable fats and sodium.

[4]high in salt (sodium)

Carbohydrate

Fruit/Juice
One serving contains 40 calories
(10 grams of carbohydrates)
Count one large fruit as 2 portions (80 calories)

Eat

Fresh, frozen, or canned fruit or fruit juice without sugar or syrup; cranberries can be used as desired if no sugar is added.

Apple	½ (4″ diameter) or 1 (2″ diameter)
Applesauce	½ cup
Apricots[2]	2 fresh
Apricots, dried[2]	4 halves
Banana	½ (3″ long)
Berries:	
Blackberries	½ cup
Blueberries	½ cup
Boysenberries	½ cup
Raspberries	½ cup
Strawberries[1]	¾ cup
Cherries	10 large
Dates	2

[1]high in Vitamin C

[2]high in Vitamin A

[3]high in Vitamin A and Vitamin C

Figs, fresh or dried	1
Fruit cocktail	½ cup
Grapefruit[1]	½
sections	½ cup
Grapes	12 large
Kiwi	½
Mango[1]	½ small
Melon:	
Cantaloupe[3]	¼ (6″ diameter)
Casaba[2]	¼ (6″ diameter)
Honeydew[1]	⅛ (7″ diameter)
Watermelon[2]	1 cup
Melon balls[3]	¾ cup
Nectarine	1 small
Orange[1]	1 small
Orange sections[1]	½ small
Papaya[3]	¾ cup
Peach, fresh[2]	1 medium
Pear, fresh	1 small
Pear, canned	2 halves
Pineapple, diced	½ cup
Pineapple, sliced	1½ slices
Plums	2 medium
Prunes, dried	2 medium
Raisins	2 tablespoons
Tangerine[1]	1 medium

Juices

Apple juice	⅓ cup
Cider	⅓ cup

Cranberry juice

    low-cal   ¾ cup

    regular   ¼ cup

Grapefruit juice[1]   ½ cup

Grape juice   ¼ cup

Nectar   ⅓ cup

Orange juice[1]   ½ cup

Pineapple juice   ⅓ cup

Prune juice   ¼ cup

Avoid

---

all sweetened frozen juice or canned fruit

[1]high in Vitamin C

[2]high in Vitamin A

[3]high in Vitamin A and Vitamin C

Carbohydrate

Vegetables
One serving contains 25 calories
(2 grams protein, 5 grams carbohydrate)
One serving = ½ cup

Eat

Raw, baked, broiled, steamed, boiled:

Artichoke	Eggplant	String beans
Asparagus	Green pepper[3]	green or yellow
Bean sprouts	Greens, all types[3]	Summer squash[2]
Beets	Kohlrabi	Tomatoes[3]
Broccoli[3]	Mushrooms	Tomato juice[1][4]
Brussels sprouts	Okra	Turnips
Cabbage[1]	Onions	Vegetable juice
Carrots[2]	Rhubarb	cocktail[1][4]
Cauliflower[1]	Rutabaga	Water chestnuts
Celery	Sauerkraut	Zucchini[1]

Eat these raw vegetables in any quantity:

Chicory[2]	Lettuce	Radishes
Chinese cabbage	Parsley[1]	Watercress[3]
Cucumbers	Pickles[4]	Rhubarb
Endive[2]	dill or sour	
Escarole[2]		

Avoid

Creamed or fried vegetables; vegetables with gravies, sauces

[1]high in Vitamin C

[2]high in Vitamin A

[3]high in Vitamin A and Vitamin C

[4]high in salt (sodium)

Fat

One serving contains 45 calories
(5 grams of fat)

Eat

Margarine, soft tub or stick*	1 teaspoon
Margarine, diet*	3 teaspoons
Vegetable oils* (except coconut, palm)	1 teaspoon
Mayonnaise	1 teaspoon
Diet mayonnaise	3 teaspoons
Yogannaise	2 teaspoons
Avocado	⅛
Olives[4]	5
Salad dressing without sour cream or cheese (i.e., Italian, French)*[-4]	1 tablespoon
Salad dressing (low-calorie)*[-4]	2 tablespoons
Seeds (i.e., sunflower, sesame), unsalted	1 tablespoon
Nuts, unsalted	6 small
Almonds, unsalted	6
Peanuts, unsalted	10
Pecans (whole), unsalted	2

*Made with corn, cottonseed, safflower, or sunflower oil only. Choose margarine with "liquid oil" as the first listed (predominant) ingredient on the label.

Avoid

Bacon & bacon drippings[4]	Gravies, sauces, meat drippings
Butter	Hydrogenated oils (as first ingredient)
Chicken fat	
Chocolate, cocoa butter	Ice cream
Coconut & palm oil	Lard
Commercial baked goods	Margarine (regular stick)
Commercial popcorn[4] (made w/coconut oil)	Nondairy creamers w/coconut and/or palm oil
Creamy salad dressings[4] (blue cheese, 1000 island, sour cream, etc.)	Whipped topping
	Nuts: cashew, macadamia
	Salt pork[4]
	Shortening
Cream: liquid, sour, whipping (sweet)	Sour cream
	Food labeled with nonspecific "vegetable oil"
Desserts	
Dips[4] and chips[4]	

[4]high in salt (sodium)

Meat Tips

Ways to Trim Meat Fat

1. Eat a maximum of 8 ounces meat/fish/poultry daily. Limit beef, lamb, pork to 12 to 16 ounces per week.
2. Choose only lean cuts of meat (see list page 376). Avoid cuts where fat is "hidden" or visible throughout the meat (i.e., brisket, rib, roast, prime rib).
3. Trim all visible fat; remove skin from poultry.
4. Bake, broil, barbecue meats; do not add fats (i.e., sauté, fry, add sauces, gravies, etc.).
5. Roast and bake meats with rack to allow excess fat to drain off meat.
6. Prepare eggs fat-free by poaching, boiling, scrambling, or cooking in nonstick pans or with nonstick sprays.
7. Remove fat from meat drippings: refrigerate drippings so that the cold fat will rise to the top and harden. Skim off or use a "gravy skimmer," which separates fat from hot drippings.
8. Weigh meat after cooking and without bone. A 3-ounce serving of cooked meat equals approximately ¼ pound (4 ounces) of raw meat.

Portions Count

3-ounce Portions

---

1 pork or veal chop, ¼" thick
2 rib lamb chops or 1 shoulder chop
leg-and-thigh or ½ breast of 3-pound chicken
1 meat pattie, 3" x ¼"
2 thin slices roast meat, each 3" x 3" x ¼"
3 medium-size pieces of stew meat
1 small beef filet or ½ small sirloin tip
1 fish filet, 3" x 3" x ½"
¼ cup tuna, salmon, crab, cottage cheese
12 medium shrimp (or 15 small)
3 boiled crabs, 15 oysters

Typical Portions

Meat, Poultry, Fish

---

3 ounces	= size of palm of lady's hand (don't count fingers!)
	= amount in a sandwich
	= amount in a "quarter pounder" (cooked)
	= chicken breast (3" across)

6 ounces	= restaurant chicken breast (6″ across)
	= common luncheon or cafeteria portion
8 ounces	= common evening restaurant portion

Cheese[4]

1 ounce	= 1 slice on sandwich or hamburger
	= 1″ cube or 1 wedge (airplane serving)
½ cup	= 1 scoop cottage cheese

[4]high in salt (sodium)

A Meal Plan to Combat Hypertension

These menus have been formulated according to the following specific nutritional guidelines:

- They consist of low-sodium dishes, with approximately 2 grams (2,000 mg) of sodium per day. In every case, the diets average less than 2.3 grams of sodium per day.

- They are low-fat, with fats comprising less than 30 percent of any day's calories.

  Those foods which do contain fats have been chosen with the latest understanding of how nutrition may have an impact on hypertension. Among other things, we've emphasized the inclusion of seafoods containing polyunsaturated fish oil, a substance which may lower blood pressure.

In this regard, a report in the April 20, 1989 issue of *The New England Journal of Medicine*, concludes that "high doses of fish oil can reduce blood pressure in men with essential hypertension. However, the clinical usefulness and safety of fish oil in the treatment of hypertension will require further study." (Knapp, Howard R., et al., "The antihypertensive effects of fish oil," Vol. 320, p. 1037).

- They are low-cholesterol, with all menus containing less than 300 mg of cholesterol per day. (In many cases, they have *far* less than 300 mg per day.)

- They are high-fiber diets, with a high percentage of daily calories (50 to 70 percent) from complex carbohydrate foods.

- They are high-calcium, typically providing from 1,000 to 1,500 mg of calcium per day.

- There is a 1,200-calorie-per-day program designed to help women lose weight.

Also, a 1,500-calorie-per-day plan will enable women to maintain weight, or men to lose weight. Finally, there's a 2,200-calorie-per-day plan for men to maintain an ideal weight.

- The meals are high in potassium as a result of the high proportion of complex carbohydrates.

As I've already mentioned, these menus have been designed to be used with the food exchange system. Here is a summary of sample meal plans at three calorie levels—1,200, 1,500, 2,200—that could fit into the system. The numbers under each calorie category refer to servings from each of the exchange categories.

Food Exchanges
for Sample Meal Plans

Exchanges:	*1,200 cal.*	*1,500 cal.*	*2,200 cal.*
Milk	1	1	2
Meat (including cheese)	5	7	8
Bread/Starch	5	7	12
Vegetables	3	3	4
Fruit	4	4	8
Fat	4	5	6

Although these exact exchanges haven't been used for every menu in this book, they should prove useful as a general guide if you plan to use the food exchange system.

*Basic Tips for Using the Menus and Recipes—
and for Creating Your Own Menus
with the Food Exchange System*

You've seen some of these tips before, as in the sections on strategies for sodium reduction. But I want to emphasize *all* the major principles at this point so that you'll be sure to have them in mind as you prepare to use the menus and recipes.

Tip 1. Be selective with protein foods, including dairy and meat products. Remember: These foods are naturally high in sodium.

For example, 1 cup of milk contains approximately 150 mg of sodium; 1 ounce of cheese has 100 to 400 mg; and 8 ounces of fresh fish, meat, or poultry have 150 mg of sodium. I suggest that you include no more than 8 ounces of meat or meat substitutes daily, and 2 to 3 low-fat milk products daily, to not consume excessive amounts of fat or cholesterol. (To check the precise nutrient content of various foods, see the charts in appendix IV.)

Tip 2. Eat large portions of fresh produce— especially fruit and vegetables. These foods contain virtually no sodium, are relatively free of fat and cholesterol, are rich in potassium and fiber, and are highly nutritious complex carbohydrates.

I recommend a minimum of six fruit and vegetable servings a day. Using the exchange system, you may want to substitute seasonal fruit in the menus.

All fresh, frozen, or canned fruits in the menus are sodium-free or low in sodium. Make it a point to buy unsalted or low-sodium canned vegetables (check the labels!).

Tip 3. Avoid canned or packaged processed foods. Most contain high levels of sodium.

Tip 4. Eat at least 4 to 6 starches daily. Most starches—including rice, pasta, oatmeal, potatoes, and corn—are sodium-free. Prepare them without salt, even though the package instructions may recommend cooking with salt.

Tip 5. Be aware that each slice of bread contains approximately 125 mg of sodium. Instead of bread, emphasize grains such as rice, pasta, oatmeal, or oat bran. Also, it's helpful to include plenty of starches such as potatoes, corn, peas, and beans, which contain no sodium as long as they are not canned with salt. In addition, eat unsalted crackers, and avoid dry mixes for cornbread, biscuits, or muffins.

Tip 6. Do not add salt at the table—I've said this already, but I'll say it again! In cooking, use one-half as much salt as a recipe (other than those in this book) calls for, or none at all.

Tip 7. Read cereal labels. Some cereals contain approximately 300 to 600 mg of sodium per one-cup serving.

Shredded wheat, shredded wheat with extra fiber, oatmeal, cooked oat bran, puffed wheat, puffed rice, puffed corn, and special "low-sodium" labeled cereals are your best choices. Wheat-bran cereals are excellent fiber sources, but most contain high levels of sodium, so control the portion sizes of these in your diet.

Tip 8. To limit fat and cholesterol, choose fish, poultry (skinned), and meatless dishes more often (8 to 10 servings per week), and limit red-meat dishes (0 to 4 servings per week).

Tip 9. Oil and vinegar contain no sodium and often are used as salad dressing in the menus. You can purchase sodium-free bottled salad dressings in the "diet" section of most grocery stores. Or you can make your own dressings by substituting herbs and spices and sodium-free seasonings.

Tip 10. For margarine, use regular (44 mg of sodium per teaspoon), diet (22 mg sodium per teaspoon), or unsalted (no sodium), depending on your sodium restriction.

Tip 11. Choose the following as beverages: water, mineral water, or sparkling water. Canned diet soft drinks contain a small amount of sodium—approximately 50 mg per 12-ounce can. Fruit juices are sodium-free. But V-8 and other vegetable and tomato juices are high in salt, unless you purchase the "low-sodium" varieties.

Tip 12. When cooking, avoid high-sodium condiments such as monosodium glutamate, bouillon cubes, canned broths, canned soups, meat tenderizers, garlic salt, onion salt, lemon pepper, soy sauce, teriyaki sauce, catsup, steak sauce, Worcestershire sauce, and barbecue sauce.

Instead, use herbs, spices, salt-free seasoning, blends, lemon juice, tabasco sauce, Kitchen Bouquet (a liquid seasoning blend), angostura bitters, unsalted bouillon cubes, or regular wine (not cooking wine).

Note: For further information on this subject, refer to the "How to Cook with Herbs and Spices" chart on pages 348–353 and the "Low-Sodium Commercial Seasoning Products" on pages 359–361.

Tip 13. All the recipes in this book have been kitchen-tested at the Cooper Clinic. In formulating these dishes, we've substituted lower-sodium and lower-fat ingredients, including appropriate seasonings. In some cases, our nutritionists have included *"very* low sodium" recipe variations (entitled "lower sodium" variations).

Tip 14. Simply by substituting fresh goods

for canned, and also herbal seasonings for salt, we've tried to avoid recipes that require special low-sodium-product purchases.

Tip 15. The use of "lite" salt in place of regular salt cuts the sodium in half. Or salt can be eliminated entirely with a "salt substitute" or "salt-free seasoning blend."

Tip 16. All recipes and menus have been computer-analyzed, using the Cooper Clinic Nutrition and Exercise Evaluation System.

Tip 17. A reminder about and expansion upon two food preparation tips that have already been suggested in other contexts:

1. Make homemade broth from defatted, unsalted chicken drippings, and freeze in ice-cube trays to be used later as "bouillon" or "broth" cubes. Regular bouillon cubes are excessive in salt.

2. In cooking, use regular wine, which is salt-free, rather than "cooking wine," which is high in sodium.

Tip 18. At salad bars, eat the fresh, simple vegetables, avoiding combination dishes (e.g., tuna salad, pasta salad, etc.). The combination plates contain unknown quantities of salt. Also avoid obvious high-salt selections such as canned bean salads, pickles, olives, croutons, bacon, commercial dressings, or salted nuts and seeds.

Tip 19. For snacks, make salt-free homemade popcorn, or purchase unsalted pretzels. Eat shredded wheat or homemade "trail mix" made of dried fruit, low-sodium cereals, and unsalted pretzels. In addition, fruit makes a good sodium-free antihypertensive snack.

Tip 20. For desserts, choose fruit, sherbet, fruit ice, frozen yogurt, ice milk, gelatin, and homemade desserts containing low-sodium ingredients. Avoid commercial pastries, cakes, and cookies, which are high in sodium.

Tip 21. Avoid fast foods or follow the fast food guidelines on pages 368–370. Choose mainly salad bars and baked potatoes. Top potatoes with vegetables from the salad bar, including green pepper, onions, mushrooms, and broccoli.

Tip 22. Prepare sandwiches with leftover unsalted chicken, meat, or other such foods. Avoid cured, processed luncheon meats. For example: 3 ounces of chicken contain 75 mg of sodium, while 3 ounces of salami or ham have 1,200 mg of sodium!

Go easy on or omit mayonnaise and mustard: They tend to be high in sodium. Skip the pickles and olives, and use unsalted pretzels instead of chips. Fresh fruit and raw carrot sticks are also a good antihypertensive way to fill out a sandwich meal.

Tip 23. For adequate calcium, include 2 to 3 nonfat or low-fat milk products daily (e.g., milk, yogurt, or cheese). Part-skim-milk moz-zarella is an excellent lower-sodium, low-fat, high-calcium cheese. Deli cheese counters may include many specialty low-fat, low-sodium cheeses—but read the labels to find out which ones are best.

Finally, be aware that low-fat cottage cheese is high in sodium, though it is a good source of calcium.

Tip 24. In the menus, "diet" margarine or mayonnaise refers to products labeled "low-calorie" or "50 calories per tablespoon." Tub, unsalted diet margarine is the best choice for a low-sodium, low-fat, low-calorie meal plan.

Tip 25. Prepare homemade beans from scratch. If you must use canned beans occasion-ally, rinse them first to reduce their sodium content.

Daily Menus
The Antihypertensive
Meal Plan

1,200 - Calorie Menus

Week 1—Monday

Breakfast

1 cup cooked oat bran cereal without salt (2
   Bread)
2 tablespoons raisins (1 Fruit)
1 cup skim milk (1 Milk)

Lunch

1 pita pocket sandwich:
   1 whole wheat pita pocket (2 Bread)
   1 ounce sliced turkey (1 Meat)
   ½ ounce part-skim mozzarella cheese
      (½ Meat)
   1 teaspoon mayonnaise (1 Fat)
   ½ teaspoon mustard
   shredded lettuce and ½ cup chopped
      tomatoes (1 Vegetable)
1 small apple (1 Fruit)
½ cup skim milk (½ Milk)

Dinner

¾ cup gazpacho (1½ Vegetable, ½ Fat) (24 mg Sodium), see page 471

¼ sliced avocado (2 Fat)

1 Pita Cracker (⅛ Bread) (23 mg Sodium), see page 506

1 cup Spanish Chicken and Rice (3½ Meat, 2 Bread, 1 Fat, 2 Vegetable) (375 mg Sodium), see page 482

12 large green grapes (1 Fruit)

1,200 - Calorie Menus

Week 1—Tuesday

Breakfast

½ cup fresh orange slices (1 Fruit)
1 poached egg (1 Meat)
1 slice whole wheat toast (1 Bread)
1 teaspoon unsalted margarine (1 Fat)
1 tablespoon apple butter (½ Fruit)
1 cup skim milk (1 Milk)

Lunch

1 cup Cold Pasta Salad (1½ Bread, ½ Meat, 2
    Vegetable, ½ Fat) (412 mg Sodium), see
    page 475
1 slice garlic bread:
    1 3-inch slice Italian bread (1 Bread)
    1 teaspoon unsalted   margarine (1 Fat)
    ½ teaspoon garlic powder
1 sliced kiwi (2 Fruit)

Dinner

2½ ounces Peppered Veal (2½ Meat, 1
    Vegetable, ½ Bread, ½ Fat) (208 mg
    Sodium), see page 483
1 small baked potato (1 Bread) with
1 teaspoon unsalted margarine (1 Fat)
½ cup steamed broccoli (1 Vegetable)
    seasoned with
1 teaspoon pimiento
½ cup unsweetened applesauce (1 Fruit)

1,200 - Calorie Menus

Week 1—Wednesday

Breakfast

½ cup unsweetened orange juice (1 Fruit)
½ cup bran flakes (1 Bread)
1 cup skim milk (1 Milk)
½ cup unsweetened, canned peaches (1 Fruit)

Lunch

1 grilled cheese sandwich:
    2 slices whole wheat bread (2 Bread)
    1½ ounces low-fat cheese (1½ Meat),
      grilled, using
    2 teaspoons unsalted margarine (2 Fat)
    3 slices tomato (1 Vegetable)
1½ cups fresh strawberries (2 Fruit)
½ cup skim milk (½ Milk)

Dinner

3 ounces Herbed Garlic Fish Fillets (3 Meat)
    (202 mg Sodium), see page 486
½ cup Oven French Fries (2 Bread) (5 mg
    Sodium), see page 505
1 orange romaine salad:
    2 cups romaine lettuce (2 Vegetable)
    ½ cup unsweetened mandarin oranges
      (1 Fruit)
    1 teaspoon rice vinegar
    1 teaspoon olive oil (1 Fat)
1 whole wheat dinner roll (1 Bread)
½ cup skim milk (½ Milk)

1,200 - Calorie Menus

Week 1—Thursday

Breakfast

1 cup unsweetened, canned pears (2 Fruit)
1 vegetable omelet:
    1 egg (1 Meat)
    1 slice tomato
    2 fresh sliced mushrooms
    1 chopped green onion (tomato,
    mushrooms, onion = 1 Vegetable)
1 whole wheat English muffin (2 Bread)
2 teaspoons unsalted margarine (2 Fat)
½ cup skim milk (½ Milk)

Lunch

1 "Munchie Tray":
    1 ounce sliced chicken (1 Meat)
    ½ ounce low-fat cheese (½ Meat)
    12 saltine crackers, unsalted tops (2 Bread)
    12 large green grapes (1 Fruit)
1 cup Fruit Smoothy (1½ Milk) (85 mg
    Sodium), see page 503

Dinner

1 Spicy Bean Enchilada (1 Meat, 2 Bread, ½
    Vegetable) (553 mg Sodium), see page 496
1 cup tossed dinner salad (1 Vegetable)
1½ tablespoons oil and vinegar dressing
    (1½ Fat)

1,200 - Calorie Menus

Week 1—Friday

Breakfast

1 cup cooked oatmeal or oat bran cereal
without salt (2 Bread)
½ mashed banana (1 Fruit)
1 cup skim milk (1 Milk)

Lunch

½ cup Long Grain and Wild Rice Chicken
Salad (1 Meat, 1 Bread, ½ Vegetable, ½
Fruit, 1 Fat) (250 mg Sodium), see page
476, on
¼ cup shredded lettuce
6 saltine crackers, unsalted tops (1 Bread)

Dinner

1 piece Vegetarian Lasagna (2 Bread, 2 Meat,
2½ Vegetable, ½ Fat) (350 mg Sodium),
see page 499
1 whole wheat dinner roll (1 Bread)
2 teaspoons unsalted margarine (2 Fat)
½ cup fresh fruit salad (1 Fruit)
½ cup skim milk (½ Milk)

1,200 - Calorie Menus

Week 1—Saturday

Breakfast

1 slice French Toast Puff (1 Meat, ⅛ Milk, ½ Fruit, 1 Bread) (230 mg Sodium), see page 468, with

1 teaspoon unsalted margarine (1 Fat) and

2 tablespoons Berry Syrup (1 Fruit) (0 mg Sodium), see page 507

1 cup skim milk (1 Milk)

Lunch

½ cup Tuna Salad (2 Meat, 1 Milk) (707 mg Sodium), see page 478, on

1 lettuce leaf with 3 slices tomato (1 Vegetable)

4 pieces melba toast (1 Bread)

1 medium apple (2 Fruit)

½ cup skim milk (½ Milk)

Dinner

3 Stuffed Shells (1 Meat, 2 Bread, 3 Vegetable, ½ Fat) (150 mg Sodium), see page 498

1 cup tossed dinner salad with cucumber and carrot slices (1 Vegetable)

1 tablespoon oil and vinegar dressing (1 Fat)

1,200 - Calorie Menus

Week 1—Sunday

Breakfast

1 Oatmeal Pancake (1 Bread, 1/6 Milk) (199
    mg Sodium), see page 470
1 teaspoon unsalted margarine (1 Fat)
1 tablespoon low-calorie syrup (¼ Fruit)
1 cup skim milk (1 Milk)

Lunch

1 fruit salad:
    ¾ cup fresh strawberries (1 Fruit)
    12 large green grapes (1 Fruit)
    1 sliced banana (2 Fruit)
¼ cup low-fat cottage cheese (1 Meat)
6 saltine crackers, unsalted tops (1 Bread)

Dinner

4 ounces Teriyaki Steak (4 Meat, ½
    Vegetable, ½ Fat) (472 mg Sodium), see
    page 492
¾ cup steamed rice (1½ Bread) with
1 teaspoon unsalted margarine (1 Fat)
1 cup stir-fry vegetables:
    ¼ cup julienne zucchini (½ Vegetable)
    ¼ cup julienne carrots (½ Vegetable)

¼ cup chopped red bell peppers
(½ Vegetable)
¼ cup sliced onion (½ Vegetable)
1 teaspoon safflower oil (1 Fat)
¼ teaspoon ginger powder
¼ teaspoon minced garlic
½ cup skim milk (½ Milk)

1,200 - Calorie Menus

Week 2—Monday

Breakfast

1 waffle (1 Bread, 1 Fat) topped with
½ cup unsweetened applesauce (1 Fruit) and
½ teaspoon cinnamon
1 cup skim milk (1 Milk)

Lunch

1 small baked potato (1 Bread) topped with
2 tablespoons grated cheddar cheese (½ Meat)
1 cup fresh fruit salad (2 Fruit)

Dinner

3 ounces Grilled Sesame Chicken Breast (3
    Meat, ½ Fat, ½ Fruit) (443 mg Sodium),
    see page 480
½ cup cooked corkscrew pasta (1 Bread) with
1 teaspoon unsalted margarine (1 Fat)
½ cup steamed broccoli (1 Vegetable)
1 cup marinated vegetables:
    ½ cup sliced tomato
    ½ cup sliced cucumber (tomato and
      cucumber = 1 Vegetable)
    1 tablespoon Italian dressing (1 Fat)

1,200 - Calorie Menus

Week 2—Tuesday

Breakfast

½ cup unsweetened orange juice (1 Fruit)
1 Oat Bran Muffin (½ Bread, ½ Fruit, ½ Fat)
　　(60 mg Sodium), see page 469
¼ cup scrambled egg substitute (1 Meat)
　　cooked with vegetable oil cooking spray
1 teaspoon unsalted margarine (1 Fat)

Lunch

1 cup Low-Sodium Minestrone Soup (1 Bread,
　　1 Vegetable) (57 mg Sodium), see page
　　472
1 turkey sandwich:
　　2 slices diet whole wheat bread (1 Bread)
　　1 ounce sliced turkey breast (1 Meat)
　　1 teaspoon diet mayonnaise (½ Fat)
　　¼ cup alfalfa sprouts (1 Vegetable)
1 cup plain, nonfat yogurt (1 Milk) with
1 teaspoon sugar substitute and
1 teaspoon vanilla
¾ cup fresh strawberries (1 Fruit)

Dinner

1¾ cups Low-Sodium Shrimp Creole (2 Meat,
    1½ Bread, 2 Vegetable) (291 mg Sodium),
    see page 488
1 3-inch slice French bread (1 Bread)
1 teaspoon unsalted margarine (1 Fat)
Lettuce wedge with
1 tablespoon French dressing (1 Fat)
1 small baked apple (1 Fruit)

1,200 - Calorie Menus

Week 2—Wednesday

Breakfast

1 English muffin (2 Bread)
3 teaspoons unsalted diet margarine (1 Fat)
1 fresh fruit cup:
    ¼ sliced banana (½ Fruit)
    ½ sliced orange (½ Fruit)
1 cup homemade cocoa:
    1 cup heated skim milk (1 Milk)
    1 tablespoon cocoa
    1 teaspoon sugar substitute

Lunch

1 tostada:
    1 flour tortilla (1 Bread)
    ¼ cup cooked, drained ground beef (1 Meat)
    1 tablespoon picante sauce
    2 tablespoons grated cheddar cheese (½ Meat)
    ¼ cup chopped tomato (½ Vegetable)
½ cantaloupe (2 Fruit)

Dinner

2 ounces Veal Scaloppine (2 Meat, 1 Vegetable, 1 Fat, 1 Bread) (168 mg Sodium), see page 485
½ cup cooked egg noodles (1 Bread)
½ cup steamed green beans (1 Vegetable)
1 cup romaine lettuce with
1 tablespoon oil and vinegar dressing (1 Fat)
½ cup unsweetened, canned pears (1 Fruit)

1,200 - Calorie Menus

Week 2—Thursday

Breakfast

1 Bran Muffin (1 Bread, ½ Fruit, 1 Fat) (200
    mg Sodium), see page 467
¼ cup scrambled egg substitute (1 Meat)
    cooked with vegetable oil cooking spray
½ fresh grapefruit (1 Fruit)

Lunch

½ cup cooked spaghetti (1 Bread)
½ cup Low-Sodium Italian Tomato Sauce (1½
    Vegetable) (20 mg Sodium), see page 508
1½ tablespoons grated Parmesan cheese
    (½ Meat)
1 small fresh peach (1 Fruit)

Dinner

¾ serving Low-Sodium Beef Broccoli Stir-Fry
    (3 Meat, 1 Vegetable) (408 mg Sodium),
    see page 489
½ cup cooked rice (1 Bread)
1 oriental salad:
    1 cup mixed greens
    ½ cup unsweetened mandarin oranges
      (1 Fruit)
    1 tablespoon slivered almonds (1 Fat)
    2 teaspoons oil and vinegar dressing (1 Fat)
1 cup Apple Oat Crisp (2 Fruit, 1 Bread,
    ½ Fat) (80 mg Sodium), see page 501

1,200 - Calorie Menus

Week 2–Friday

Breakfast

½ cup unsweetened grapefruit juice (1 Fruit)
¾ cup corn bran cereal (1 Bread)
1 cup skim milk (1 Milk)
1 slice whole wheat toast (1 Bread)
1 teaspoon unsalted margarine (1 Fat)

Lunch

1 serving Low-Sodium Seafood Quiche (½ Milk,
    2½ Meat) (350 mg Sodium), see page 487
½ cup steamed asparagus (1 Vegetable)
½ cup Apple Waldorf Salad (1 Fruit, 1 Fat)
    (76 mg Sodium), see page 474
1 whole wheat dinner roll (1 Bread)
1 teaspoon unsalted margarine (1 Fat)

Dinner

2 tacos:
    2 taco shells (1 Bread, 1 Fat)
    ½ cup cooked, seasoned ground chicken
      (2 Meat)
    ¼ cup chopped tomato (½ Vegetable)
    shredded lettuce
    picante sauce
½ cup steamed zucchini (1 Vegetable)
½ cup sugar-free vanilla pudding (½ Milk) with
½ sliced banana (1 Fruit) and
4 vanilla wafers (1 Bread)

1,200 - Calorie Menus

Week 2—Saturday

Breakfast

½ cup unsweetened orange juice (1 Fruit)
½ cup cooked oatmeal without salt (1 Bread)
1 cup skim milk (1 Milk)

Lunch

1 serving Ricotta-Parmesan Torte (1 Fat, ½
    Vegetable, 1½ Bread, 1 Meat) (365 mg
    Sodium), see page 493
1 cup steamed, mixed vegetables (2 Vegetable)
1 teaspoon unsalted margarine (1 Fat)
12 large green grapes (1 Fruit)
1 cup skim milk (1 Milk)

Dinner

4 ounces Low-Sodium Southern Fried Chicken
    (4 Meat, ½ Bread, ½ Fat) (98 mg
    Sodium), see page 481
½ cup mashed potatoes (1 Bread)
½ cup steamed French-cut green beans
    (1 Vegetable)
½ cup fresh pineapple (1 Fruit)
1 teaspoon unsalted margarine (1 Fat)

1,200 - Calorie Menus

Week 2—Sunday

Breakfast

½ cup unsweetened grapefruit juice (1 Fruit)
½ English muffin (1 Bread) topped with
½ small sliced apple (½ Fruit) and
2 tablespoons grated cheddar cheese (½ Meat)
¾ cup bran flakes (1 Bread)
1 cup skim milk (1 Milk)

Lunch

1 chicken salad sandwich:
    2 slices diet whole wheat bread (1 Bread)
    ¼ cup cooked, chopped chicken (1 Meat)
    2 tablespoons diet mayonnaise (2 Fat)
6 raw carrot sticks (1 Vegetable)
1 small fresh pear (1 Fruit)
¾ cup skim milk (¾ Milk)

Dinner

2 ounces Shishkabob (2 Meat, 1 Vegetable)
    (196 mg Sodium), see page 491
1 small baked potato (1 Bread) with
1 tablespoon sour cream (1 Fat) and
1 teaspoon chives
½ cup steamed broccoli (1 Vegetable)
¼ honeydew melon (2 Fruit)

1,500 - Calorie Menus

Week 1—Monday

Breakfast

1 cup cooked oat bran cereal without salt
   (2 Bread)
2 tablespoons raisins (1 Fruit)
½ cup skim milk (½ Milk)

Lunch

1 pita pocket sandwich:
   1 whole wheat pita pocket (2 Bread)
   1 ounce sliced turkey (1 Meat)
   ½ ounce part-skim mozzarella cheese
      (½ Meat)
   1 teaspoon mayonnaise (1 Fat)
   ½ teaspoon mustard
   shredded lettuce and ½ cup chopped
      tomatoes (1 Vegetable)
1 large apple (3 Fruit)

Dinner

¾ cup Gazpacho (1½ Vegetable, ½ Fat) (24
   mg Sodium), see page 471, with
¼ sliced avocado (2 Fat)
1 Pita Cracker (⅛ Bread) (23 mg Sodium), see
   page 506

1 cup Spanish Chicken and Rice (3½ Meat, 2 Bread, 2 Vegetable, 1 Fat), (375 mg Sodium), see page 482
24 large green grapes (2 Fruit)

Snack

1 cup plain, nonfat yogurt (1 Milk)
½ cup unsweetened, crushed pineapple (1 Fruit)
2 vanilla wafers (½ Bread)

1,500 - Calorie Menus

Week 1—Tuesday

Breakfast

½ cup fresh orange slices (1 Fruit)
1 poached egg (1 Meat)
1 slice whole wheat toast (1 Bread)
1 teaspoon unsalted margarine (1 Fat)
1 tablespoon apple butter (½ Fruit)
1 cup skim milk (1 Milk)

Lunch

1½ cups Cold Pasta Salad (2¼ Bread, ¾ Meat, 3 Vegetable, ¾ Fat) (618 mg Sodium), see page 475
2 slices garlic bread:
    2 3-inch slices Italian bread (1 Bread)
    1 teaspoon unsalted margarine (1 Fat)
    ½ teaspoon garlic powder
1 sliced kiwi (2 Fruit)

Dinner

2½ ounces Peppered Veal (2½ Meat, 1 Vegetable, ½ Bread, ½ Fat) (208 mg Sodium), see page 483
1 small baked potato (1 Bread) with
1 teaspoon unsalted margarine (1 Fat) and
¼ cup plain, nonfat yogurt (¼ Milk)
½ cup steamed broccoli (1 Vegetable) seasoned with
1 teaspoon pimiento
½ cup unsweetened applesauce (1 Fruit)

1,500 - Calorie Menus

Week 1—Wednesday

Breakfast

½ cup unsweetened orange juice (1 Fruit)
½ cup shredded wheat biscuits (1 Bread)
1 cup skim milk (1 Milk)
1 cup unsweetened, canned peaches (2 Fruit)

Lunch

1 grilled cheese sandwich:
    2 slices whole wheat bread (2 Bread)
    2 ounces low-fat cheese (2 Meat), grilled, using
    2 teaspoons unsalted margarine (2 Fat)
    3 slices tomato (1 Vegetable)
1½ cups fresh strawberries (2 Fruit)
½ cup skim milk (½ Milk)

Dinner

3 ounces Herbed Garlic Fish Fillets (3 Meat) (202 mg Sodium), see page 486
1 cup Oven French Fries (4 Bread) (10 mg Sodium), see page 505
1 orange romaine salad:
    2 cups romaine lettuce (2 Vegetable)
    ½ cup unsweetened mandarin oranges (1 Fruit)
    1 teaspoon rice vinegar
    1 teaspoon olive oil (1 Fat)

1 whole wheat dinner roll (1 Bread)
1 teaspoon unsalted margarine (1 Fat)

Snack

½ cup ice milk (1 Milk)

1,500 - Calorie Menus

Week 1—Thursday

Breakfast

1 cup unsweetened, canned pears (2 Fruit)
1 vegetable omelet:
    1 whole egg, plus 2 egg whites (2 Meat)
    3 slices tomato
    2 fresh sliced mushrooms
    1 chopped green onion
    (tomato, mushrooms, onion = 1½ Vegetable)
1 whole wheat English muffin (2 Bread)
2 teaspoons unsalted margarine (2 Fat)

Lunch

1 "Munchie Tray":
    1 ounce sliced chicken (1 Meat)
    ½ ounce low-fat cheese (½ Meat)
    9 saltine crackers, unsalted tops (1½ Bread)
    12 large green grapes (1 Fruit)
1 cup Fruit Smoothy (1½ Milk) (85 mg
    Sodium), see page 503

Dinner

1 Spicy Bean Enchilada (1 Meat, 2 Bread, ½
    Vegetable) (553 mg Sodium), see page 496
1 cup steamed rice (2 Bread) mixed with
¼ cup tomato sauce (1 Vegetable)
1 cup tossed dinner salad (1 Vegetable)
2 tablespoons oil and vinegar dressing (2 Fat)

Snack

1 large orange (2 Fruit)

1,500 - Calorie Menus

Week 1—Friday

Breakfast

1 cup cooked oatmeal or oat bran cereal
without salt (2 Bread)
½ mashed banana (1 Fruit)
1 cup skim milk (1 Milk)

Lunch

1 cup Long Grain and Wild Rice Chicken Salad
(2 Meat, 2 Bread, 1 Vegetable, 1 Fruit, 2
Fat) (500 mg Sodium), see page 476 on
¼ cup shredded lettuce
6 saltine crackers, unsalted tops (1 Bread)

Dinner

1 piece Vegetarian Lasagna (2 Bread, 2 Meat,
2½ Vegetable, ½ Fat) (350 mg Sodium),
see page 499
1 whole wheat dinner roll (1 Bread)
2 teaspoons unsalted margarine (2 Fat)
1 cup fresh fruit salad (2 Fruit)
1 cup skim milk (1 Milk)

1,500 - Calorie Menus

Week 1—Saturday

Breakfast

½ cup orange juice (1 Fruit)
1 slice French Toast Puff (1 Meat, ⅛ Milk, ½ Fruit, 1 Bread) (230 mg Sodium), see page 468, with
1 teaspoon unsalted margarine (1 Fat) and
½ cup plain, nonfat yogurt (½ Milk) and
4 tablespoons Berry Syrup (2 Fruit) (0 mg Sodium), see page 507
½ cup skim milk (½ Milk)

Lunch

½ cup Tuna Salad (2 Meat, 1 Milk) (707 mg Sodium), see page 478, on
1 lettuce leaf with 3 slices tomato (1 Vegetable)
4 pieces melba toast (1 Bread)
1 large apple (3 Fruit)
½ cup skim milk (½ Milk)

Dinner

3 Stuffed Shells (1 Meat, 2 Bread, 3 Vegetable, ½ Fat) (150 mg Sodium), see page 498
½ cup steamed broccoli (1 Vegetable) with
1 teaspoon unsalted margarine (1 Fat)
1 cup tossed dinner salad with cucumber and carrot slices (1 Vegetable)

1 tablespoon oil and vinegar dressing (1 Fat)

Snack

1 small oatmeal cookie (1 Bread)

1,500 - Calorie Menus

Week 1—Sunday

Breakfast

2 Oatmeal Pancakes (2 Bread, ⅓ Milk) (398
    mg Sodium), see page 470
1 teaspoon unsalted margarine (1 Fat)
2 tablespoons low-calorie syrup (½ Fruit)
1 cup skim milk (1 Milk)

Lunch

1 fruit salad:
    ¾ cup fresh strawberries (1 Fruit)
    12 large green grapes (1 Fruit)
    1 sliced banana (2 Fruit)
    1 small sliced apple (1 Fruit)
½ cup low-fat cottage cheese (2 Meat)
6 saltine crackers, unsalted tops (1 Bread)

Dinner

4 ounces Teriyaki Steak (4 Meat, ½ Vegetable,
    ½ Fat) (472 mg Sodium), see page 492
1 cup steamed rice (2 Bread) with
1 teaspoon unsalted margarine (1 Fat)
1 cup stir-fry vegetables:
    ¼ cup julienne zucchini (½ Vegetable)
    ¼ cup julienne carrots (½ Vegetable)
    ¼ cup chopped red bell peppers
        (½ Vegetable)

¼ cup sliced onion (½ Vegetable)
1 teaspoon safflower oil (1 Fat)
¼ teaspoon ginger powder
¼ teaspoon minced garlic
1 cup skim milk (1 Milk)

Snack

½ cup unsalted pretzel sticks (1 Bread)

1,500 - Calorie Menus

Week 2—Monday

Breakfast

¾ cup unsweetened orange-grapefruit juice
    (1½ Fruit)
1 waffle (1 Bread, 1 Fat) topped with
½ cup unsweetened applesauce (1 Fruit) and
1 teaspoon cinnamon
1 cup skim milk (1 Milk)

Lunch

1 small baked potato (1 Bread) topped with
2 tablespoons grated cheddar cheese (½ Meat)
1 cup fresh fruit salad (2 Fruit) with
¼ cup low-fat cottage cheese (1 Meat)

Dinner

3 ounces Grilled Sesame Chicken Breast (3
    Meat, ½ Fat, ½ Fruit) (443 mg Sodium),
    see page 480
1 cup cooked corkscrew pasta (2 Bread) with
1 teaspoon unsalted margarine (1 Fat)
½ cup steamed broccoli (1 Vegetable)
1 cup marinated vegetables:
    ½ cup sliced tomato
    ½ cup sliced cucumber
    (tomato and cucumber = 1 Vegetable)
    1 tablespoon Italian dressing (1 Fat)
¼ cantaloupe (1 Fruit)

1,500 - Calorie Menus

Week 2—Tuesday

Breakfast

½ cup unsweetened orange juice (1 Fruit)
1 Oat Bran Muffin (½ Bread, ½ Fruit, ½ Fat)
    (60 mg Sodium), see page 469
¼ cup scrambled egg substitute (1 Meat)
    cooked with vegetable oil cooking spray
1 teaspoon unsalted margarine (1 Fat)
1 cup skim milk (1 Milk)

Lunch

1 cup Low-Sodium Minestrone Soup (1 Bread, 1
    Vegetable) (57 mg Sodium), see page 472
1 turkey sandwich:
    2 slices whole wheat bread (2 Bread)
    2 ounces sliced turkey breast (2 Meat)
    1 teaspoon diet mayonnaise (½ Fat)
    ¼ cup alfalfa sprouts (1 Vegetable)
    1 slice tomato (½ Vegetable)
1 cup plain, nonfat yogurt (1 Milk) with
1 teaspoon sugar substitute and
1 teaspoon vanilla
¾ cup fresh strawberries (1 Fruit)

Dinner

2½ cups Low-Sodium Shrimp Creole (3 Meat,
   2 Bread, 3 Vegetable) (436 mg Sodium),
   see page 488
1 3-inch slice French bread (1 Bread)
1 teaspoon unsalted margarine (1 Fat)
Lettuce wedge with
1 tablespoon French dressing (1 Fat)
1 small baked apple (1 Fruit)

1,500 - Calorie Menus

Week 2—Wednesday

Breakfast

1 English muffin (2 Bread)
3 teaspoons unsalted diet margarine (1 Fat)
1 fresh fruit cup:
    ¼ sliced banana (½ Fruit)
    ½ sliced orange (½ Fruit)
1 cup homemade cocoa:
    1 cup heated skim milk (1 Milk)
    1 tablespoon cocoa
    1 teaspoon sugar substitute

Lunch

2 tostadas:
    2 flour tortillas (2 Bread)
    ¼ cup cooked, drained ground beef (1 Meat)
    2 tablespoons picante sauce
    2 tablespoons grated cheddar cheese
        (½ Meat)
    ½ cup chopped tomato (1 Vegetable)
¼ cantaloupe (1 Fruit)

Dinner

3 ounces Veal Scaloppine (3 Meat, 1½
    Vegetable, 1 Fat, 1 Bread) (252 mg
    Sodium), see page 485
½ cup cooked egg noodles (1 Bread)

½ cup steamed green beans (1 Vegetable)
1 cup romaine lettuce with
1 tablespoon oil and vinegar dressing (1 Fat)
½ cup unsweetened, canned pears (1 Fruit)
1 cup skim milk (1 Milk)

1,500 - Calorie Menus

Week 2—Thursday

Breakfast

1 Bran Muffin (1 Bread, ½ Fruit, 1 Fat) (200 mg Sodium), see page 467

1 teaspoon unsalted margarine (1 Fat)

¼ cup scrambled egg substitute (1 Meat) cooked with vegetable oil cooking spray

½ fresh grapefruit (1 Fruit)

1 cup skim milk (1 Milk)

Lunch

¾ cup cooked spaghetti (1½ Bread)

½ cup Low-Sodium Italian Tomato Sauce (1½ Vegetable) (20 mg Sodium), see page 508

1½ tablespoons grated Parmesan cheese (½ Meat)

1 3-inch slice French bread (1 Bread)

1 small fresh peach (1 Fruit)

1 cup skim milk (1 Milk)

Dinner

1 serving Low-Sodium Beef Broccoli Stir-Fry (4 Meat, 2 Vegetable, ½ Fat) (544 mg Sodium), see page 489

½ cup cooked rice (1 Bread)

1 oriental salad:
    1 cup mixed greens

½ cup unsweetened mandarin oranges
(1 Fruit)
1 tablespoon slivered almonds (1 Fat)
1 tablespoon oil and vinegar dressing (1 Fat)
1 cup Apple Oat Crisp (2 Fruit, 1 Bread,
½ Fat) (80 mg Sodium), see page 501

1,500 - Calorie Menus

Week 2—Friday

Breakfast

½ cup unsweetened grapefruit juice (1 Fruit)
¾ cup corn bran cereal (1 Bread)
½ cup fresh blueberries (1 Fruit)
1 cup skim milk (1 Milk)
1 slice whole wheat toast (1 Bread)
1 teaspoon unsalted margarine (1 Fat)

Lunch

1 serving Low-Sodium Seafood Quiche (½
    Milk, 2½ Meat) (350 mg Sodium), see page
    487
½ cup steamed asparagus (1 Vegetable)
½ cup Apple Waldorf Salad (1 Fruit, 1 Fat)
    (76 mg Sodium), see page 474
2 whole wheat dinner rolls (2 Bread)
1 teaspoon unsalted margarine (1 Fat)

Dinner

2 tacos:
    2 taco shells (1 Bread, 1 Fat)
    ½ cup cooked, seasoned ground chicken
        (2 Meat)
    ¼ cup chopped tomato (½ Vegetable)
    shredded lettuce
    picante sauce

½ cup steamed zucchini (1 Vegetable)
½ cup sugar-free vanilla pudding (½ Milk) with
½ sliced banana (1 Fruit) and
4 vanilla wafers (1 Bread)

1,500 - Calorie Menus

Week 2—Saturday

Breakfast

½ cup unsweetened orange juice (1 Fruit)
½ cup cooked oatmeal without salt (1 Bread)
1 slice whole wheat toast (1 Bread)
3 teaspoons unsalted diet margarine (1 Fat)
1 cup skim milk (1 Milk)

Lunch

1 serving Ricotta-Parmesan Torte (1 Fat, ½
    Vegetable, 1½ Bread, 1 Meat) (365 mg
    Sodium), see page 493
2 4-inch breadsticks (1 Bread)
1 cup steamed, mixed vegetables (2 Vegetable)
1 teaspoon unsalted margarine (1 Fat)
½ cup Turkey-Fruit Salad (1 Meat, 1 Fruit, ½
    Vegetable) (75 mg Sodium), see page 479
6 large green grapes (½ Fruit)
1 cup skim milk (1 Milk)

Dinner

3 ounces Low-Sodium Southern Fried Chicken
    (3 Meat, ½ Bread, ½ Fat) (195 mg
    Sodium), see page 481
½ cup mashed potatoes (1 Bread)
½ cup steamed French-cut green beans (1
    Vegetable)
1 cup fresh pineapple (2 Fruit)
1 teaspoon unsalted margarine (1 Fat)

1,500 - Calorie Menus

Week 2—Sunday

Breakfast

½ cup unsweetened grapefruit juice (1 Fruit)
1 English muffin (2 Bread) topped with
1 small sliced apple (1 Fruit) and
1 tablespoon grated cheddar cheese (¼ Meat)
¾ cup bran flakes (1 Bread)
1 cup skim milk (1 Milk)

Lunch

1 chicken salad sandwich:
    2 slices whole wheat bread (2 Bread)
    ¼ cup cooked, chopped chicken (1 Meat)
    2 tablespoons diet mayonnaise (2 Fat)
6 raw carrot sticks (1 Vegetable)
1 small fresh pear (1 Fruit)
1 cup skim milk (1 Milk)

Dinner

3 ounces Shishkabob (3 Meat, 2 Vegetable)
    (295 mg Sodium), see page 491
1 small baked potato (1 Bread) with
1 tablespoon sour cream (1 Fat) and
1 teaspoon chives
½ cup steamed broccoli (1 Vegetable)
¼ honeydew melon (2 Fruit)

2,200 - Calorie Menus

Week 1—Monday

Breakfast

1 cup orange juice (2 Fruit)
1 cup cooked oat bran cereal without salt
   (2 Bread)
2 tablespoons raisins (1 Fruit)
1 cup skim milk (1 Milk)

Lunch

1 pita pocket sandwich:
   1 whole wheat pita pocket (2 Bread)
   1 ounce sliced turkey (1 Meat)
   ½ ounce part-skim mozzarella cheese
      (½ Meat)
   2 teaspoons mayonnaise (2 Fat)
   ½ teaspoon mustard
   shredded lettuce and
   ½ cup chopped tomatoes (1 Vegetable)
1 large apple (3 Fruit)
½ cup skim milk (½ Milk)

Dinner

1½ cups Gazpacho (3 Vegetable, 1 Fat)
   (48 mg Sodium), see page 471, with
¼ sliced avocado (2 Fat)
4 Pita Crackers (½ Bread) (92 mg Sodium),
   see page 506

1½ cups Spanish Chicken and Rice (5¼ Meat, 3 Bread, 3 Vegetable, 1½ Fat), (563 mg Sodium), see page 482
24 large green grapes (2 Fruit)

Snack

1 cup plain, nonfat yogurt (1 Milk)
½ cup unsweetened, crushed pineapple (1 Fruit)
4 vanilla wafers (1 Bread)

2,200 - Calorie Menus

Week 1—Tuesday

Breakfast

1 cup fresh orange slices (2 Fruit)
¼ cup scrambled egg substitute (1 Meat)
    cooked with vegetable oil cooking spray
2 slices whole wheat toast (2 Bread)
1 teaspoon unsalted margarine (1 Fat)
1 tablespoon apple butter (½ Fruit)
1 cup skim milk (1 Milk)

Lunch

2 cups Cold Pasta Salad (3 Bread, 1 Meat, 4
    Vegetable, 1 Fat) (824 mg Sodium), see
    page 475
2 slices garlic bread:
    2 3-inch slices Italian bread (2 Bread)
    2 teaspoons unsalted margarine (2 Fat)
    ½ teaspoon garlic powder
1 sliced kiwi (2 Fruit)

Dinner

5 ounces Peppered Veal (5 Meat, 2 Vegetable, 1
    Bread, 1 Fat) (416 mg Sodium), see page
    483
1 small baked potato (1 Bread) with
1 teaspoon unsalted margarine (1 Fat) and
¼ cup plain, nonfat yogurt (¼ Milk)

½ cup steamed broccoli (1 Vegetable)
½ cup unsweetened applesauce (1 Fruit)

Snack

½ cup plain, nonfat yogurt (½ Milk) with
½ cup fresh blueberries (1 Fruit)

2,200 - Calorie Menus

Week 1—Wednesday

Breakfast

1 cup unsweetened orange juice (2 Fruit)
½ cup shredded wheat biscuits (1 Bread)
1 cup skim milk (1 Milk)
1 cup unsweetened, canned peaches (2 Fruit)

Lunch

1 grilled tuna melt:
    2 slices whole wheat bread (2 Bread)
    ½ cup tuna, packed in water, low-sodium
    (2 Meat) mixed with
    2 teaspoons mayonnaise (2 Fat)
    2 ounces American cheese (2 Meat),
    grilled using
    1 teaspoon unsalted margarine (1 Fat)
3 slices tomato (1 Vegetable)
1 cup raw broccoli and cauliflower (1 Vegetable)
1½ cups fresh strawberries (2 Fruit)
½ cup skim milk (½ Milk)

Dinner

6 ounces Herbed Garlic Fish Fillets (6 Meat)
    (404 mg Sodium), see page 486
1 cup Oven French Fries (4 Bread) (10 mg
    Sodium), see page 505
1 orange romaine salad:

2 cups romaine lettuce (2 Vegetable)
1 cup unsweetened mandarin oranges
   (2 Fruit)
1 teaspoon rice vinegar
1 teaspoon olive oil (1 Fat)
1 whole wheat dinner roll (1 Bread)
1 teaspoon unsalted margarine (1 Fat)

Snack

½ cup ice milk (1 Milk)
½ cup fresh raspberries (1 Fruit)
25 small unsalted pretzel sticks (1 Bread)

2,200 - Calorie Menus

Week 1—Thursday

Breakfast

1 cup unsweetened, canned pears (2 Fruit)
1 vegetable omelet:
    ¾ cup egg substitute (3 Meat)
    3 slices tomato
    2 fresh sliced mushrooms
    1 chopped green onion
    (tomato, mushrooms, onion =
      1½ Vegetable)
    ¼ teaspoon dried oregano
1 whole wheat English muffin (2 Bread)
2 teaspoons unsalted margarine (2 Fat)

Lunch

1 "Munchie Tray":
    4 ounces sliced chicken (4 Meat)
    12 saltine crackers, unsalted tops (2 Bread)
    24 large green grapes (2 Fruit)
    ½ cup raw carrot sticks (½ Vegetable)
    ½ cup raw celery sticks (½ Vegetable)
1 cup Fruit Smoothy (1½ Milk) (85 mg
    Sodium), see page 503

Dinner

1 Spicy Bean Enchilada (1 Meat, 2 Bread, ½
    Vegetable) (553 mg Sodium), see page 496

1½ cups steamed rice (3 Bread) mixed with
⅜ cup tomato sauce (1 Vegetable)
1 corn tortilla (1 Bread)
2 cups tossed dinner salad (2 Vegetable)
2 tablespoons oil and vinegar dressing (2 Fat)

Snack

1 large orange (2 Fruit)
1 cup plain, nonfat yogurt (1 Milk)
½ cup unsweetened fruit cocktail (1 Fruit)

2,200 - Calorie Menus

Week 1—Friday

Breakfast

½ cup orange juice (1 Fruit)
1½ cups cooked oatmeal or oat bran cereal
    without salt (3 Bread)
1 mashed banana (2 Fruit)
1 cup skim milk (1 Milk)

Lunch

1½ cups Long Grain and Wild Rice Chicken
    Salad (3 Meat, 3 Bread, 1½ Vegetable,
    1½ Fruit, 3 Fat) (750 mg Sodium), see
    page 476, on
½ cup shredded lettuce
12 saltine crackers, unsalted tops (2 Bread)

Dinner

1 piece Vegetarian Lasagna (2 Bread, 2 Meat,
    2½ Vegetable, ½ Fat) (350 mg Sodium),
    see page 499
1 cup cooked green beans (2 Vegetable) with
1 teaspoon unsalted margarine (1 Fat)
1 whole wheat dinner roll (1 Bread) with
2 teaspoons unsalted margarine (2 Fat)
1 cup fresh fruit salad (2 Fruit)
½ cup skim milk (½ Milk)

Snack

1 cup raw celery sticks (1 Vegetable)
1 tablespoon cream cheese (1 Fat)

2,200 - Calorie Menus

Week 1—Saturday

Breakfast

½ cup orange juice (1 Fruit)
3 slices French Toast Puff (3 Meat, ⅜ Milk,
    1½ Fruit, 3 Bread) (690 mg Sodium), see
    page 468, with
2 teaspoons unsalted margarine (2 Fat) and
½ cup plain, nonfat yogurt (½ Milk) and
4 tablespoons Berry Syrup (2 Fruit) (0 mg
    Sodium), see page 507
½ cup skim milk (½ Milk)

Lunch

½ cup Tuna Salad (2 Meat, 1 Milk) (707 mg
    Sodium), see page 478, on
1 lettuce leaf
1 cup chopped cucumbers and tomatoes
    (1 Vegetable) mixed with
1 tablespoon oil and vinegar dressing (1 Fat)
1 large apple (3 Fruit)

Dinner

3 Stuffed Shells (1 Meat, 2 Bread, 3
    Vegetable, ½ Fat) (150 mg Sodium), see
    page 498
½ cup steamed broccoli (1 Vegetable) with
1 teaspoon unsalted margarine (1 Fat)

1 cup tossed dinner salad with cucumber and carrot slices (1 Vegetable)

1 tablespoon oil and vinegar dressing (1 Fat)

Snack

2 small oatmeal cookies (2 Bread)

1 cup skim milk (1 Milk)

2,200 - Calorie Menus

Week 1—Sunday

Breakfast

½ grapefruit (1 Fruit)
3 Oatmeal Pancakes (3 Bread, ½ Milk) (597
    mg Sodium), see page 470
2 teaspoons unsalted margarine (2 Fat)
4 tablespoons low-calorie syrup (1 Fruit)
⅔ cup skim milk (⅔ Milk)

Lunch

1 fruit salad:
    ¾ cup fresh strawberries (1 Fruit)
    24 large green grapes (2 Fruit)
    1 sliced banana (2 Fruit)
    1 sliced small apple (1 Fruit)
¾ cup low-fat cottage cheese (3 Meat)
12 saltine crackers, unsalted tops (2 Bread)

Dinner

4 ounces Teriyaki Steak (4 Meat, ½ Vegetable,
    ½ Fat) (472 mg Sodium), see page 492
1 cup steamed rice (2 Bread) with
1 teaspoon unsalted margarine (1 Fat)
2 cups stir-fry vegetables:
    ½ cup julienne zucchini (1 Vegetable)
    ½ cup julienne carrots (1 Vegetable)
    ½ cup chopped red bell pepper (1 Vegetable)

½ cup sliced onion (1 Vegetable)
2 teaspoons safflower oil (2 Fat)
½ teaspoon ginger powder
½ teaspoon minced garlic

Snack

1 cup frozen yogurt (2 Milk)
1 cup unsalted pretzel sticks (2 Bread)

2,200 - Calorie Menus

Week 2—Monday

Breakfast

1 cup unsweetened orange juice (2 Fruit)
2 waffles (2 Bread, 2 Fat) topped with
½ cup unsweetened applesauce (1 Fruit) and
1 teaspoon cinnamon
1 cup skim milk (1 Milk)

Lunch

3 ounces grilled tuna steak (3 Meat)
1 large baked potato (3 Bread) topped with
2 tablespoons grated cheddar cheese (½ Meat)
    and
2 teaspoons unsalted margarine (2 Fat)
1 cup fresh fruit salad (2 Fruit) with
¼ cup low-fat cottage cheese (1 Meat)
1 whole wheat dinner roll (1 Bread)
1 teaspoon unsalted margarine (1 Fat)

Dinner

3 ounces Grilled Sesame Chicken Breast (3
    Meat, ½ Fat, ½ Fruit) (443 mg Sodium),
    see page 480
1 cup cooked corkscrew pasta (2 Bread) with
1 teaspoon unsalted margarine (1 Fat)
1 cup steamed broccoli (2 Vegetable)
1 cup marinated vegetables:

½ cup sliced tomato
½ cup sliced cucumber
(tomato and cucumber = 1 Vegetable)
2 tablespoons oil and vinegar dressing
    (2 Fat)
½ cantaloupe (2 Fruit)
1 cup skim milk (1 Milk)

2,200 - Calories Menus

Week 2—Tuesday

Breakfast

½ cup unsweetened orange juice (1 Fruit)
2 Oat Bran Muffins (1 Bread, 1 Fruit, 1 Fat)
 (120 mg Sodium), see page 469
¼ cup scrambled egg substitute (1 Meat)
 cooked with vegetable oil cooking spray
2 teaspoons unsalted margarine (2 Fat)
1 cup skim milk (1 Milk)

Lunch

1½ cups Low-Sodium Minestrone Soup (1½
 Bread, 1½ Vegetable) (86 mg Sodium),
 see page 472
1 turkey sandwich:
 2 slices whole wheat bread (2 Bread)
 4 ounces sliced turkey breast (4 Meat)
 1 teaspoon diet mayonnaise (½ Fat)
 ¼ cup alfalfa sprouts (1 Vegetable)
 1 slice tomato (½ Vegetable)
1 cup plain, nonfat yogurt (1 Milk) with
1 teaspoon sugar substitute and
1 teaspoon vanilla
¾ cup fresh strawberries (1 Fruit)
1 slice (¹⁄₂₄, angel food cake (1 Bread)

Dinner

2½ cups Low-Sodium Shrimp Creole (3 Meat, 2 Bread, 3 Vegetable) (436 mg Sodium), see page 488

2 3-inch slices French bread (2 Bread)

2 teaspoons unsalted margarine (2 Fat)

Lettuce wedge with

1 tablespoon French dressing (1 Fat)

1 large baked apple (3 Fruit)

Snack

3 cups air-popped popcorn (1 Bread)

1 cup apple juice (3 Fruit)

2,200 - Calorie Menus

Week 2—Wednesday

Breakfast

2 English muffins (4 Bread)
2 teaspoons unsalted margarine (2 Fat)
1 fresh fruit cup:
    ½ sliced banana (1 Fruit)
    1 sliced orange (1 Fruit)
1 cup homemade cocoa:
    1 cup heated skim milk (1 Milk)
    1 tablespoon cocoa
    1 teaspoon sugar substitute

Lunch

2 tostadas:
    2 flour tortillas (2 Bread)
    ½ cup cooked, drained ground beef (2 Meat)
    2 tablespoons picante sauce
    ¼ cup grated cheddar cheese (1 Meat)
    ½ cup chopped tomato (1 Vegetable)
½ cantaloupe (2 Fruit)

Dinner

3 ounces Veal Scaloppine (3 Meat, 1½
    Vegetable, 1 Fat, 1 Bread) (252 mg
    Sodium), see page 485
1 cup cooked egg noodles (2 Bread)
½ cup steamed green beans (1 Vegetable)

1 cup romaine lettuce with
1 tablespoon oil and vinegar dressing (1 Fat)
1 3-inch slice Italian Bread (1 Bread)
1 teaspoon unsalted margarine (1 Fat)
½ cup unsweetened, canned pears (1 Fruit)

Snack

1 small apple (1 Fruit)

2,200 - Calorie Menus

Week 2—Thursday

Breakfast

2 Bran Muffins (2 Bread, 1 Fruit, 2 Fat)
   (400 mg Sodium), see page 467
2 teaspoons unsalted margarine (2 Fat)
¼ cup scrambled egg substitute (1 Meat)
   cooked with vegetable oil cooking spray
½ fresh grapefruit (1 Fruit)

Lunch

2 cups cooked spaghetti (4 Bread)
1 cup Low-Sodium Italian Tomato Sauce
   (3 Vegetable) (40 mg Sodium), see page 508
2 3-inch slices Italian bread (2 Bread)
2 teaspoons unsalted margarine (2 Fat)
1 small fresh peach (1 Fruit)

Dinner

1 serving Low-Sodium Beef Broccoli Stir-Fry
   (4 Meat, 2 Vegetable, ½ Fat) (544 mg
   Sodium), see page 489
¾ cup cooked rice (1½ Bread)
1 oriental salad:
   1 cup mixed greens
   ½ cup unsweetened mandarin oranges
      (1 Fruit)
   1 tablespoon slivered almonds (1 Fat)

1 tablespoon oil and vinegar dressing
   (1 Fat)
1 cup Apple Oat Crisp (2 Fruit, 1 Bread,
   ½ Fat) (80 mg Sodium), see page 501
1 cup skim milk (1 Milk)

Snack

¼ cup low-fat cottage cheese (1 Meat)
½ cup unsweetened, canned pears (1 Fruit)

2,200 - Calorie Menus

Week 2—Friday

Breakfast

1 cup unsweetened grapefruit juice (2 Fruit)
1½ cups corn bran cereal (2 Bread)
½ cup fresh blueberries (1 Fruit)
1 cup skim milk (1 Milk)
1 slice whole wheat toast (1 Bread)
1 teaspoon unsalted margarine (1 Fat)

Lunch

2 servings Low-Sodium Seafood Quiche
   (1 Milk, 5 Meat) (700 mg Sodium),
   see page 487
½ cup steamed asparagus (1 Vegetable)
½ cup Apple Waldorf Salad (1 Fruit, 1 Fat)
   (76 mg Sodium), see page 474
2 whole wheat dinner rolls (2 Bread)

Dinner

2 tacos:
   2 taco shells (1 Bread, 1 Fat)
   ½ cup cooked, seasoned ground chicken
    (2 Meat)
   ¼ cup chopped tomato (½ Vegetable)
   shredded lettuce
   picante sauce
1 cup steamed zucchini (2 Vegetable)

1 cup sugar-free vanilla pudding (1 Milk) with
1 sliced banana (2 Fruit) and
8 vanilla wafers (2 Bread)

Snack

1 chicken sandwich:
    2 slices rye bread (2 Bread)
    ¼ cup cooked, diced chicken (1 meat)
    1 small chopped apple (1 Fruit)
    3 teaspoons diet mayonnaise (1 Fat)
½ cup unsweetened orange juice (1 Fruit)

2,200 - Calorie Menus

Week 2—Saturday

Breakfast

1 cup unsweetened orange juice (2 Fruit)
2 large shredded wheat biscuits (2 Bread)
1 slice whole wheat toast (1 Bread)
1 teaspoon unsalted margarine (1 Fat)
1 cup skim milk (1 Milk)

Lunch

1½ servings Ricotta-Parmesan Torte (1½ Fat,
    1 Vegetable, 2 Bread, 1½ Meat) (547 mg
    Sodium), see page 493
2 4-inch breadsticks (1 Bread)
1 cup steamed, mixed vegetables (2 Vegetable)
1 teaspoon unsalted margarine (1 Fat)
½ cup Turkey-Fruit Salad (1 Meat, 1 Fruit,
    ½ Vegetable) (75 mg Sodium), see page
    479
12 large green grapes (1 Fruit)

Dinner

3 ounces Low-Sodium Southern Fried Chicken
    (3 Meat, ½ Bread, ½ Fat) (195 mg Sodium),
    see page 481

1½ cups mashed potatoes (3 Bread)
½ cup steamed French-cut green beans
　(1 Vegetable)
1 cup fresh pineapple (2 Fruit)
2 teaspoons unsalted margarine (2 Fat)

Snack

1 cup skim milk (1 Milk)
8 vanilla wafers (2 Bread)
1 small fresh peach (1 Fruit)

2,200 - Calorie Menus

Week 2—Sunday

Breakfast

1 cup unsweetened grapefruit juice (2 Fruit)
1 English muffin (2 Bread) topped with
1 small sliced apple (1 Fruit) and
2 tablespoons grated cheddar cheese (½ Meat)
1½ cups bran flakes (2 Bread)
1 cup skim milk (1 Milk)

Lunch

1 chicken salad sandwich:
    2 slices whole wheat bread (2 Bread)
    ½ cup cooked, chopped chicken (2 Meat)
    2 tablespoons diet mayonnaise (2 Fat)
    ¼ cup chopped celery (½ Vegetable)
6 raw carrot sticks (1 Vegetable)
1 small fresh pear (1 Fruit)

Dinner

4 ounces Shishkabob (4 Meat, 3 Vegetable)
    (392 mg Sodium), see page 491
1 medium baked potato (2 Bread) with
1 tablespoon sour cream (1 Fat) and
2 teaspoons unsalted margarine and
1 teaspoon chives

½ cup steamed broccoli (1 Vegetable)
¼ honeydew melon (2 Fruit)

Snack

1 cup plain, nonfat yogurt (1 Milk)
½ cup frozen or fresh unsweetened raspberries
   (1 Fruit)

Recipes
The Antihypertensive
Meal Plan

Breakfasts

Bran Muffins

Yields: 14 muffins
1 serving (1 muffin):

Calories   = 127
Cholesterol = 18 mg
Fat   = 5 gm
Sodium   = 200 mg

Exchanges =
1 Bread +
½ Fruit +
1 Fat

¾ cup all-purpose flour
½ cup whole wheat flour
1 tablespoon baking powder
½ teaspoon "lite" salt
¼ cup sugar
2½ cups bran flakes cereal
1¼ cups skim milk
1 egg
¼ cup safflower oil

Preheat oven to 400° F. Stir together flour, baking powder, salt, and sugar. Set aside. Measure bran flakes and milk into large mixing bowl. Let stand 1 to 2 minutes while cereal softens. Add egg and oil. Beat well. Add flour mixture. Stir only until combined. Spoon batter evenly into 14 greased muffin tins. Bake for 18 to 20 minutes or until done.

French Toast Puff

Yields: 4 servings
1 serving (1 slice):

Calories	*= 215*	*Exchanges =*
Cholesterol	*= 2 mg*	*1 Meat +*
Fat	*= 8 gm*	*1 Bread +*
Sodium	*= 230 mg*	*½ Fruit +*
		⅛ Milk

 1 cup egg substitute
½ cup evaporated skimmed milk
 1 tablespoon honey
½ teaspoon ground cinnamon
¼ teaspoon ground mace
 4 1-ounce slices cinnamon-raisin bread,
   cut diagonally in half
   nonstick vegetable cooking spray

Preheat oven to 350 °F. Spray a 9-inch pie plate with cooking spray. In medium bowl, whisk together all ingredients except bread. Place bread in prepared plate; pour milk mixture over bread. Cover with plastic wrap and refrigerate at least 1 hour or overnight. Bake 25 to 30 minutes, until puffy and golden brown. Serve at once.

Optional:
Sprinkle with confectioner's sugar or Berry Syrup, see page 507

Oat Bran Muffins

Yields: 24 1-inch muffins
1 serving (1 muffin):

Calories	*= 66*	*Exchanges =*	
Cholesterol	*= 0 mg*	*½ Bread +*	
Fat	*= 1 gm*	*½ Fruit +*	
Sodium	*= 60 mg*	*½ Fat*	

1¼ cups oat bran cereal
1 cup whole wheat flour
⅓ cup raisins
1 tablespoon baking powder
½ cup skim milk
½ cup unsweetened orange juice
¼ cup honey
2 tablespoons safflower oil
3 egg whites

Preheat oven to 425° F. Mix together dry ingredients. Add skim milk, orange juice, honey, oil, and egg whites. Mix. Divide mixture into mini-muffin tins. Bake for 15 minutes or until lightly browned.

Oatmeal Pancakes

Yields: 12 5-inch diameter pancakes
1 serving (1 pancake):

Calories	*= 98*	*Exchanges =*	
Cholesterol	*= 1 mg*		*1 Bread +*
Fat	*= 1 gm*		*⅙ Milk*
Sodium	*= 199 mg*		

1½ cups uncooked oatmeal
2 cups buttermilk
2 egg whites
1 cup whole wheat flour
2 teaspoons baking soda
1 mashed banana

Combine oatmeal, buttermilk, and egg whites and let stand for at least ½ hour or refrigerate up to 24 hours. Add remaining ingredients and stir the batter just until the dry ingredients are moistened. Cook on each side on a hot, lightly oiled griddle.

Soups

Gazpacho

Yields: 6 servings
1 serving (¾ cup):

Calories	*= 60*	*Exchanges =*
Cholesterol	*= 0 mg*	*1½ Vegetable +*
Fat	*= 3 gm*	*½ Fat*
Sodium	*= 24 mg*	

4 cups low-sodium tomato juice
½ cup unpeeled chopped cucumber
¼ cup chopped green pepper
¼ cup finely chopped onion
1 tablespoon olive oil
2 tablespoons wine vinegar
½ teaspoon pepper
1 teaspoon dried oregano
2 teaspoon chopped fresh basil
1 minced garlic clove

Combine all ingredients. Cover and chill overnight.

Minestrone Soup

Yields: 8 servings
1 serving (1 cup):
Calories = 100   *Exchanges =*
Cholesterol = 0 mg   *1 Bread +*
Fat = 1 gm   *1 Vegetable*
Sodium = 170 mg

   1 diced onion
 1½ cups chopped celery
   ¼ cup homemade vegetable stock or low-sodium broth
*14½- or 16-ounce can tomatoes with juice
   3 cups homemade vegetable stock or low-sodium broth
   3 cups water
   ¼ cup chopped parsley
     dash of pepper
   2 bay leaves
   1 teaspoon oregano
   2 teaspoons basil
   ½ teaspoon rosemary
   1 minced garlic clove
   ½ cup chopped carrot
   ½ cup diced zucchini
   ½ cup diced potato
   ¼ cup chopped green pepper
   ¼ cup fresh frozen corn
   1 cup sliced fresh mushrooms

½ cup uncooked spaghetti
1 cup canned and rinsed garbanzo beans
½ cup cooked barley

Sauté onion and celery in vegetable stock until soft. Add the tomatoes, vegetable stock, water, parsley, seasonings, and vegetables. Simmer soup for 30 minutes. Add spaghetti, garbanzo beans, and cooked barley. Continue cooking over medium heat for 10 minutes.

*Lower-Sodium Variation:
Substitute low-sodium canned tomatoes.
1 serving: Sodium = 57 mg

Salads

Apple Waldorf Salad

Yields: 4 servings
1 serving (½ cup):

Calories	*= 90*	*Exchanges =*
Cholesterol	*= 0 mg*	*1 Fruit +*
Fat	*= 4 gm*	*1 Fat*
Sodium	*= 76 mg*	

 1 chopped Granny Smith apple
 1 chopped red delicious apple
 1 tablespoon fresh lemon juice
½ cup chopped celery
 1 tablespoon coarsely chopped pecan halves
¼ cup plain, nonfat yogurt
   dash ground cinnamon
   dash ground nutmeg
 2 tablespoons diet mayonnaise

Sprinkle apples with lemon juice. Add all other ingredients and combine gently. Serve on purple cabbage leaf or lettuce leaf.

Cold Pasta Salad

Yields: 4 servings
1 serving (1 cup):

Calories   *= 240*   *Exchanges =*
Cholesterol = 14 mg   *1½ Bread +*
Fat   *= 7 gm*   *½ Meat +*
Sodium   *= 412 mg*   *2 Vegetable +*
                                 ½ Fat

     6 ounces (3 cups) cooked pasta
   *½ cup feta cheese
   *⅓ cup low-calorie Italian dressing
    ¼ cup chopped green onion
    2 tablespoons sliced, pitted black olives
6 to 8 cherry tomatoes, cut in half
    6 cups fresh spinach, washed and stems cut

Combine all ingredients except spinach. Arrange spinach on serving platter and arrange pasta salad on top.

*Lower-Sodium Variation:
Substitute part-skim mozzarella cheese and vinegar and oil dressing.
1 serving:

Calories   = 265
Cholesterol = 8 mg
Fat   = 10 gm
Sodium   = 163 mg

Long Grain and Wild Rice Chicken Salad

Yields: 10 servings
1 serving (½ cup):

Calories	*= 260*	*Exchanges =*
Cholesterol	*= 30 mg*	*1 Meat +*
Fat	*= 11 gm*	*1 Bread +*
Sodium	*= 250 mg*	*1 Fat +*
		½ Vegetable +
		½ Fruit

¾ cup uncooked long grain brown rice
¼ cup uncooked wild rice
2½ cups water
½ cup diet mayonnaise
½ cup skim milk
½ cup lemon juice
1 small (¼ cup) grated onion
1 teaspoon chopped chives
12 ounces cooked chicken, cubed
1 can (8 ounces) drained and chopped water chestnuts
½ teaspoon curry powder
½ teaspoon pepper
½ pound seedless green grapes, cut in half
½ cup chopped nuts (optional)

Combine rice and water in saucepan and heat to boiling. Lower heat and cover. Simmer 1 hour or until tender. Combine mayonnaise, milk, lemon juice, onion, and chives in large bowl, blending well. Stir in chicken, water chestnuts, curry powder, and pepper, mixing well. Stir in cooked rice. Refrigerate two hours or until chilled. At serving time, fold in halved grapes. Spoon salad on serving platter, lined with lettuce. Top with chopped nuts, if desired.

Tuna Salad

Yields: 2 servings
1 serving (½ cup):

Calories = 190	*Exchanges =*
Cholesterol = 65 mg	*2 Meat +*
Fat = 2 gm	*1 Milk*
Sodium = 707 mg	

6½-ounce can (1 cup) water-packed,
low-sodium tuna, drained
4 teaspoons diet Miracle Whip
4 tablespoons plain, low-fat yogurt
2 cooked, chopped egg whites
*½ chopped dill pickle
onion powder, to taste
pepper, to taste
1 to 2 tablespoons chopped apple (optional)

Combine all ingredients and mix well.

Lower-Sodium Variation:
Omit dill pickle.
1 serving: Sodium = 225 mg

Turkey-Fruit Salad

Yields: 4 servings
1 serving (1 cup):

Calories	*= 185*	*Exchanges =*
Cholesterol	*= 30 mg*	*½ Meat +*
Fat	*= 4 gm*	*2 Fruit +*
Sodium	*= 150 mg*	*1 Vegetable*

⅓ cup plain, low-fat yogurt
1 tablespoon diet mayonnaise
1 tablespoon honey
½ teaspoon finely shredded orange peel
⅛ teaspoon salt
1 cup cooked, cubed turkey
1 cup halved fresh strawberries
1 small banana, cut in ½-inch slices
½ cup sliced celery
2 medium peeled and sliced oranges
   lettuce leaves

Blend first five ingredients together and set aside. Combine remaining ingredients in a separate bowl. Fold the first mixture into the salad ingredients. Chill.

Main Courses

Grilled Sesame Chicken Breasts

Yields: 4 servings
1 serving (4 ounces):

Calories	*= 265*	*Exchanges =*
Cholesterol	*= 73 mg*	*3½ Meat +*
Fat	*= 11 gm*	*½ Fruit +*
Sodium	*= 590 mg*	*1 Fat +*
		½ Bread

½ cup unsweetened white grape juice
¼ cup low-sodium "lite" soy sauce
¼ cup dry white wine
1 tablespoon sesame seeds
2 tablespoons safflower oil
¼ teaspoon garlic powder
¼ teaspoon ground ginger
1 teaspoon liquid smoke flavoring
16 ounces skinless, boneless chicken breasts

Combine all ingredients except chicken in a shallow dish; mix well. Add chicken, turning to coat; cover and marinate in refrigerator at least 4 hours. Remove chicken from marinade, reserving marinade. Grill 4 to 5 inches from medium-hot flame or coals for 15 minutes, turning and basting frequently with marinade.

Southern Fried Chicken

Yields: 6 servings
1 serving (⅙ recipe):

Calories	*= 262*	*Exchanges =*
Cholesterol	*= 101 mg*	*4 Meat +*
Fat	*= 11 gm*	*½ Bread +*
Sodium	*= 260 mg*	*½ Fat*

24 ounces skinless, boneless chicken
1 tablespoon safflower oil
⅓ cup white flour
*1 teaspoon "lite" salt
½ teaspoon paprika
¼ teaspoon poultry seasoning
¼ teaspoon garlic powder
⅛ teaspoon pepper
½ cup water

Select a large nonstick skillet with a closely fitting lid. Remove all skin and visible fat from chicken. Combine flour and spices in plastic bag or bowl. Shake or roll chicken, one or two pieces at a time in seasoned flour. Set aside on waxed paper. Coat all chicken with flour before heating oil. Heat 1 tablespoon oil in the skillet, then add chicken. Brown over medium heat, about 10 to 12 minutes per side, until golden brown on all sides. Add ½ cup water to chicken.

Cover tightly, cook over low heat for 30 minutes. Remove cover, turn up heat, and cook off any remaining liquid. Continue frying chicken until reddish-brown, 1 to 2 minutes.

*Lower-Sodium Variation:
Omit "lite" salt.
1 serving: Sodium = 98 mg

Spanish Chicken and Rice

Yields: 2 servings
1 serving (1 cup):

Calories	*= 421*	*Exchanges =*
Cholesterol	*= 75 mg*	*3½ Meat +*
Fat	*= 12 gm*	*2 Bread +*
Sodium	*= 375 mg*	*2 Vegetable +*
		1 Fat

 2 teaspoons olive oil
½ cup diced onion
½ cup chopped green pepper
 2 minced garlic cloves
½ cup canned low-sodium tomato sauce
⅓ cup water
½ cup low-sodium chicken broth
¼ teaspoon ground cumin
    dash pepper
 6 ounces cooked skinless, boneless chicken
 1 cup cooked long grain rice

2 ounces cooked pinto beans
1 tablespoon chopped fresh parsley

In a 10-inch skillet, heat oil; then add onion, green pepper, and garlic. Sauté over low heat until tender, about 5 minutes. Add tomato sauce, water, broth, and seasonings and bring to a boil. Reduce heat and let simmer 5 minutes; stir in remaining ingredients and cook until thoroughly heated.

Peppered Veal

Yields: 6 servings
1 serving (2½ ounces):

Calories	*= 225*	*Exchanges =*
Cholesterol	*= 58 mg*	*2½ Meat +*
Fat	*= 12 gm*	*1 Vegetable +*
Sodium	*= 208 mg*	*½ Bread +*
		½ Fat

  1 pound veal cutlets
¼ teaspoon freshly ground pepper
  1 crushed garlic clove
  2 teaspoons olive oil
  1 medium onion, cut into strips
  2 green peppers, seeded and cut into strips
½ cup dry white wine
½ cup water
*1 teaspoon beef-flavored bouillon granules

½ teaspoon dried whole basil
¼ teaspoon dried whole oregano
1½ teaspoons cornstarch
 2 tablespoons water
12 cherry tomatoes, cut in half

Trim excess fat from veal cutlets; cut into 1-inch strips. Sprinkle with pepper. Sauté garlic in olive oil in a large skillet over medium-high heat until tender. Add cutlets and cook until browned. Stir in next 7 ingredients and bring to a boil. Cover; reduce heat and simmer 5 minutes or until vegetables are crisp-tender. Combine cornstarch and water, stirring until blended; stir into veal mixture. Bring to a boil and cook 1 minute or until slightly thickened. Stir in tomatoes. Serve over corkscrew pasta, rice, or noodles.

*Lower-Sodium Variation:
  Substitute low-sodium bouillon granules
  1 serving: Sodium = 50 mg

Veal Scaloppine

Yields: 4 servings
1 serving (3 ounces):

Calories	*= 290*	*Exchanges =*
Cholesterol	*= 65 mg*	*3 Meat +*
Fat	*= 15 gm*	*1½ Vegetable +*
Sodium	*= 252 mg*	*1 Fat +*
		1 Bread

  8 ounces (2 cups) sliced fresh mushrooms
⅛ teaspoon pepper
½ cup dry white wine
12 ounces (4 3-ounce pieces) veal scaloppine
  2 tablespoons flour
  1 tablespoon olive oil
¾ cup minced onion
  1 cup chicken broth

Place mushrooms, pepper and wine in a small saucepan. Simmer uncovered for about 10 minutes until mushrooms are tender. Pound the veal with flat side of meat mallet or with a rolling pin to half the original thickness. Sprinkle with "lite" salt, if desired, then dredge with flour. Heat olive oil in a large nonstick skillet over high heat. Add onion and shake pan to distribute onion evenly. Arrange breaded cutlets on bed of onion in skillet and cook for 1 or 2 minutes over high heat until meat begins to brown. Turn and cook for 1 or 2 minutes to brown other side. Reduce heat to low, add broth, and simmer for 2 minutes. Turn veal and add the mushroom mixture. Increase the heat and cook for 3 to 5 minutes until fluid is reduced and sauce is slightly thickened.

Variation:
Turkey Scaloppine: Substitute turkey cutlets (sliced raw breast meat) for veal.

Herbed Garlic Fish Fillets
(microwave recipe)

Yields: 4 servings
1 serving (3 ounces):
Calories	*= 146*	*Exchanges = 3 Meat*
Cholesterol	*= 47 mg*	
Fat	*= 6 gm*	
Sodium	*= 202 mg*	

  1 tablespoon water
  1 teaspoon grated orange peel
  ½ teaspoon crushed dried rosemary leaves
  ¼ teaspoon crushed dried thyme leaves
  1 minced garlic clove
  ¼ cup chopped fresh parsley
  12 ounces fish fillets, about ½ inch thick,
    cut into 4 serving-size pieces

In a small ceramic bowl, combine water, orange peel, rosemary, thyme, and garlic. Cover with plastic wrap. Microwave at HIGH for 1 minute. Stir in parsley. Arrange fillets in a 9-inch square baking dish with thickest portions toward outside of dish. Top with parsley mixture. Cover with wax paper. Microwave at HIGH for 5 to 7 minutes, or until fish flakes easily with fork, rotating dish once. Let stand, covered, for 3 minutes.

Seafood Quiche

Yields: 8 servings
1 serving (⅛ of quiche):

Calories = *185*	*Exchanges* =
Cholesterol = *70 mg*	*½ Milk* +
Fat = *7 gm*	*2½ Meat*
Sodium = *475 mg*	

2 eggs or equivalent egg substitute
4 egg whites, beaten well
6 ounces precooked shrimp
*6 ounces crab meat
2 chopped green onions
10 to 12 (about 4 ounces) thinly sliced medium mushrooms
1¼ cups evaporated skimmed milk
2 cups grated part-skim mozzarella cheese
nonstick vegetable cooking spray

Preheat oven to 350° F. Mix all ingredients and pour into a 9-inch pan sprayed with nonstick vegetable cooking spray. Bake for 30 to 40 minutes until firm and lightly browned.

*Lower-Sodium Variation:
Omit crab and add 6 ounces more shrimp.
1 serving:
Calories   = 169
Cholesterol = 77 mg
Fat   = 5 gm
Sodium   = 350 mg

Shrimp Creole

Yields: 6 servings
1 serving (1¾ cup):

Calories	*= 282*	*Exchanges =*
Cholesterol	*= 106 mg*	
Fat	*= 3 gm*	*2 Meat +*
Sodium	*= 450 mg*	*1½ Bread +*
		2 Vegetable

  2 tablespoons diet margarine
½ cup diced onion
½ cup diced celery
½ cup diced green pepper
  1 minced garlic clove
  2 8-ounce cans low-sodium tomato sauce
⅛ teaspoon pepper
¼ teaspoon chili powder

*¾ teaspoon "lite" salt
 1 pound cooked shrimp, cut in pieces
 4 cups cooked rice

Melt margarine in skillet. Sauté vegetables and garlic in melted margarine. Blend together tomato sauce, pepper, chili powder and "lite" salt. Add tomato mixture to vegetables and simmer for 15 minutes. Add cooked shrimp and heat thoroughly. Serve over cooked rice.

Lower-Sodium Variation:
  Omit "lite" salt.
  1 serving: Sodium = 291 mg

Beef Broccoli Stir-Fry

Yields: 4 servings
1 serving (¼ recipe):
Calories   = 349   Exchanges =
Cholesterol = 76 mg   4 Meat +
Fat   = 13 gm   2 Vegetable +
Sodium   = 736 mg   ½ Fat

1 pound lean flank steak or top round, trimmed
  of fat
1 large bunch (approximately 2 pounds) fresh
  broccoli
2 teaspoons safflower oil
2 minced garlic cloves
2 tablespoons water

Marinade

2 teaspoons sake (rice wine) or cooking sherry
½ teaspoon baking soda
2 tablespoons low-sodium "lite" soy sauce
1½ teaspoons cornstarch
2 teaspoons safflower oil
½ teaspoon sugar
½ teaspoon ground ginger

Sauce

2 teaspoons cornstarch
*1 cup beef broth
1 teaspoon low-sodium "lite" soy sauce
¼ to ½ teaspoon pepper

Trim beef of all fat, then slice across the grain into ⅛-inch strips. Combine marinade ingredients in medium bowl. Add beef strips and mix well. Let stand 20 to 30 minutes to tenderize. Trim tough stems and leaves from broccoli. Break tops into bite-sized florets and cut stems into ½-inch slices. Combine sauce ingredients in small bowl and set aside. Heat a large nonstick skillet or wok until very hot. Add beef strips with marinade. Stir-fry over highest possible heat until lightly browned. Remove beef from skillet and set aside. Heat the 2 teaspoons safflower oil in the same skillet. Add minced garlic and prepared broccoli. Stir-fry over high heat for 3 to 5 minutes until broccoli is crisp-tender. Add water, cover tightly, and steam over medium heat for 3 minutes. Remove lid. Add sauce ingredients. Stir until sauce bubbles. Add beef, heat through, and serve immediately.

Lower-Sodium Variation:
Substitute low-sodium beef broth.
1 serving: Sodium = 544 mg

Shishkabob

Yields: 4 servings
Per serving (3 ounces meat):
Calories   = 257   Exchanges =
Cholesterol = 60 mg   3 Meat +
Fat   = 9 gm   2 Vegetable
Sodium   = 295 mg

1 pound lean meat (flank), cut in chunks and
   trimmed of fat
½ cup commercial oil-free Italian salad dressing
½ cup red wine
8 cherry tomatoes
½ medium onion, cut in 8 chunks
½ green pepper, cut in 8 chunks
1 zucchini, cut in 8 chunks
4 skewers

Marinate meat overnight in salad dressing and wine, turning once. On each skewer, alternate ¼ of the meat chunks, 2 cherry tomatoes, 2 chunks of onion, 2 chunks of green pepper, and 2 chunks of zucchini. On a charcoal grill or in an oven broiler, cook shishkabobs 10 to 15 minutes each side, turning as needed to cook evenly throughout.

Teriyaki Steak

Yields: 6 servings
1 serving (4 ounces):

Calories	*= 280*	*Exchanges =*
Cholesterol	*= 76 mg*	*4 Meat +*
Fat	*= 10 gm*	*½ Fat +*
Sodium	*= 472 mg*	*½ Vegetable*

1½ pounds lean flank steak, trimmed of fat
  1 tablespoon olive oil
  ¼ cup low-sodium "lite" soy sauce
  ¼ cup pineapple juice
  2 tablespoons vinegar
1½ teaspoons ground ginger
  2 tablespoons finely chopped green onion
  1 minced garlic clove
  1 tablespoon cooking sherry

Trim excess fat from steak. Score steak with ⅛-inch deep diagonal cuts on both sides. Combine remaining ingredients in large, shallow dish; add steak, turning to coat well with marinade. Cover and marinate in refrigerator 4 hours or overnight, turning occasionally. Remove steak from marinade. Broil steak 4 to 5 inches from heat, 5 to 7 minutes on each side or until desired degree of doneness. Transfer steak to a cutting board; cut in thin slices across grain.

Note: May also be cooked over hot coals.

Ricotta-Parmesan Torte

Yields: 8 servings
1 serving (1 piece):

		Exchanges =
Calories	*= 250*	
Cholesterol	*= 144 mg*	*1 Fat +*
Fat	*= 12 gm*	*½ Vegetable +*
Sodium	*= 365 mg*	*1½ Bread +*
		1 Meat

Dough
¾ cup all-purpose white flour
 3 tablespoons warm water
 1 tablespoon plus 1 teaspoon safflower oil
 ⅛ teaspoon salt

Filling

1 tablespoon plus 1 teaspoon margarine
1 cup minced scallions (green onion)
1 cup grated zucchini
½ cup grated carrots
2 minced garlic cloves
2 cups cooked long-grain rice
1 cup part-skim ricotta cheese
4 eggs (or 8 egg whites)
3 tablespoons grated part-skim Parmesan
cheese, divided
⅛ teaspoon salt
⅛ teaspoon freshly ground pepper

To Prepare Dough:

In a small mixing bowl, combine flour, water, oil, and salt. Using your hands, knead dough into a smooth ball (dough should hold together but not be sticky; if necessary, add up to 1 more tablespoon warm water to adjust consistency). Wrap dough in plastic wrap and set aside while preparing filling (plastic wrap will prevent dough from cracking).

To Prepare Filling:

In a 10-inch nonstick skillet, heat margarine until bubbly and hot. Add vegetables and garlic and sauté over medium-low heat, stirring occasionally until vegetables are soft, about 3 minutes. Set aside and let cool. In large mixing bowl, combine rice, ricotta cheese, 3 eggs, 2 tablespoons Parmesan cheese, salt and pepper; beat until smooth. Add cooled vegetables and stir to combine.

To Prepare Torte:

Preheat oven to 350° F. Between 2 sheets of wax paper roll dough, forming a rectangle about ⅛ inch thick. Remove paper and lift dough into a 10 x 6 x 2-inch baking dish so that edges of dough extend slightly over sides of dish. Spoon cheese mixture over dough and bring up sides of dough over edges of filling, leaving center uncovered. In small bowl, beat remaining egg with remaining tablespoon Parmesan cheese. Pour over entire surface of torte. Bake until brown, about 1 hour. Remove from oven and let stand until set, about 15 minutes. Serve warm or at room temperature.

Spicy Bean Enchiladas

Yields: 8 servings
1 serving (1 enchilada):

Calories = 200	*Exchanges =*
Cholesterol = 3 mg	*1 Meat +*
Fat = 2 gm	*2 Bread +*
Sodium = 553 mg	*½ Vegetable*

¾ pound dried pinto beans
8 cups water
2 minced garlic cloves
1 bay leaf
*¾ teaspoon salt
1 recipe Spicy Tomato Sauce, see page 510
½ teaspoon chili powder
¼ teaspoon pepper
8 6-inch corn tortillas
  nonstick vegetable cooking spray
1 cup (4 ounces) shredded low-fat cheddar
  cheese
½ cup plain, low-fat yogurt
2 tablespoons chopped green onion
  shredded lettuce (optional)

Sort and wash beans. Cover with water 2 inches above top of beans and let stand 8 hours; drain. Preheat oven to 350° F. Combine beans, 8 cups water, garlic, bay leaf, and salt in Dutch oven; bring to a boil. Cover, reduce heat to medium, and cook 1½ hours or until tender. Drain and discard bay leaf. Mash beans; add ½ cup Spicy Tomato Sauce, chili powder, and pepper, stirring well. Spread ½ cup bean mixture over each tortilla. Roll up; place seam-side down in a 13 x 9 x 2-inch baking dish coated with cooking spray. Spoon remaining Spicy Tomato Sauce over tortillas; cover and bake for 20 minutes. Top with cheese and bake uncovered an additional 5 minutes or until cheese melts. Serve with a spoonful of yogurt for each serving and sprinkle with green onions. Garnish with lettuce, if desired.

Note: If corn tortillas crack or are hard to roll up, soften by steaming. To steam, place 2 or 3 tortillas at a time in a strainer, and place over boiling water. Cover and steam 2 to 3 minutes or until softened and pliable.

*Lower-Sodium Variation:
  Omit salt.
  1 serving: Sodium = 354 mg

Stuffed Shells

Yields: 7 servings
1 serving (3 shells):

Calories = 320	*Exchanges* =
Cholesterol = 55 mg	*2 Bread +*
Fat = 9 gm	*3 Vegetable +*
Sodium = 150 mg	*1 Meat +*
	½ Fat

¾ of a 12-ounce package large shells, cooked
  according to package directions (21 shells)
1 box (10 ounces) frozen chopped spinach
1 tablespoon chopped onion
2 teaspoons diet margarine
2 beaten egg whites
⅔ cup part-skim ricotta cheese
½ cup grated Parmesan cheese
½ teaspoon ground nutmeg
1 recipe Original Tomato Sauce, see page 509

Preheat oven to 350° F. Defrost and squeeze
excess water from spinach. In skillet, cook
onion in margarine until tender. Add spinach;
heat through. Combine eggs, ricotta cheese,
Parmesan cheese, nutmeg, and spinach mixture.
Pour half the sauce in a baking dish. Stuff shells
with filling. Arrange in dish and top with remaining sauce. Bake for 30 minutes.

Vegetarian Lasagna

Yields: 8 servings
1 serving (1 piece):
Calories   = 350   *Exchanges =*
Cholesterol = 50 mg   *2 Bread +*
Fat   = 11 gm   *2 Meat +*
Sodium   = 350 mg   *2½ Vegetable +*
                                 ½ Fat

1 large chopped onion
2 minced garlic cloves
¼ pound sliced, fresh mushrooms
4 medium diced eggplant (or zucchini)
1 8-ounce package lasagna noodles, cooked
     according to package directions
1 recipe Original Tomato Sauce, see page 509
2 cups low-fat cottage cheese
8 ounces grated part-skim mozzarella cheese
½ cup grated Parmesan cheese
1 tablespoon safflower oil

Preheat oven to 350° F. Sauté onion and garlic in oil in nonstick skillet until soft. Add mushrooms and eggplant (or zucchini). Cook lasagna noodles. Mix vegetable mixture with sautéd tomato sauce. Mix 5½ ounces mozzarella cheese with Parmesan cheese, reserving 1½ ounces. To prepare lasagna, layer ½ noodles on bottom of 13 x 9-inch casserole dish; then ½ vegetable mixture; then cheese, repeat. Sprinkle the reserved 1½ ounces of cheeses mixture over top; then sprinkle with Parmesan cheese to complete. Bake for 45 minutes.

Side Dishes

Apple Oat Crisp

Yields: 4 servings
1 serving (1 cup):

Calories	*= 165*	*Exchanges =*
Cholesterol	*= 0 mg*	*1 Bread +*
Fat	*= 3 gm*	*2 Fruit +*
Sodium	*= 80 mg*	*½ Fat*

Fruit

3 small cored and sliced apples
½ cup unsweetened applesauce
1½ teaspoons lemon juice
½ teaspoon grated lemon rind
1 teaspoon sugar
¼ teaspoon ground cinnamon

Topping

1 ounce quick-cooking oats
2 tablespoons whole wheat flour
2 tablespoons firmly packed brown sugar
¼ teaspoon ground cinnamon
1 tablespoon plus 1 teaspoon diet margarine

Preheat oven to 350° F. In medium non-aluminum bowl, combine all fruit ingredients. Pour into an 8-inch baking dish. Prepare topping in a small bowl by combining oats, flour, brown sugar, and cinnamon. Cut margarine into topping mixture with a pastry blender until crumbly. Sprinkle topping evenly over apple mixture. Bake for 35 to 40 minutes until apples are tender and topping is browned. Serve hot.

Optional:
Top each with ½ cup ice milk.
1 serving with ½ cup ice milk:

		Exchanges =
Calories	= 260	
Cholesterol	= 13 mg	1 Milk +
Fat	= 6 gm	1 Bread +
Sodium	= 145 mg	2 Fruit +
		½ Fat

Fruit Smoothy

Yields: 4 servings
1 serving (1 cup):
Calories = 100   *Exchanges =*
Cholesterol = 4 mg   *1½ Milk*
Fat = 0 gm
Sodium = 85 mg

1 8-ounce can "lite" fruit cocktail, chilled
1 cup skim milk
¼ cup nonfat dry powdered milk
¼ cup plain, low-fat yogurt
½ teaspoon vanilla
½ cup ice cubes (3 to 4 large ice cubes)
   few dashes ground cinnamon
1 package sugar substitute (optional)

In a blender container, combine undrained fruit cocktail and remaining ingredients except the ice cubes and the cinnamon. Cover and blend until combined. Add ice cubes; cover and blend until smooth. Sprinkle with cinnamon. Serve immediately.

Italian Rice and Peas

Yields: 8 servings
1 serving (½ cup):
Calories = *134*   *Exchanges* =
Cholesterol = *3 mg*   *1½ Bread* +
Fat = *2 gm*   *½ Fat*
Sodium = *206 mg*

1 tablespoon diet margarine
1 small chopped onion
1 10-ounce package frozen peas
2 cups water
1 cup uncooked rice
*1 teaspoon instant chicken bouillon granules
¼ cup grated Parmesan cheese

In a 2-quart saucepan, heat margarine, stir in onion, and cook until tender. Stir in remaining ingredients except cheese. Heat to boiling, stirring once or twice. Cover, reduce heat, and simmer 14 minutes. (Do NOT lift cover or stir). Remove from heat. Fluff rice lightly with fork; cover and let steam 5 to 10 minutes. Stir in cheese lightly with fork.

*Lower-Sodium Variation:
  Substitute low-sodium bouillon cube.
  1 serving: Sodium = 87 mg

Oven French Fries

Yields: 6 servings
1 serving (½ cup):
Calories = 100   *Exchanges = 2 Bread*
Cholesterol = 0 mg
Fat = 0 gm
Sodium = 5 mg

3 to 4 (about 1 pound) thinly sliced medium
    baking potatoes
    nonstick vegetable cooking spray
¼ cup minced chives
3 tablespoons minced fresh parsley
½ teaspoon pepper
½ teaspoon paprika
1 teaspoon minced rosemary

Preheat oven to 350° F. Layer ⅓ of potatoes in
an 8-inch square baking pan, coated with cooking spray. Sprinkle with ⅓ of chives, parsley,
pepper, paprika, and rosemary. Repeat layers
until all ingredients are used. Cover with foil.
Bake for 45 minutes or until done.

Pita Crackers

Yields: 32 crackers
1 serving (1 cracker):
Calories   = 10   Exchanges =
Cholesterol = 0 mg   ⅛ Bread
Fat   = 0 gm
Sodium   = 23 mg

whole wheat pita pockets
nonstick vegetable cooking spray

Preheat oven to 300° F. Spray baking sheet with nonstick cooking spray. Cut 4 1-ounce pita pockets into quarters; split each apart. Place wedges on prepared baking sheet. Bake 10 minutes, or until well toasted. Cool. Crackers can be stored in an airtight container.

Sauces and Toppings

Berry Syrup

Yields: 8 servings
1 serving (1 tablespoon):
Calories   = 20   Exchanges = ½ Fruit
Cholesterol = 0 mg
Fat   = 0 gm
Sodium   = 0 mg

2 cups berries (blueberries, strawberries, raspberries)
2 tablespoons pineapple juice concentrate
½ teaspoon vanilla

Blend berries in a food processor. Combine all ingredients in a heavy saucepan. Bring to a boil and simmer for 25 to 30 minutes. Cool before serving.

Italian Tomato Sauce

Yields: 14 servings
1 serving (½ cup):
Calories   = 40   Exchanges =
Cholesterol = 0 mg   1½ Vegetable
Fat   = 0 gm
Sodium   = 150 mg

2 large cans (28-ounce each) crushed Italian
   tomatoes
1 teaspoon dried basil
½ teaspoon dried oregano
*1 6-ounce can tomato paste
1 bay leaf
10 minced garlic cloves
½ teaspoon pepper

Mix all ingredients and simmer on stove for 2
hours. Use for lasagna, stuffed shells, or any
other recipe you desire.

Lower-Sodium Variation:
   Substitute low-sodium tomato paste.
   1 serving: Sodium = 20 mg

Original Tomato Sauce

Yields: 6 servings
1 serving (¾ cup):

Calories	*= 100*	*Exchanges =*
Cholesterol	*= 0 mg*	*2½ Vegetable +*
Fat	*= 3 gm*	*½ Fat*
Sodium	*= 10 mg*	

½ to 1 minced garlic clove
1 tablespoon olive oil
4 pounds fresh Italian tomatoes
1 small chopped onion
½ chopped pablano pepper, seeded
½ teaspoon "lite" salt
½ chopped green pepper (optional)
  tabasco sauce (optional)

Lightly brown garlic in olive oil. Cut tomatoes in small chunks. Add tomatoes to garlic along with onion, pablano pepper, salt, and green pepper, if used. Cook on high until tomatoes soften; then lower heat and cook 20 minutes. Add tabasco sauce to taste, if desired. Use as desired.

Spicy Tomato Sauce

Yields: 8 servings
1 serving (4 tablespoons):
Calories = 28   *Exchanges =*
Cholesterol = 0 mg   *1 Vegetable*
Fat = 0 gm
Sodium = 340 mg

2 8-ounce cans low-sodium tomato sauce
1 4-ounce can chopped green chiles, undrained
1 minced garlic clove
¾ cup chopped green onion
2 teaspoons chili powder
1 teaspoon ground cumin
¼ teaspoon dried whole oregano

Combine all ingredients in saucepan; simmer, uncovered, for 5 minutes.

10

Watch the Way
You Respond—
and Learn to Relax!

Practically everyone has anxious, worried, or otherwise tense reactions to highly stressful situations. But *not* everyone experiences a significant rise in blood pressure as a result of stress.

The blood pressure in some people rises only slightly, if at all, under extreme emotional pressure—though there will typically be a marked increase in the heart rate. Others experience a moderate rise in pressure, perhaps into the mild hypertensive range just above 140/90 mm Hg. Still others—who are called "vascular reactors"— undergo a major "spike" in their measurements, well up into the moderate or even severe range, in excess of 200/110.

There is evidence, as we saw in chapter 3 on risk factors related to hypertension, that people who are under constant stress are more likely to develop sustained hypertension than are those in tranquil environments. Furthermore, this risk seems greatest among the vascular reactors—those whose blood pressure increases rapidly under stress.

The periodic expansion of the vessels through temporarily high readings finally takes its toll: The muscles in the vessel walls thicken, and the tissue on the inner lining of the vessel walls becomes scarred and vulnerable to the buildup of fatty or atherosclerotic deposits. The end result of these and other influences is an increase in the resistance of the vessels to the pressure of the flowing blood—and permanent hypertension.

In many cases, this reactor response to stress is probably related to genetic factors. It's been suggested, for example, that some people inherit a sympathetic nervous system that responds more sensitively to stress than is the case with other people. Also, genetic problems in the sodium excretion mechanism may contribute to higher blood pressure readings.

A 1983 study of young men with normal blood pressure was reported in *Science* by researcher K. C. Light and several colleagues. A major finding: Stress can trigger disturbances in the sodium excretion mechanism in the children of hypertensives.

Specifically, in a majority of the young male participants with hypertensive parents, one hour of emotional stress caused a fall in their sodium excretion. Such a decline in sodium loss will automatically encourage greater sodium retention in the blood, a higher blood volume—and a concomitant rise in blood pressure.

But among the participants whose parents had *normal* blood pressure, sodium excretion actually *increased* with stress—a result that tends to decrease blood volume and be protective against the development of hypertension.

Finally, those with the lower excretion levels of sodium during the stressful hour tended also to have the greatest increases in heart rate under stress. This response was important because, as we know, another major factor in regulating blood pressure is the pumping action of the heart.

To summarize: The elevated blood pressure in the participants in this study occurred as a result of (1) the increase in blood volume due to excess sodium retention, and (2) the increase in the heart rate. Furthermore, both the sodium excretion deficiency *and* the greater rise in heart rate during stress seem to be inherited or genetically related.

However, this doesn't mean that a person

who has inherited some undesirable traits must be destined to a life of hypertension. On the contrary, there are a number of effective ways to combat the impact of stress, which I've classified under two general headings: (1) relaxation techniques, and (2) lifestyle habits.

Combating Stress Through Relaxation Techniques

A number of studies have shown that various relaxation techniques—including various forms of meditation, biofeedback programs, and muscle-relaxing strategies—can help lower both diastolic and systolic readings, at least temporarily.

For example, in a 1981 study reported in the *British Medical Journal*, medical researcher Chandra Patel and two colleagues found that eight weeks of relaxation therapy, reinforced by biofeedback techniques, could lower average systolic pressure from more than 160 mm Hg to 142 mm Hg, and diastolic readings from 100 mm Hg to less than 90 mm Hg.

In a later investigation in 1988 in the *British Medical Journal*, using similar relaxation and biofeedback approaches, Patel and Michael Marmot reported similar results: After one year of treatment, average systolic pressure dropped more than 12 mm Hg lower for those on relaxation treatment, in comparison with a control group not on such treatment. Also, diastolic pressures dropped more than 4 mm Hg on average for those on relaxation therapy.

Generally speaking, relaxation therapy is also helpful when used with antihypertensive medications. A study by Dr. Rolf G. Jacob and five colleagues, published in the *Archives of Internal Medicine* in 1986, explored the effect of using relaxation techniques with a beta blocker (100 mg per day of atenolol) and also with a diuretic (50 mg per day of chlorthalidone).

The researchers concluded that the long-term effects of relaxation were beneficial, independent of the medication therapy. At the same time, although relaxation enhanced the action of both drugs, it worked best with the diuretic in lowering blood pressure.

Why did the diuretic, combined with relaxation, work best? The researchers suggest that relaxation therapy may somehow enhance the effect of diuretic drugs on the kidneys and sympathetic nervous system. But they indicate that further exploration of the biological mechanisms is necessary before any definite explanation can be offered.

A number of hypertension experts have concluded that for the average patient, the impact of relaxation therapy is "modest." Also, they note that the benefits often are limited, lasting for only a short time.

On the other hand, some highly motivated patients find that they can achieve significant, lasting drops in their blood pressure with regular relaxation therapy. These people have discovered that relaxation therapy can play a key role in controlling hypertensive conditions *without* drugs.

In general, I recommend a systematic relaxation technique for anyone who has hypertension. It's not uncommon for those who are diligent with this approach to see drops of 10 mm Hg or more in both their diastolic and systolic readings.

If you decide to try relaxation therapy, what approach should you use? Some of the techniques, such as those using sophisticated biofeedback machines, are too expensive and complicated for the average patient. But the following method—based on several concepts, including the classic "relaxation response" approach popularized by Dr. Herbert Benson of Harvard Medical School—is easy to use and produces beneficial results in many people:

- Find a quiet room or corner; sit comfortably, with your back straight, feet flat on the floor, and eyes closed. Your arms should rest loosely and comfortably in your lap.

- For about one minute, concentrate on relaxing all the muscles in your body. Begin by tensing and then relaxing your feet and legs, your trunk muscles, your neck and shoulder muscles, and your arms and hands.

- For another ten minutes, breathe regularly. Every time you exhale, repeat silently a particular word or phrase that makes you feel comfortable or secure. Many people choose a meaningful word or two from their religious faith.

- When outside thoughts threaten to interrupt this relaxation exercise—as they always will—don't fight them. Simply push them gently aside and return to your "focus word," as Dr. Benson calls it.

- Include one or two of these relaxation therapy sessions in your schedule each day, and you might be surprised to discover what happens to your blood pressure.

- Another possibility is what Dr. Benson calls a "mini-meditation." That is, in addition to your lengthier relaxation sessions, try doing your regular breathing with your focus word or phrase for much shorter periods—even a few seconds, if that's all the time you have.

As I've said, this approach doesn't work for everyone, and it may not work for you. However, it *has* succeeded quite well in helping control hypertension in many people, and it *may* work for you. So why not try it?

You may find that these relaxation sessions become the cornerstone to the next approach to stress management—combating the pressures in your life through certain lifestyle strategies.

Combating Stress Through Creative Lifestyle Strategies

The first way to control your response to stress is to develop a basic relaxation technique, such as the one described in the preceding section. Next, it's important to learn to apply shortened forms of that technique and also other, simple relaxation devices, such as taking a deep breath, during your most stressful times.

Here's an easy-to-use daily stress management strategy, based on those employed by Chandra Patel and other investigators in their research on relaxation therapy and hypertension:

Step 1. Identify those times of day when you're under the greatest stress. You probably already know when your anxiety levels are most likely to rise and when feelings of being out of control are most likely to occur.

Even better, if you have a home blood pressure device, use it to determine those times during a typical day when your blood pressure peaks. If possible, take your blood pressure before, after, or even during your high-pressure situations. (Obviously, you can't strap a cuff around your upper arm during a business meeting. But you may be able to take your pressure during a phone conversation in the privacy of your office.)

By evaluating your feelings or actually determining your blood pressure, you'll be in a better position to answer these questions:

- Are you under the greatest stress when you're on the telephone, trying to negotiate a business deal or make a sale?

- How about the encounters you have with your boss, or presentations you are required to make to committees or colleagues?

- Do your worst on-the-job experiences involve conducting interviews with strangers? Getting your office organized in preparation for a trip? Making the transition back into the office after you've been away for a few days?

Researchers have found that for many people, the most stressful times occur when they are *outside* the office—such as driving to and from work; waiting for red lights to change; dealing with air or rail travel; or waiting for a dental appointment. Some find that they experience the most stress in encounters with their spouse or children, or even at church or synagogue meetings.

Whatever your worst times for stress, write down the precise situations and the hours of the day when they most often occur. This way, they won't catch you by surprise, and you'll be in a better position to prepare for them and meet them with greater equanimity.

Step 2. Formulate a response strategy to meet these difficult situations.

An approach that has helped many hypertensives is to employ a brief relaxation technique (e.g., a "mini-meditation") just before and after the event. So, if you're expecting a particularly difficult phone conversation, take a minute or so beforehand to relax your muscles; concentrate on your breathing; and silently repeat your focus word or phrase. Then, proceed with the conversation. Finally, *immediately* after you hang up, employ the relaxation technique again for a minute or so.

If you can discipline yourself to follow this strategy, you'll likely be pleased with the results. Many people find that they feel calmer, are

able to handle themselves more effectively during stressful encounters, and blood pressure
readings taken on home devices reveal that their
measurements are lower.

Step 3. Condition yourself to engage in
relaxation techniques *during* stressful situations
that you may not be able to anticipate.

Many times, high-pressure encounters are
impossible to foresee. In those circumstances—
and even when you *are* able to anticipate a
source of stress—you may find it helpful to close
your eyes for a second or two and concentrate on
regular breathing and on silently repeating your
focus word. In fact, just a deep breath or two
may be enough to calm you down and reduce
your stress level.

Step 4. Learn to *detach* yourself from the
stress in your life.

For example, if you begin to get into an
argument with a business associate, you might
imagine yourself in another office, or in an
airplane flying over the city, or even on a quiet
tropical beach.

It also may be helpful to say to yourself,
"This isn't that important. It's silly for me to get
so excited about a little problem that's bound to
pass."

Achieving detachment will enable you to put

the pressure you're feeling in proper perspective. In fact, when you think about it, *almost nothing* that we do in our daily lives is so important that it justifies our getting excessively anxious, angry, or tense.

Certainly, some level of anger or anxiety is inevitable for busy, ambitious, high-achieving people. But when these emotions paralyze, immobilize, or upset a person to any extent, the emotional and physical fallout may be unacceptable. The patient will most likely find that it's impossible to function effectively—and blood pressure levels are much more likely to increase.

So, learning to watch the way you respond to stress is a very personal endeavor. Some people have the ability and discipline to develop a relaxation strategy, and others don't. A few may find that no relaxation technique helps. But *most* should discover that a systematic approach to relaxation is a valuable tool in controlling hypertension.

The ultimate question is simply this: How willing are you to make a commitment to use a regular relaxation technique—and to make some significant adjustments in your lifestyle? Such commitments and adjustments are required to minimize the impact of stress in your life. And don't forget what I've said many times previously: Aerobic exercise performed regularly is nature's best physiological tranquilizer.

11

The Challenge of Secondary Hypertension

In many respects, hypertension is a rather mysterious disease. At least 90 to 95 percent of all high blood pressure disorders are classified as "primary" or "essential" hypertension. That is, nobody is absolutely sure of the underlying cause (or, in medical terms, the "etiology"). Those are the cases we've been concentrating on up to now.

But in about 5 to 10 percent of all cases of hypertension, which involve an estimated 3 to 6 million Americans, we *do* know the precise cause. These high blood pressure conditions are a byproduct of some other illness, condition, practice, or habit.

Known as "secondary hypertension," this disorder may appear as a result of such factors as:

- The use of oral contraceptive pills
- Pregnancy
- Kidney problems and disease
- Hormonal problems, including those linked to the adrenal glands
- Acute stress responses
- Reactions to surgery
- Use and abuse of "street drugs," such as amphetamines, heroin, and cocaine
- Use of over-the-counter drugs, such as phenylpropanolamine
- Brain tumors
- Acute strokes
- Head injuries

The physician should always examine and question the patient first to eliminate from consideration possible secondary causes of hypertension. Then, he may move on to prescribe treatment more appropriate for those with the primary form of the disease.

As a kind of "patient's aid" in the process of identifying secondary hypertension, let me provide you now with an overview of some of the main types of the disease—and brief explanations of possible medical responses to them.

Hypertension Related to Kidney Disease

The cause of up to 5 percent of all cases of hypertension can be traced to some underlying problem with the kidneys. In general, injury, damage, or disease in the kidneys can interfere with their capacity to get rid of sodium and fluids. The result may be excessive sodium and fluid retention, a higher fluid volume in the circulatory system, and increased pressure on the vessels.

In one type of kidney disorder—which presents a kind of "chicken or egg" situation—patients who already have severe hypertension may suffer damage to key kidney tissue as a result of existing high blood pressure. In such cases, the hypertension may be the cause of the kidney damage, which in turn aggravates the hypertension still more. Or the kidney damage may have come first—it's often not easy to tell.

In another relatively common situation, polycystic kidneys (kidneys with multiple cysts) may cause the damage that triggers hypertension.

Kidney damage may also result from diabetes mellitus, especially among those who suffer from juvenile or "brittle" diabetes.

The treatments for these types of kidney-related secondary hypertension are similar to those for some forms of primary hypertension: prescription of loop diuretics; a sodium-restricted diet; and, in the most extreme cases, dialysis.

Note: There's another kind of secondary hypertension that may arise from diseases of the blood vessels in the kidneys. This variety of hypertension occurs most commonly in two groups of people: (1) young women before about age 30 who for unknown reasons develop scar tissue in the arteries going into the kidneys (the renal arteries), and (2) those over age 50 with atherosclerosis (obstruction due to fatty deposits and plaque) in the renal arteries.

Many times, surgery or balloon dilation (angioplasty) is necessary for those with this disease.

Hypertension from Disorders of the Adrenal Glands

This kind of secondary hypertension represents less than 1 percent of all hypertension seen in adults, according to Dr. Norman Kaplan.

The specific problem may be tumors on the gland (pheochromucytoma) that cause extreme fluctuations in blood pressure. The usual treatment: alpha blockers, and if that fails, surgery.

Also, the condition called Cushing's disease may be the cause of the hypertension. This disorder involves a tumorous overgrowth and hyperactivity of one or both of the adrenal glands, with accompanying symptoms such as high blood pressure and obesity.

The treatment, once more, may be surgical removal of the tumorous gland.

Finally, tumors on an adrenal gland may trigger the condition known as aldosteronism. This disorder is characterized by excessive loss of potassium from the blood, possible paralysis—and hypertension.

Again, the usual treatment is surgery. In addition, medications should be prescribed to counter the loss of potassium, and a thiazide diuretic may be required for the treatment of hypertension.

Hypertension as a Result of Oral Contraceptives

Judy, a 34-year-old mother of two, was using oral contraceptives under the supervision of her obstetrician. When the doctor had put her on the pill shortly after the birth of her second child, her blood pressure was 125/80 mm Hg. But when Judy came back for a checkup six months later, the reading was up to 145/90.

Thinking that the rise could be related to the pill, the physician took her off the pill and put her on another contraceptive.

Sure enough, when she came in for a follow-up exam two months later, her measurements were down to an almost normal level of 130/82.

In Judy's case, which is typical of many women on estrogen-constituted oral contraceptives, the pill acted as a trigger to elevate her blood pressure.

Interestingly, estrogen-replacement therapy, which is used for postmenopausal women to combat osteoporosis, doesn't cause hypertension. But the situation is different for women taking the pill: The blood pressure of about 5 percent of those on oral contraceptives rises above 140/90 within five years.

The reasons for this increase in blood pressure are unknown, though many experts feel that the pill may somehow promote an increase in renin levels in the kidneys. The increase in renin may in turn lead to a rise in angiotensin II, and an accompanying elevation in blood pressure.

Among women who *stop* taking the pill, as Judy did, blood pressure declines in about two-thirds of the 5 percent. But the other one-third continue to have problems with hypertension, perhaps because they are already predisposed to the disorder. Or the reason may be that they've sustained damage to their vessels as a result of the pill.

Dr. Norman Kaplan recommends that women over age 35 not use oral contraceptives, especially if they smoke cigarettes. Younger women may use the pill safely, but their physicians should check them every three to six months to be sure they are in good health and are not developing hypertension.

Hypertension in Pregnancy

During pregnancy, a woman's blood pressure usually declines in the first six months to relatively low levels (e.g., 100/60 mm Hg). In the last three months of pregnancy, however, blood pressure may rise as a result of the condition known as "pregnancy-induced hypertension" (PIH).

This pregnancy-related hypertension typically involves an increase of the normal blood pressure by 30/15 mm Hg or more, and measurements may rise above the standard hypertension limit of 140/90.

There are a number of serious dangers involved with this type of hypertension. For example, the rate of fetal death increases when the mother's diastolic pressure goes higher than 85. Yet, medications usually are prescribed only if the diastolic pressure exceeds 100 mm Hg. The reason: The risk to the fetus is considered less with a mild increase in the mother's blood pressure than with the possibility of lowering the blood pressure too much through drugs. Excessive drops in the mother's pressure can result in too little blood flow to the fetus and impairment of fetal development.

Hypertension from Surgery or Other Physical Trauma

Immediately after surgery, blood pressure may increase for a number of reasons, including an inadequate supply of oxygen to the lungs and blood; an increase in the amount of fluids in the body; or simply the tension and stress that accompany pain. The phenomenon of surgically induced hypertension is especially common after coronary bypass surgery.

Medications used to treat this type of hypertension include the vasodilator nitroprusside, which acts immediately when the drug is given in large doses. But there's a danger: cyanide poisoning may occur with extended administration of high doses. So it's essential for those on this drug to be monitored closely in an intensive-care environment.

Other drugs that may help with surgery-related hypertension are the alpha-beta blocker labetalol and the vasodilator hydralazine.

Another related cause of hypertension can be severe burns. Dr. Kaplan notes that those with third-degree burns over more than one-fifth of the body will most likely develop hypertension that requires therapy.

Hypertension from "Street" Drugs

One frequently overlooked danger of using drugs such as cocaine, amphetamines, and heroin is that they may lead to problems with hypertension.

In general, blood pressure goes up significantly with cocaine use, but then it comes back down again rather quickly when the drug leaves the body. Despite the fact that the effect is usually temporary, cocaine may aggravate an underlying problem with hypertension.

Amphetamines may cause rises in blood pressure and can work against antihypertensive medications that the person is taking.

Intravenous drugs, such as heroin, may cause serious kidney damage, with a resulting elevation in blood pressure.

There are a number of other conditions that may trigger secondary hypertension, including hormonal problems such as hypothyroidism. Because hypertension may accompany so many other disorders, it's important for doctors to perform a thorough physical exam on hypertensive patients. In the end, the doctor may determine that the person's high blood pressure must be classified as "primary" and treated as such. But sometimes it's necessary to treat only the underlying disease or condition—and the hypertension will disappear.

12

A Future Without Hypertension?

Because of the effective work of many physicians and other health professionals, as well as the National High Blood Pressure Program—an effort by the National Heart, Lung and Blood Institute, which was launched in 1972—a great deal of progress has been made in recent years in combating the ravages of hypertension.

The public has been given access to free blood pressure measurements in shopping malls and on street corners; literature showing how to lower the risks of hypertension has been disseminated on a large scale; and physicians have been alerted as never before to the gravity of the problem.

The results of this public-information campaign have been dramatic. Since 1972, there has been a 50 percent decline in the national age-adjusted stroke mortality rate (stroke, as you know, is one of the major lethal complications of hypertension). Also, the death rate from coronary artery disease has declined by 35 percent during that period.

But much more needs to be done. There are currently *at least* 40 million adult Americans whose average blood pressure exceeds 140/90 mm Hg. By definition, these people are hypertensives, and their disease *could* eventually place them at serious risk to their health or their lives.

Fortunately, a growing percentage of these hypertensives—a majority, by most estimates—are on appropriate drugs or under regular medical care. Increasing numbers of those who have high blood pressure, or are at significant risk for the disease, are watching their diets, exercising, trying to manage stress more effectively, and seeing their physicians regularly.

Still, I continue to be profoundly concerned about getting the word out to those who, for whatever reason, aren't aware of the danger they face. I'm also deeply disturbed by those who may be aware but have failed to take decisive action against hypertension.

I frequently encounter patients who tell me,

in effect, "I know I have a *little* hypertension, but it's not *that* bad. Besides, I know it takes years for complications to develop." Or, "I simply don't have the discipline to stay on an exercise program." Or, "My schedule just doesn't allow for a serious commitment to a low-salt diet." Or, "I keep forgetting to take my blood pressure medication."

How do you motivate such patients? It's frustrating for doctors to diagnose the problem or identify multiple risk factors in a patient during an exam, and to communicate that danger clearly, and then have that patient disregard all your medical advice.

I don't believe in using scare tactics, though certainly there *is* reason for a patient to be deeply concerned if a set of blood pressure measurements reveals a high level of risk. But the main motivator, in my estimation, should be the promise of good future health and an enhanced quality of life.

If you have normal blood pressure, but you know you're at risk, why not act *now* through nondrug measures to lower your risk? Why wait and possibly have to go on medications or, worse, suffer a stroke or kidney damage?

If you have mild hypertension, why not be diligent *now* in following your physician's advice about changing your diet, exercise habits, and response to stress?

If you have more serious hypertension, why not be conscientious *now* about staying on your prescribed medication and *also* pursuing non-drug approaches to treatment? If you do, you may be able to reduce your drug dosage and perhaps even go off the medication completely at some point.

Likely, there will never be a future entirely without hypertension. But if we get more serious about making the best use of the medical tools at hand—and they are powerful tools, indeed—most people should eventually find that high blood pressure is a condition that *should* and *can* be brought completely under control.

References

Chapter 1

Kaplan, Norman M., M.D. *Clinical Hypertension.* Baltimore: Williams & Wilkins, fourth edition, 1986.

————. *Management of Hypertension.* Durant, Oklahoma: Creative Infomatics, Inc., second edition, 1987.

"The 1988 Report of the Joint National Committee on Detection, Evaluation, and Treatment of High Blood Pressure." *Archives of Internal Medicine,* vol. 148, May 1988, pp. 1023–37.

Chapter 2

"Blood-Pressure Monitors." *Consumer Reports,* May 1987, pp. 314–19.

Evans, C. Edward, et al. "Home Blood Pressure Measuring Devices: A Comparative Study of Accuracy." *Journal of Hypertension,* vol. 7, 1989, pp. 133–42.

Hampton, J. R. "Mild Hypertension: To Treat or Not to Treat?" *Comparative Studies in Hypertension.* Nephron 47: suppl. 1, pp. 57–61 (1987).

Hunt, James C., et al. "Devices Used for Self-Measurement of Blood Pressure." *Archives of Internal Medicine,* vol. 145, December 1985, pp. 2231–34.

Kaplan, Norman M., M.D. *Clinical Hypertension.* Baltimore: Williams & Wilkins, fourth edition, 1986.

———. *Management of Hypertension.* Durant, Oklahoma: Creative Infomatics, Inc., second edition, 1987.

———. "Misdiagnosis of Systemic Hypertension and Recommendations for Improvement." *American Journal of Cardiology,* vol. 60, December 1, 1987, pp. 1383–86.

"The 1988 Report of the Joint National Committee on Detection, Evaluation, and Treatment of High Blood Pressure." *Archives of Internal Medicine,* vol. 148, May 1988, pp. 1023–37.

Pickering, Thomas G., et al. "How Common Is White Coat Hypertension?" *Journal of the American Medical Association,* vol. 259, no. 2, January 8, 1988, pp. 225–28.

Chapter 3

"Alcohol and Blood Pressure." *Nutrition and the M.D.*, July 1985.

"Alcohol and Hypertension: Implications for Prevention and Treatment." *Annals of Internal Medicine,* Editorials, vol. 105, no. 1, July 1986.

Arakawa, Kikuo. "Nonpharmacological Treatment of Hypertension." *Seminars in Nephrology,* vol. 8, no. 2, June 1988, pp. 169–75.

Beard, Trevor C., and Richard F. Heller. "Relevance of the Salt-Hypertension Hypothesis to the Community Control of Hypertension." *Medical Journal of Australia,* vol. 147, July 6, 1987, pp. 29–33.

"Childhood Obesity." *The Aerobics News,* vol. 1, no. 4, August 1986.

Dannenberg, Andrew L., et al. "Progress in the Battle Against Hypertension: Changes in Blood Pressure Levels in the United States from 1960–1980." *Hypertension,* vol. 10, no. 2, August 1987, pp. 226–33.

"An Epidemiological Approach to Describing Risk Associated with Blood Pressure Levels, Final Report of the Working Group on Risk and High Blood Pressure." *Hypertension,* special report, vol. 7, no. 4, July–August 1985, pp. 641–51.

Falkner, Bonita, M.D. "Sodium Sensitivity: A Determinant of Essential Hypertension." *Journal of the American College of Nutrition,* vol. 7, no. 1, 1988, pp. 35–41.

Gillum, Richard F., M.D. "The Epidemiology of Resting Heart Rate in a National Sample of Men and Women: Associations with Hypertension, Coronary Heart Disease, Blood Pressure, and Other Cardiovascular Risk Factors." *American Heart Journal,* vol. 116, no. 1, part 1, July 1988, pp. 163–74.

"Hypertension." 1988 Consensus Conference on Exercise, Fitness, and Health, held in Toronto, Canada. Section D, paragraph 309.

"Hypertension: The Patient at Risk. A Panel Discussion with William B. Kannel, M.D., Robert M. Graham, M.D., Ingvar Hjermann, M.D., J. Caulie Gunnells, Jr., M.D." A Minipress Publication, October 1980.

"Is There a Black Hypertension?" *Hypertension,* Editorial, vol. 11, 1987.

Kannel, William B., M.D. "Cardiovascular Risk Factors and 'Preventive Management.'" *Hospital Practice,* October 15, 1987, pp. 119–35.

———. "Hypertension and Other Risk Factors in Coronary Heart Disease." *American Heart Journal,* vol. 114, no. 4, part 2, October 1987, pp. 918–25.

———. "New Perspectives on Cardiovascular Risk Factors." *American Heart Journal,* vol. 114, no. 4, part 2, 1987, p. 213.

Kaplan, Norman M., M.D. *Clinical Hypertension.* Baltimore: Williams & Wilkins, fourth edition, 1986.

———. "The Deadly Quadrangle: Upper Body Obesity, Glucose Intolerance, Hypertriglyceridemia and Hypertension." Medical Grand Rounds, University of Texas Southwestern Medical School in Dallas, Unpublished, February 4, 1988.

———. "Hypertension: Prevalence, Risks, and Effects of Therapy." *Annals of Internal Medicine,* vol. 98, no. 5, part 2, May 1983, pp. 705–709.

———. *Management of Hypertension.* Durant, Oklahoma: Creative Infomatics, Inc., second edition, 1987.

———. "Nondrug Treatment of Hypertension." *Texas Medicine,* vol. 78, October 1982, pp. 52–54.

Khaw, Kay-Tee, et al. "Dietary Potassium and Stroke-Associated Mortality." *New England Journal of Medicine,* vol. 316, no. 5, January 29, 1987.

Levy, Daniel, M.D., and William B. Kannel, M.D. "Cardiovascular Risks: New Insights from Framingham." *American Heart Journal,* vol. 116, no. 1, part 2, July 1988.

Light, Kathleen C., et al. "Effects of Race and Marginally Elevated Blood Pressure on Responses to Stress." *Hypertension,* vol. 10, 1987, pp. 555–63.

MacMahon, Stephen. "Alcohol Consumption and Hypertension." *Hypertension,* vol. 9, 1987, pp. 111–21.

Messerli, Franz H., M.D. "Obesity, Hypertension, and Cardiovascular Disease." *Journal of the American Medical Association,* Letters to the Editor, vol. 257, no. 12, March 27, 1987, p. 1598.

Myers, Martin G., M.D., FRCPC. "Effects of Caffeine on Blood Pressure." *Archives of Internal Medicine,* vol. 148, May 1988, pp. 1189–93.

"The 1988 Report of the Joint National Committee on Detection, Evaluation, and Treatment of High Blood Pressure." *Archives of Internal Medicine,* vol. 148, May 1988, pp. 1023–37.

Nissinen, Aulikki, et al. "Predictors of Blood Pressure Change in a Series of Controlled Dietary Intervention Studies." *Journal of Human Hypertension,* vol. 1, 1987, pp. 167–73.

Phillips, Stephen J., M.B., B.S., et al. "A Community Blood Pressure Survey: Rochester, Minnesota, 1986." *Mayo Clinic Proceedings,* vol. 63, July 1988, pp. 691–99.

Ribeiro, Artur B., and Myriam B. Debert Ribeiro. "Epidemiological and Demographic Considerations: Hypertension in Underdeveloped Countries." *Drugs* 31, suppl. 4, 1986, pp. 23–28.

Rutan, Gale H. "Mortality Associated with Diastolic Hypertension and Isolated Systolic Hypertension Among Men Screened for the Multiple Risk Factor Intervention Trial." *Circulation,* vol. 77, no. 3, March 1988, pp. 504–14.

"Salt and Hypertension." *Journal of the American Medical Association,* vol. 250, no. 3, July 15, 1983, pp. 388–89.

"Salt, Sodium and Blood Pressure: Piecing Together the Puzzle." Chicago Heart Association, an affiliate of the American Heart Association, 1979.

Shaper, A. Gerald, et al. "Blood Pressure and Hypertension in Middle-Aged British Men." *Journal of Hypertension,* vol. 6, no. 5, 1988, pp. 367–74.

"Should Mild Hypertension Be Treated?" *New England Journal of Medicine,* Letter to the Editor, December 9, 1982, p. 1522.

Slattery, M. L., and D. R. Jacobs. "Physical Fitness and Cardiovascular Disease Mortality: The U.S. Railroad Study." *American Journal of Epidemiology,* vol. 127, no. 3, 1988, pp. 571–80.

Stokes III, Joseph, M.D., et al. "The Relative Importance of Selected Risk Factors for Various Manifestations of Cardiovascular Disease Among Men and Women from 35 to 65 Years Old: 30 Years of Follow-up in the Framingham Study." *Circulation,* vol. 75, suppl. V, June 1987, pp. 65–73.

Williams, Paul T., Ph.D., et al. "Associations of Dietary Fat, Regional Adiposity, and Blood Pressure in Men." *Journal of the American Medical Association,* vol. 257, no. 23, 1987, pp. 3251–56.

Chapter 4

"About High Blood Pressure." American Heart Association, National Center, Dallas, Texas.

Amery, A., et al. "Mortality and Morbidity Results from the European Working Party on High Blood Pressure in the Elderly Trial." *The Lancet,* vol. 1, June 15, 1985, pp. 1349–54.

"Disease Prevention/Health Promotion: The Facts." Prepared by the Office of Disease Prevention and Health Promotion, U.S. Public Health Service, U.S. Department of Health and Human Services. Palo Alto, California: Bull Publishing Company, 1988, Chapter 11.

"Facts About Strokes." American Heart Association, National Center, Dallas, Texas.

"Facts About Women: Heart Disease and Stroke." U.S. Department of Health and Human Services, National Institutes of Health, Public Health Service, 1986.

"The Fight Against Stroke." *Medical Times,* vol. 115, no. 6, June 1987, pp. 59–66.

Gould, B. A., et al. "Is the Blood Pressure the Same in Both Arms?" *Clinical Cardiology,* vol. 8, August 1985, pp. 423–26.

"How You Can Help Your Doctor Treat Your High Blood Pressure." American Heart Association, National Center, Dallas, Texas, 1974.

Kaplan, Norman M., M.D. *Clinical Hypertension.* Baltimore: Williams & Wilkins, fourth edition, 1986.

————. *Management of Hypertension.* Durant, Oklahoma: Creative Infomatics, Inc., second edition, 1987.

Mancia, Giuseppe, et al. "Effects of Blood-Pressure Measurement by the Doctor on Patient's Blood Pressure and Heart Rate." *The Lancet,* September 24, 1983, pp. 695–98.

Mason, Dean, M.D., and Ralph Cutler, M.D. *Cardiorenal Considerations in Hypertension.* Science & Medicine, Inc., Pfizer Inc., 1980.

"The 1988 Report of the Joint National Committee on Detection, Evaluation, and Treatment of High Blood Pressure." *Archives of Internal Medicine,* vol. 148, May 1988, pp. 1023–37.

Pickering, George. *High Blood Pressure.* New York: Grune & Stratton, Inc., second edition, 1968.

"Statement on Hypertension in the Elderly." National High Blood Pressure Education Program Coordinating Committee, National Institutes of Health. Bethesda, Maryland: September 20, 1985.

Zamula, Evelyn. "Stroke: Fighting Back Against America's No. 3 Killer." Department of Health and Human Services, Public Health Service, Food and Drug Administration, Office of Public Affairs, July/August 1986.

Chapter 5

"Drugs for Hypertension." *The Medical Letter,* vol. 29, no. 730, January 2, 1987, pp. 1–6.

"Enalapril for Hypertension." *The Medical Letter,* vol. 28, no. 714, May 23, 1983, pp. 53–56.

"Famotidine (PEPCID)." *The Medical Letter,* vol. 29, no. 733, February 13, 1987, pp. 17–20.

Kaplan, Norman M., M.D. *Clinical Hypertension.* Baltimore: Williams & Wilkins, fourth edition, 1986.

———. *Management of Hypertension.* Durant, Oklahoma: Creative Infomatics, Inc., second edition, 1987.

"Labetalol for Hypertension." *The Medical Letter,* vol. 26, no. 670, September 14, 1984, pp. 83–86.

"The 1988 Report of the Joint National Committee on Detection, Evaluation, and Treatment of High Blood Pressure." *Archives of Internal Medicine,* vol. 148, May 1988, pp. 1023–37.

"Verapamil for Hypertension." *The Medical Letter,* vol. 29, no. 737, April 10, 1987, pp. 37–40.

Chapter 6

Kaplan, Norman M., M.D. *Clinical Hypertension.* Baltimore: Williams & Wilkins, fourth edition, 1986.

———. *Management of Hypertension.* Durant, Oklahoma: Creative Infomatics, Inc., second edition, 1987.

"The 1988 Report of the Joint National Committee on Detection, Evaluation, and Treatment of High Blood Pressure." *Archives of Internal Medicine,* vol. 148, May 1988, pp. 1023–37.

Rossman, Isadore, M.D., Ph.D. *Clinical Geriatrics.* Philadelphia: Lippincott, second edition, 1979.

———. *Clinical Geriatrics.* Philadelphia: Lippincott, third edition, 1986.

Chapter 7

"Drugs That Cause Sexual Dysfunction." *The Medical Letter,* vol. 29, no. 744, July 17, 1987, pp. 65–70.

Kaplan, Norman M., M.D. *Clinical Hypertension.* Baltimore: Williams & Wilkins, fourth edition, 1986.

———. *Management of Hypertension.* Durant, Oklahoma: Creative Infomatics, Inc., second edition, 1987.

"The 1988 Report of the Joint National Committee on Detection, Evaluation, and Treatment of High Blood Pressure." *Archives of Internal Medicine,* vol. 148, May 1988, pp. 1023–37.

Chapter 8

Arakawa, Kikuo, et al. "The Beneficial Effect of Exercise Therapy for Essential Hypertension and a Probable Mechanism: A Preliminary Report." *Nutritional Prevention of Cardiovascular Disease,* 1984, pp. 349–55.

"Diuretics, Hypokalemia, and Ventricular Ectopy: The Controversy Continues." *Archives of Internal Medicine,* vol. 145, July 1985, pp. 1185–87.

Duncan, John J., et al. "The Effects of Aerobic Exercise on Plasma Catecholamines and Blood Pressure in Patients with Mild Essential Hypertension." *Journal of the American Medical Association,* vol. 254, no. 18, November 8, 1985, pp. 2609–13.

el-Dean, Salah, M.D., et al. "Physical Exercise and Health: A Review Study." *Medical Times,* vol. 113, no. 12, December 1985, pp. 57–64.

"Hypertension." 1988 Consensus Conference on Exercise, Fitness and Health, held in Toronto, Canada, section D, paragraph 309.

Jingu, Sumie, M.D., et al. "Exercise Training Augments Cardiopulmonary Baroreflex Control of Forearm Vascular Resistance in Middle-Aged Subjects." *Japanese Circulation Journal,* vol. 52, February 1988.

Kaplan, Norman M., M.D. "Calcium and Potassium in the Treatment of Essential Hypertension." *Seminars in Nephrology,* vol. 8, no. 2, June 1988, pp. 176–84.

————. *Clinical Hypertension.* Baltimore: Williams & Wilkins, fourth edition, 1986.

————. *Management of Hypertension.* Durant, Oklahoma: Creative Infomatics, Inc., second edition, 1987.

————. "Non-Drug Treatment of Hypertension." *Annals of Internal Medicine,* vol. 102, no. 3, March 1985, pp. 359–73.

Khaw, Kay-Tee, and Elizabeth Barrett-Connor. "Dietary Fiber and Reduced Ischemic Heart Disease Mortality Rates in Men and Women: A 12-year Prospective Study." *American Journal of Epidemiology,* vol. 126, no. 6, 1987, pp. 1093–1102.

Kiyonaga, Akira, et al. "Blood Pressure and Hormonal Responses to Aerobic Exercise." *Hypertension,* vol. 7, no. 1, January–February 1985, pp. 125–31.

Larson, Eric B., and Robert A. Bruce. "Health Benefits of Exercise in an Aging Society." *Archives of Internal Medicine,* vol. 147, February 1987, pp. 353–56.

Liao, Youlian, et al. "Cardiovascular Responses to Exercise of Participants in a Trial on the Primary Prevention of Hypertension." *Journal of Hypertension,* vol. 5, no. 3, 1987, pp. 317–21.

McNutt, Robert A., M.D., et al. "Acute Myocardial Infarction in a 22-year-old World Class Weight Lifter Using Anabolic Steroids." *American Journal of Cardiology,* vol. 62, July 1, 1988, p. 164.

"The 1988 Report of the Joint National Committee on Detection, Evaluation, and Treatment of High Blood Pressure." *Archives of Internal Medicine,* vol. 148, May 1988, pp. 1023–37.

Ravussin, Eric, Ph.D., et al. "Reduced Rate of Energy Expenditure as a Risk Factor for Body-Weight Gain." *New England Journal of Medicine,* vol. 318, no. 8, February 25, 1988, pp. 467–72.

Slattery, Martha L. and David R. Jacobs, Jr. "Physical Fitness and Cardiovascular Disease Mortality: The U.S. Railroad Study." *American Journal of Epidemiology,* vol. 127, no. 3, 1988, pp. 571–80.

Urata, Hidenori, et al. "Antihypertensive and Volume-Depleting Effects of Mild Exercise on Essential Hypertension." *Hypertension,* vol. 9, no. 3, March 1987, pp. 245–52.

Chapter 9

Altura, Burton M., and Bella T. Altura. "Interactions of Mg and K on Blood Vessels—Aspects in View of Hypertension. Review of Present Status and New Findings." *Magnesium,* vol. 3, 1984, pp. 175–94.

Beilin, Lawrence J. "State of the Art Lecture, Diet and Hypertension: Critical Concepts and Controversies." *Journal of Hypertension,* vol. 5, suppl. 5, 1987, pp. S447–57.

"Calcium and Hypertension." *Nutrition and the M.D.,* July 1985.

Fregley, Melvin J. "Estimates of Sodium and Potassium Intake." *Annals of Internal Medicine,* vol. 98, May 1983, pp. 792–99.

Kaplan, Norman M., M.D. *Clinical Hypertension.* Baltimore: Williams & Wilkins, fourth edition, 1986.

————. *Management of Hypertension*. Durant, Oklahoma: Creative Infomatics, Inc., second edition, 1987.

Kostas, G., and K. Glasgow. "Limit Your Sodium!" *The Balancing Act*. Dallas: 1984.

Kroenke, Kurt, et al. "The Value of Serum Magnesium Determination in Hypertensive Patients Receiving Diuretics." *Archives of Internal Medicine,* vol. 147, September 1987, pp. 1553–56.

"Magnesium Aspartate and 'Jogger's Heart.'" *Health News,* May–July 1982.

"The 1988 Report of the Joint National Committee on Detection, Evaluation, and Treatment of High Blood Pressure." *Archives of Internal Medicine,* vol. 148, May 1988, pp. 1023–37.

Resnick, Lawrence M. "Dietary Calcium and Hypertension." *Journal of Nutrition,* vol. 117, 1987, pp. 1806–08.

Siani, Alfonso, et al. "Controlled Trial of Long-Term Oral Potassium Supplements in Patients with Mild Hypertension." *British Medical Journal,* vol. 294, June 6, 1987, pp. 1453–56.

Solum, T. T., et al. "The Influence of a High-Fibre Diet on Body Weight, Serum Lipids, and Blood Pressure in Slightly Overweight Persons." *International Journal of Obesity,* vol. 11, suppl. 1, 1987, pp. 67–71.

Stamier, Rose, M.A., et al. "Nutritional Therapy for High Blood Pressure, Final Report of a Four-Year Randomized Controlled Trial—The Hypertension Control Program." *Journal of the American Med-*

ical Association, vol. 257, no. 11, March 20, 1987, pp. 1484–91.

Weinberger, Myron H., M.D. "Salt Intake and Blood Pressure in Humans." *Contemporary Nutrition,* vol. 13, no. 8, 1988.

Williams, Paul T., Ph.D., et al. "Associations of Dietary Fat, Regional Adiposity, and Blood Pressure in Men." *Journal of the American Medical Association,* vol. 257, no. 23, June 19, 1987, pp. 3251–56.

Chapter 10

Benson, Herbert, M.D. *Beyond the Relaxation Response.* New York: Berkley, 1984.

———. *The Relaxation Response.* New York: Avon, 1976.

———. *Your Maximum Mind.* New York: Avon, 1987.

Ewart, Craig K., et al. "Feasibility and Effectiveness of School-Based Relaxation in Lowering Blood Pressure." *Health Psychology,* vol. 6, 1987, pp. 399–416.

Goleman, Daniel. "Hypertension? Relax." *New York Times Magazine,* December 11, 1988.

Jacob, Rolf G., et al. "The Behavioral Treatment of Hypertension: Long-Term Effects." *Behavior Therapy,* vol. 18, 1987, pp. 325–52.

———. "Relaxation Therapy for Hypertension: Comparison of Effects with Concomitant Placebo, Diuretic, and B-Blocker." *Archives of Internal Medicine,* vol. 146, December 1986, pp. 2335–40.

Kaplan, Norman M., M.D. *Clinical Hypertension.* Baltimore: Williams & Wilkins, fourth edition, 1986.

————. *Management of Hypertension.* Durant, Oklahoma: Creative Infomatics, Inc., second edition, 1987.

"The 1988 Report of the Joint National Committee on Detection, Evaluation, and Treatment of High Blood Pressure." *Archives of Internal Medicine,* vol. 148, May 1988, pp. 1023–37.

Patel, Chandra, and Michael Marmot. "Can General Practitioners Use Training in Relaxation and Management of Stress to Reduce Mild Hypertension?" *British Medical Journal,* vol. 296, January 2, 1988, pp. 21–24.

Warner, Greg. "Blood Pressure Was 'Up.' " *Baptist Standard,* November 17, 1982.

Chapter 11

Kaplan, Norman M., M.D. *Clinical Hypertension.* Baltimore: Williams & Wilkins, fourth edition, 1986.

————. *Management of Hypertension.* Durant, Oklahoma: Creative Infomatics, Inc., second edition, 1987.

"The 1988 Report of the Joint National Committee on Detection, Evaluation, and Treatment of High Blood Pressure." *Archives of Internal Medicine,* vol. 148, May 1988, pp. 1023–37.

Chapter 12

"The 1988 Report of the Joint National Committee on Detection, Evaluation, and Treatment of High Blood Pressure." *Archives of Internal Medicine,* vol. 148, May 1988, pp. 1023–37.

Appendix I

Sodium, Potassium, Calcium, and Fiber Content of Selected Foods

Sodium

0–140 mg Sodium	*141–400 mg Sodium*	*401 + mg Sodium*

FRUIT and VEGETABLE
(½ cup or 1 small serving)

0–140 mg	141–400 mg	401 + mg
Fruit, fresh or frozen or canned— 1–50 mg	Beets, canned— 200 mg	Pork and beans, canned— 590 mg
Frozen lima beans— 125 mg	Cream-style corn— 300 mg	Sauerkraut, canned— 880 mg
Frozen peas— 90 mg	Tomato juice— 243 mg	Spaghetti sauce— 925 mg
Tomato paste— 50 mg		Tomato sauce— 656 mg
Vegetables, canned— 300 mg		Vegetable soup, canned— 505 mg
Vegetables, plain, frozen— 10–30 mg		

Sodium (continued)

0–140 mg Sodium	141–400 mg Sodium	401 + mg Sodium

BREAD/STARCH (½ cup or 1 piece)

0–140 mg Sodium	141–400 mg Sodium	401 + mg Sodium
Graham crackers— 95 mg	Biscuit— 270 mg	
Noodles— 2 mg	Bran flakes— 182 mg	
Rice—2 mg	Corn flakes— 163 mg	
Saltine crackers (4)—125 mg	Cornbread— 265 mg	
Shredded Wheat— 1 mg	Cream of wheat— 175 mg	
Wheat bread— 130 mg	Instant oatmeal— 350 mg	
	Waffle— 340 mg	
	Wheaties— 158 mg	

Sodium (continued)

0–140 mg Sodium	141–400 mg Sodium	401 + mg Sodium

MILK
(8 ounces milk or yogurt or 1 ounce cheese)

0–140 mg Sodium	141–400 mg Sodium	401 + mg Sodium
Low-fat yogurt, fruit— 120 mg	Buttermilk— 318 mg	American processed cheese— 405 mg
Low-sodium cheese— 90 mg	Cheddar cheese— 175 mg	Low-fat cottage cheese (½ cup)— 455 mg
Mozzarella cheese— 104 mg	Chocolate milk— 150 mg	
Skim milk— 125 mg	Chocolate pudding— 320 mg	
Swiss cheese— 75 mg	Low-fat milk, 2%— 145 mg	
Whole milk— 120 mg	Low-fat yogurt, plain— 159 mg	

Sodium (continued)

0–140 mg Sodium	*141–400 mg Sodium*	*401 + mg Sodium*
MEAT (3 ounces or as specified)		
Beef—52 mg	Beef liver— 155 mg	Baked ham— 800 mg
Chicken— 74 mg	Peanut butter (2 tablespoons) —190 mg	Bologna— 1036 mg
Egg (1)— 60 mg		Corned beef— 808 mg
Pork chop— 54 mg		Frankfurter (1) —477 mg
		Sausage— 788 mg
		Tuna—727 mg

Sodium (continued)

0–140 mg Sodium	*141–400 mg Sodium*	*401 + mg Sodium*
COMBINATION FOODS		
Fresh fruit salad (1 cup)— 10 mg	Homemade soup (1 cup)— 400 mg	Chicken noodle soup, canned (1 cup)— 1999 mg
Tossed salad (1 cup) with oil and vinegar (1 tablespoon) —12 mg		Beef stew, canned (1 cup)— 980 mg
		Spaghetti and meatballs, canned (1½ cup)— 985 mg
		Chicken pot pie (1)— 863 mg
		Chili with beans and beef (1 cup)— 1355 mg
		Chow mein (1 cup)— 725 mg
		Fast food fish sandwich— 800 mg

Sodium (continued)

0–140 mg Sodium	141–400 mg Sodium	401 + mg Sodium

COMBINATION FOODS (continued)

		Fast food hamburger— 774 mg
		Frozen beef dinner— 938 mg
		Pizza with sausage (1 slice)— 720 mg

OTHER FOODS
(½ cup or 1 piece or as specified)

0–140 mg Sodium	141–400 mg Sodium	401 + mg Sodium
Beer—8 mg	Cake-type doughnut— 216 mg	Apple pie— 482 mg
Coffee—2 mg		Dill pickle— 1930 mg
Cola—2 mg	Potato chips (10)— 200 mg	
Ice cream— 90 mg		
Oatmeal cookie— 69 mg	Salted popcorn— 233 mg	
Sherbet— 20 mg	Sweet pickle— 200 mg	
Wine—5 mg		

Sodium (continued)

0–140 mg Sodium	141–400 mg Sodium	401 + mg Sodium

FATS and CONDIMENTS
(1 tablespoon or as specified)

0–140 mg Sodium	141–400 mg Sodium	401 + mg Sodium
Barbecue sauce— 130 mg	Bacon (3 slices)— 303 mg	Baking power (1 teaspoon)— 405 mg
Butter— 120 mg	Catsup— 155 mg	Baking soda (1 teaspoon)— 821 mg
Cooking wine— 133 mg	French dressing— 220 mg	Bouillon cube (1 teaspoon)— 960 mg
Herbs and spices (1 teaspoon)— 1 mg	Horseradish— 165 mg	Garlic salt (1 teaspoon)— 1850 mg
Margarine— 150 mg	Italian dressing— 315 mg	Green olives (5)— 465 mg
Margarine, unsalted— 0 mg	Low-sodium soy sauce— 300 mg	Lite salt (1 teaspoon)— 1100 mg
Mayonnaise— 85 mg	Worcestershire sauce— 157 mg	Meat tenderizer (1 teaspoon)— 1750 mg
Oil—0 mg		
Parsley— 12 mg		
Picante sauce— 74 mg		

Sodium (continued)

0–140 mg Sodium	*141–400 mg Sodium*	*401 + mg Sodium*
FATS and CONDIMENTS (continued) **(1 tablespoon or as specified)**		
Prepared mustard— 65 mg Salt substitute— 0 mg Tartar sauce— 50 mg		Monosodium glutamate (MSG) (1 teaspoon)— 492 mg Onion salt (1 teaspoon)— 1590 mg Soy sauce— 1332 mg Table salt (1 teaspoon)— 2132 mg

Potassium

401 + mg Potassium	*200–400 mg Potassium*	*0–199 mg Potassium*

MILK
(8 ounces milk or yogurt or 1 ounce cheese)

Chocolate milk— 417 mg	Buttermilk— 342 mg	American cheese— 45 mg
Low-fat milk— 450 mg	Skim milk— 381 mg	Cheddar cheese— 30 mg
Low-fat yogurt, plain— 530 mg	Whole milk— 370 mg	Chocolate pudding— 170 mg
	Yogurt, fruit— 400 mg	Cottage cheese— 95 mg
		Swiss cheese— 30 mg

FRUIT and VEGETABLE
(½ cup or 1 small serving)

Baked potato— 780 mg	Broccoli— 205 mg	Apple juice— 125 mg
Banana— 440 mg	Carrots, raw— 245 mg	Apple sauce— 100 mg
Cantaloupe— 401 mg	Mashed potato— 260 mg	Collard greens— 170 mg
Figs (2)— 640 mg		

Potassium (continued)

401 + mg Potassium	*200–400 mg Potassium*	*0–199 mg Potassium*

FRUIT and VEGETABLE (continued)
(½ cup or 1 small serving)

Prunes— 528 mg	Nectarine— 294 mg Orange juice— 370 mg	Fruit cocktail— 25 mg Green beans— 95 mg Pear, canned— 130 mg

BREAD/STARCH (½ cup or 1 piece)

Bran Buds— 700 mg Wheat bran (1 table- spoon)— 460 mg	Bran flakes— 248 mg Bran Chex— 228 mg Kidney beans— 335 mg Lentils— 250 mg Navy beans— 360 mg	Corn flakes— 24 mg Farina—10 mg Graham cracker— 55 mg Noodles— 45 mg Oatmeal— 75 mg Rice—40 mg Saltines (4)— 15 mg Wheat bread— 70 mg White bread— 25 mg

Potassium (continued)

401 + mg Potassium	*200–400 mg Potassium*	*0–199 mg Potassium*

MEAT (3 ounces or as specified)

401 + mg Potassium	200–400 mg Potassium	0–199 mg Potassium
Cod—420 mg	Beef liver—325 mg	Bacon (3 slices)—92 mg
Scallops—455 mg	Chicken—243 mg	Beef—185 mg
Sole—585 mg	Ham, canned—304 mg	Bologna (1 ounce)—65 mg
	Pork chop—287 mg	Egg (1)—65 mg
	Tuna fish—275 mg	Frankfurter (1)—95 mg
	Turkey—350 mg	Peanut butter (1 tablespoon)—100 mg
		Sausage (1 ounce)—105 mg
		Shrimp—105 mg

Potassium (continued)

401 + mg *Potassium*	*200–400 mg* *Potassium*	*0–199 mg* *Potassium*

COMBINATION FOODS

Beef stew, canned (1 cup)— 615 mg	Fast food fish sandwich— 250 mg	Chicken noodle soup, canned (1 cup)—
Burrito, bean and cheese (1)— 479 mg	Spaghetti with meatballs, canned (1 cup)—	55 mg Chicken pot pie (1)— 172 mg
Chow mein (1 cup)— 420 mg	355 mg Stuffed pepper (1)— 270 mg	Pizza with sausage (1 slice)—
Fast food hamburger, jumbo— 454 mg		160 mg
Frozen beef dinner— 655 mg		
Lasagna (1 cup)— 740 mg		
Spaghetti with meat sauce (1 cup)— 592 mg		

Potassium (continued)

401 + mg Potassium	*200–400 mg Potassium*	*0–199 mg Potassium*

OTHER FOODS
(1 cup or 1 piece or as specified)

Avocado (½)— 680 mg	Danish pastry— 275 mg	Beer (12 ounces)— 90 mg
Banana pudding (½ cup)— 403 mg	Dill pickle— 270 mg	Butter (1 tea- spoon)— 1 mg
Ice cream (1 cup)— 520 mg	Peanuts (2 table- spoons)— 200 mg	Coffee—80 mg
Postum (1 tea- spoon)— 896 mg	Potato chips (10)— 225 mg	Cola (12 ounces)— trace
		Margarine (1 tea- spoon)— 1 mg
		Oatmeal cookie— 20 mg
		Orange sherbet— 21 mg

Potassium (continued)

401 + mg Potassium	*200–400 mg Potassium*	*0–199 mg Potassium*

OTHER FOODS (continued)
(1 cup or 1 piece or as specified)

		Pretzels (1 cup)— 39 mg
		Vanilla ice cream— 130 mg
		Vanilla wafers (3)—51 mg
		Wine (4 ounces)— 95 mg

CONDIMENTS (1 tablespoon or as specified)

Black strap molasses— 585 mg	Parsley— 219 mg	Italian dressing— 2 mg
Tomato sauce (½ cup)— 463 mg		Mayonnaise— 15 mg
		Oregano— 99 mg
		Paprika— 147 mg
		Pepper—75 mg

Potassium (continued)

401 + mg Potassium	*200–400 mg Potassium*	*0–199 mg Potassium*

CONDIMENTS (1 tablespoon or as specified) (continued)

		Prepared mustard— 15 mg Sage—33 mg Thyme— 150 mg

Calcium

270 + mg Calcium	*150–269 mg Calcium*	*80–149 mg Calcium*

MILK
(8 ounces milk or yogurt or 1 ounce cheese)

Buttermilk— 285 mg	American cheese— 175 mg
Chocolate milk— 285 mg	Blue cheese— 150 mg
Skim milk— 300 mg	Brick cheese— 204 mg
Low-fat milk, 1%— 300 mg	Cheddar cheese— 204 mg

Calcium (continued)

270 + mg Calcium	*150–269 mg Calcium*	*80–149 mg Calcium*

MILK (continued)
(8 ounces milk or yogurt or 1 ounce cheese)

Low-fat milk, 2%— 300 mg	Colby cheese— 195 mg	
Whole milk— 290 mg	Edam cheese— 207 mg	
Low-fat yogurt, fruit— 345 mg	Monterey cheese— 212 mg	
Low-fat yogurt, plain— 415 mg	Mozzarella cheese, part-skim— 180 mg	
Swiss cheese— 270 mg	Mozzarella cheese— 150 mg	
	Muenster cheese— 203 mg	
	Ricotta cheese, part-skim (1 ounce = ¼ cup)— 170 mg	

Calcium (continued)

270 + mg Calcium	150–269 mg Calcium	80–149 mg Calcium

FRUIT and VEGETABLE (½ cup or 1 small serving)

	Collards—180 mg	Bokchoy—125 mg
	Kale—150 mg	Mustard greens—100 mg
	Turnip greens—169 mg	

BREAD/STARCH (½ cup or 1 piece)

		Cornbread—135 mg
		Pancake—115 mg
		Waffle—130 mg

MEAT (3 ounces)

Sardines, with bones—370 mg	Salmon, with bones—170 mg	Beans dried, cooked—90 mg
		Oysters, raw—130 mg
		Tofu, processed with calcium sulfate—108 mg

Calcium (continued)

270 + mg Calcium	150–269 mg Calcium	80–149 mg Calcium

COMBINATION FOODS

270 + mg Calcium	150–269 mg Calcium	80–149 mg Calcium
Macaroni and cheese (1 cup)— 360 mg	Cream of mush- room soup with milk (1 cup)— 178 mg	Cheese pizza (1 piece)— 145 mg
	Cream of tomato soup with milk (1 cup)— 159 mg	Chili with beans (1 cup)— 43 mg
	Taco, bean and cheese (1)— 260 mg	Spaghetti, meatballs, tomato sauce, and cheese (1 cup)— 131 mg

OTHER FOODS (½ cup or as specified)

270 + mg Calcium	150–269 mg Calcium	80–149 mg Calcium
Chocolate milkshake— 198 mg	Custard, baked— 150 mg	Ice cream— 90 mg
Vanilla milkshake— 229 mg		Ice milk— 140 mg
		Molasses, blackstrap (¼ cup)— 135 mg
		Pudding, chocolate— 133 mg

Note: To consume 1,000 mg of calcium daily, try to eat 2 to 3 foods daily from left column and 2 to 3 foods daily from center and right columns.

Fiber

5 + gm Fiber	2–4 gm Fiber	0–1 gm Fiber

FRUIT
(½ cup or 1 small serving or as specified)

5 + gm Fiber	2–4 gm Fiber	0–1 gm Fiber
Blackberries— 5.2 gm	Apple with peel (1)—3.1 gm	Grapefruit (½)—.6 gm
Prunes, dried (5)— 7.8 gm	Apricots, dried (5)—3.2 gm	Peach with skin—1 gm
	Banana (1)— 2 gm	Pineapple— 1.2 gm
	Dried dates (5)— 4 gm	Raisins (2 tablespoons)— 1.3 gm
	Orange (1)— 2.6 gm	
	Pear with peel (1)—4.4 gm	
	Raspberries— 3.3 gm	

VEGETABLE (½ cup or 1 small serving)

5 + gm Fiber	2–4 gm Fiber	0–1 gm Fiber
	Broccoli, cooked— 3.2 gm	Asparagus, cooked— 1.3 gm
	Brussels sprouts, cooked— 2.3 gm	Bean sprouts— 1.7 gm
		Cauliflower, cooked— 1.5 gm

Fiber (continued)

5 + gm Fiber	2–4 gm Fiber	0–1 gm Fiber

VEGETABLE (½ cup or 1 small serving) (continued)

5 + gm Fiber	2–4 gm Fiber	0–1 gm Fiber
	Cabbage, cooked—3.3 gm	Carrots, cooked—1.3 gm
	Corn, cooked—3.3 gm	Celery (1 stalk)—.5 gm
	Potato with skin, baked—3.8 gm	Green beans, cooked—1.2 gm
	Sweet potato—3 gm	Onion—.8 gm
		Spinach, cooked—1.7 gm
		Tomato—1.1 gm

BREAD/STARCH (½ cup or 1 piece)

5 + gm Fiber	2–4 gm Fiber	0–1 gm Fiber
All-Bran—12 gm	Bran muffin—3 gm	Nutri-Grain—1.2 gm
All-Bran with Extra Fiber—13 gm	Whole wheat bread—2.1 gm	Rye bread—1.2 gm
Bran Buds—12 gm	Bran Chex—3.4 gm	Whole wheat pasta—1.3 gm
	Corn Bran—4 gm	

Fiber (continued)

---

5 + gm Fiber   *2–4 gm Fiber*   *0–1 gm Fiber*

BREAD/STARCH (½ cup or 1 piece)
(continued)

Fiber One—
 13 gm
100% Bran—
 14 gm
Wheat bran—
 10.2 gm
Kidney
 beans—
 10 gm
Navy beans—
 6 gm

40% Bran
 Flakes—
 3.2 gm
Oat bran,
 cooked—
 3.3 gm
Oatmeal,
 cooked—
 2 gm
Raisan bran—
 2.7 gm
Shredded
 Wheat—
 2.4 gm
Brown rice,
 cooked—
 2.4 gm
Lentils,
 cooked—
 2.8 gm
Lima beans,
 cooked—
 3.6 gm
Peas,
 cooked—
 3.2 gm

Fiber (continued)

---

5 + gm Fiber   *2–4 gm Fiber*   *0–1 gm Fiber*

COMBINATION FOODS
(serving size as specified)

Baked beans
    (½ cup)—
    7 gm
Lentil soup
    (1 cup)—
    7 gm

Bean soup
    (1 cup)—
    4.5 gm

MISCELLANEOUS FOODS
(½ cup or as specified)

Almonds—
    10.3 gm
Peanuts—
    6.7 gm
Sunflower
    seeds—
    5 gm

Popcorn
    (3 cups)—
    4.8 gm
Walnuts—
    2.6 gm

Computer Analyses of Sample Menus and Recipes

1,200-Calorie Menus

Day	Calo- ries	Pro- tein gm	Fat gm	Car- bohy- drate gm	Cho- les- terol mg	Cal- cium mg	Sodium mg
Week 1							
Monday	1202	71	34	153	116	854	770
Tuesday	1252	66	40	157	336	997	1220
Wednesday	1163	70	27	160	67	1152	2046
Thursday	1187	65	39	144	338	899	1588
Friday	1225	58	37	165	100	696	1662
Saturday	1218	73	34	155	135	1073	1361
Sunday	1177	75	29	154	103	661	1248
AVERAGE	**1203**	**68** **23%**	**34** **25%**	**155** **52%**	**170**	**905**	**1414**
Week 2							
Monday	1222	65	37	171	171	944	1655
Tuesday	1182	65	36	169	154	930	1771
Wednesday	1255	57	36	166	112	826	1056
Thursday	1253	62	30	174	77	751	979
Friday	1239	65	35	162	133	1061	1629
Saturday	1234	71	40	150	270	972	1470
Sunday	1258	69	27	186	95	909	1376
AVERAGE	**1234**	**65** **21%**	**34** **25%**	**168** **54%**	**144**	**913**	**1419**

1,500-Calorie Menus

Day	Calo-ries	Pro-tein gm	Fat gm	Car-bohy-drate gm	Cho-les-terol mg	Cal-cium mg	Sodium mg
Week 1							
Monday	1524	76	40	215	134	1007	839
Tuesday	1485	69	45	201	343	911	1491
Wednesday	1540	77	36	227	80	1239	2180
Thursday	1500	68	40	217	305	871	1882
Friday	1576	77	48	209	132	899	1980
Saturday	1496	79	44	196	146	1233	1456
Sunday	1556	93	32	224	112	942	1741
AVERAGE	**1525**	**77** 20%	**41** 24%	**213** 56%	**179**	**1014**	**1653**
Week 2							
Monday	1508	80	38	224	132	1073	1799
Tuesday	1457	84	34	212	193	1129	1654
Wednesday	1502	75	47	190	141	1160	1495
Thursday	1530	88	36	207	99	1029	1395
Friday	1442	80	39	192	165	1110	1858
Saturday	1513	87	46	214	286	1011	1801
Sunday	1489	85	33	216	112	1078	1633
AVERAGE	**1491**	**82** 21%	**39** 24%	**207** 55%	**161**	**1084**	**1662**

2,200-Calorie Menus

Day	Calories	Protein gm	Fat gm	Carbohydrate gm	Cholesterol mg	Calcium mg	Sodium mg
				Week 1			
Monday	2134	106	54	306	189	1402	1304
Tuesday	2086	104	62	278	164	1295	2136
Wednesday	2132	125	60	273	279	1323	2261
Thursday	2226	124	50	320	146	1369	1779
Friday	2180	95	72	288	187	978	1926
Saturday	2261	113	77	279	163	1900	2118
Sunday	2122	105	46	322	124	868	2150
AVERAGE	**2163**	**110** 20%	**60** 25%	**295** 55%	**179**	**1305**	**1953**
				Week 2			
Monday	2240	124	71	299	238	1321	2439
Tuesday	2147	112	50	317	215	1184	2015
Wednesday	2243	101	71	303	204	1511	1932
Thursday	2193	116	68	323	142	919	2146
Friday	2224	123	56	285	278	1683	2480
Saturday	2142	93	64	320	347	1020	2417
Sunday	2248	123	58	311	195	1386	2397
AVERAGE	**2205**	**113** 20%	**62** 25%	**308** 55%	**231**	**1289**	**2260**

Recipe Analysis Per Serving

Recipes	Amount	Calories	Sodium (mg)	Exchanges
Apple Oat Crisp	1 cup	165	80	2 Fruit 1 Bread ½ Fat
Apple Waldorf Salad	½ cup	90	76	1 Fruit 1 Fat
Beef Broccoli Stir-Fry	¼ recipe	349	736	4 Meat 2 Vegetable ½ Fat
Low-Sodium Beef Broccoli Stir-Fry	¼ recipe	349	544	4 Meat 2 Vegetable ½ Fat
Berry Syrup	1 table-spoon	20	0	½ Fruit
Bran Muffins	1 muffin	127	200	1 Bread ½ Fruit 1 Fat
Cold Pasta Salad	1 cup	240	412	1½ Bread ½ Meat 2 Vegetable ½ Fat
Low-Sodium Cold Pasta Salad	1 cup	265	163	1½ Bread ½ Meat 3 Vegetable ½ Fat

Recipes	Amount	Calories	Sodium (mg)	Exchanges
French Toast Puff	1 slice	215	230	1 Meat ⅛ Milk 1 Bread ½ Fruit
Fruit Smoothy	1 cup	100	85	1½ Milk
Gazpacho	¾ cup	60	24	1½ Vegetable ½ Fat
Grilled Sesame Chicken Breasts	4 ounces	265	590	3½ Meat ½ Fruit 1 Fat ½ Bread
Herbed Garlic Fish Fillets	3 ounces	146	202	3 Meat
Italian Rice and Peas	½ cup	134	206	1½ Bread ½ Fat
Low-Sodium Italian Rice and Peas	½ cup	134	87	1½ Bread ½ Fat
Italian Tomato Sauce	½ cup	40	150	1½ Vegetable
Low-Sodium Italian Tomato Sauce	½ cup	40	20	1½ Vegetable

Recipes	Amount	Calories	Sodium (mg)	Exchanges
Long Grain and Wild Rice Chicken Salad	½ cup	260	250	1 Meat 1 Bread 1 Fat ½ Vege- table ½ Fruit
Minestrone Soup	1 cup	100	170	1 Bread 1 Vege- table
Low-Sodium Minestrone Soup	1 cup	100	57	1 Bread 1 Vege- table
Oat Bran Muffins	1 mini-muffin	66	60	½ Bread ½ Fruit ½ Fat
Oatmeal Pancakes	1 5-inch	98	199	1 Bread ⅙ Milk
Original Tomato Sauce	¾ cup	100	10	2½ Vege- table ½ Fat
Oven French Fries	½ cup	100	5	2 Bread
Peppered Veal	2½ ounces	225	208	2½ Meat 1 Vege- table ½ Bread ½ Fat

Recipes	Amount	Calories	Sodium (mg)	Exchanges
Low-Sodium Peppered Veal	2½ ounces	225	50	2½ Meat 1 Vegetable ½ Bread ½ Fat
Pita Crackers	1 cracker	10	23	⅛ Bread
Ricotta-Parmesan Torte	1 piece	250	365	1½ Bread 1 Meat ½ Vegetable 1 Fat
Seafood Quiche	⅛ pie	184	475	2½ Meat ½ Milk
Low-Sodium Seafood Quiche	⅛ pie	169	350	2½ Meat ½ Milk
Shishkabob	3 ounces	257	295	3 Meat 2 Vegetable
Shrimp Creole	1¾ cup	282	450	2 Meat 1½ Bread 2 Vegetable
Low-Sodium Shrimp Creole	1¾ cup	282	291	2 Meat 1½ Bread 2 Vegetable

Recipes	Amount	Calories	Sodium (mg)	Exchanges
Southern Fried Chicken	⅙ recipe	262	260	4 Meat ½ Bread ½ Fat
Low-Sodium Southern Fried Chicken	⅙ recipe	262	98	4 Meat ½ Bread ½ Fat
Spanish Chicken and Rice	1 cup	421	375	3½ Meat 2 Bread 1 Fat 2 Vegetable
Spicy Bean Enchiladas	1 piece	200	553	1 Meat 2 Bread ½ Vegetable
Low-Sodium Spicy Bean Enchiladas	1 piece	200	354	1 Meat 2 Bread ½ Vegetable
Spicy Tomato Sauce	4 tablespoons	28	340	1 Vegetable
Stuffed Shells	3 shells	320	150	2 Bread 3 Vegetable 1 Meat ½ Fat

Recipes	Amount	Calories	Sodium (mg)	Exchanges
Teriyaki Steak	4 ounces	280	472	4 Meat ½ Fat ½ Vegetable
Tuna Salad	½ cup	190	707	2 Meat 1 Milk
Low-Sodium Tuna Salad	½ cup	190	225	2 Meat 1 Milk
Turkey Fruit Salad	1 cup	185	150	1½ Meat 2 Fruit 1 Vegetable
Veal Scaloppine	3 ounces	290	252	3 Meat 1½ Vegetable 1 Fat 1 Bread
Vegetarian Lasagna	⅛ recipe	350	350	2 Bread 2 Meat 2½ Vegetable ½ Fat

Appendix III

Nutritional
Contents
of Fast Foods

Fast Foods

	Calories	Fat (gm)	Chol* (mg)	Sodium (mg)	% Fat
Arby's					
Junior Roast Beef	218	9	20	345	37
Regular Roast Beef	353	15	39	588	38
Giant Roast Beef	531	23	65	908	39
Philly Beef'N Swiss	460	28	107	1300	55
King Roast Beef	467	19	49	766	37
Super Roast Beef	501	22	40	798	40
Beef'N Cheddar	455	27	63	955	53
Bac'N Cheddar Deluxe	526	37	83	1672	63
Chicken Breast Sandwich	509	29	83	1082	51
Turkey Deluxe	375	17	39	1047	41

* Chol = Cholesterol

N.A. = Not Available

	Calories	Fat (gm)	Chol* (mg)	Sodium (mg)	% Fat
(cont'd)					
Hot Ham'N Cheese	292	14	45	1350	43
Fish Fillet Sandwich	580	32	70	928	50
Potato Cakes	201	13	13	397	58
Burger King					
Whopper Sandwich	628	36	90	880	52
w/cheese	711	43	113	1164	54
Bacon Double Cheese- burger	510	31	104	728	55
Whopper Junior Sandwich	322	17	41	486	48
w/cheese	364	20	52	628	49
Hamburger	275	12	37	509	39
Cheeseburger	317	15	48	651	43
Ham & Cheese Sandwich	471	23	70	1534	44

* Chol = Cholesterol

N.A. = Not Available

	Calories	*Fat (gm)*	*Chol* (mg)*	*Sodium (mg)*	*% Fat*
(cont'd)					
Chicken Sandwich	688	40	82	1423	52
Chicken Tenders (6 pcs.)	204	10	47	636	44
Whaler Fish Sandwich	488	27	77	592	50
Garden Salad	110	6	10	170	49
Side Salad	20	0	0	10	0
Chef Salad	180	11	120	610	55
Chunky Chicken Salad	140	4	50	440	26
Breakfast Crois- san'wich	304	19	243	637	56
w/bacon	355	24	248	762	61
w/sausage	538	41	293	1042	69
w/ham	335	20	262	987	54
Bagel, Egg & Cheese					
w/bacon	438	19	273	905	39
w/ham	418	15	286	1130	32
w/sausage	621	36	317	1185	52

* Chol = Cholesterol

N.A. = Not Available

	Calories	Fat (gm)	Chol* (mg)	Sodium (mg)	% Fat
(cont'd)					
Scrambled Egg Platter	468	30	370	808	58
w/sausage	700	52	420	1213	67
w/bacon	536	58	378	975	97
French Toast Sticks	499	29	74	498	52
Great Danish	500	36	6	288	65
Cookies & Cream Spooners	270	10	N.A.	210	33

Church's Fried Chicken

	Calories	Fat (gm)	Chol* (mg)	Sodium (mg)	% Fat
Breast	278	17	N.A.	560	55
Wing Breast	303	20	N.A.	583	59
Thigh	306	22	N.A.	448	65
Leg	147	9	N.A.	286	55
Corn-on-the-Cob, buttered	237	9	N.A.	20	34

Dairy Queen

	Calories	Fat (gm)	Chol* (mg)	Sodium (mg)	% Fat
Single Hamburger	360	16	45	630	40
w/cheese	410	20	50	790	44

* Chol = Cholesterol

N.A. = Not Available

	Calories	*Fat (gm)*	*Chol* (mg)*	*Sodium (mg)*	*% Fat*
(cont'd)					
Double Hamburger	530	28	85	660	48
w/cheese	650	37	95	980	51
Chicken Sandwich	640	41	75	870	58
Fish Sandwich	400	17	50	875	38
w/cheese	440	21	60	1035	43
Hot Dog	280	16	45	830	51
w/chili	320	20	55	985	56
w/cheese	330	21	55	990	57
Super Hot Dog	520	27	80	1365	47
w/chili	570	32	100	1595	51
w/cheese	580	34	100	1605	53
DQ Dip Cone, small	190	9	10	55	42
regular	340	16	20	100	42
large	510	24	30	145	42
DQ Banana Split	540	11	30	150	18
Hot Fudge Brownie Delight	600	25	20	225	38

* Chol = Cholesterol

N.A. = Not Available

	Calories	Fat (gm)	Chol* (mg)	Sodium (mg)	% Fat
Jack-in-the-Box					
Hamburger	267	11	26	556	37
Cheeseburger	315	14	41	746	40
Double Cheese-burger	467	27	72	842	52
Jumbo Jack	584	34	73	733	52
Jumbo Jack w/cheese	677	40	102	1090	53
Bacon Cheese-burger	705	39	85	1127	50
Swiss & Bacon Burger	678	47	92	1458	62
Ultimate Cheese-burger	942	69	127	1176	66
Chicken Supreme	575	36	62	1525	56
Grilled Chicken Sandwich	447	19	N.A.	845	38

* Chol = Cholesterol

N.A. = Not Available

	Calories	Fat (gm)	Chol* (mg)	Sodium (mg)	% Fat
(cont'd)					
Chicken Strips (6 pcs.)	523	20	103	1122	34
Fish Supreme	554	32	66	1047	52
Shrimp (10 pcs.)	270	16	84	669	53
Beef Fajita Pita	333	14	45	635	38
Chicken Fajita Pita	292	8	34	703	25
Club Pita w/o sauce	277	8	43	931	26
Hot Club Supreme	524	28	82	1467	48
Taco	191	11	21	406	51
Super Taco	288	17	37	765	53
Guacamole	55	5	0	130	81
Egg Rolls (3 pcs.)	405	19	30	903	42
Chef Salad	325	18	142	900	50
Mexican Chicken Salad	443	21	104	1530	43
Taco Salad	641	38	91	1670	53
Side Salad	51	3	4	84	53

* Chol = Cholesterol

N.A. = Not Available

	Calories	*Fat (gm)*	*Chol* (mg)*	*Sodium (mg)*	*% Fat*
(cont'd)					
Supreme Crescent	547	40	178	1053	66
Sausage Crescent	584	43	187	1012	66
Canadian Crescent	452	31	226	851	62
Breakfast Jack	307	13	203	871	38
Scrambled Egg Platter	662	40	354	1188	54
Hash Browns	116	7	3	211	54
Pancake Platter	612	22	99	888	32
Cheesecake	309	18	63	208	52

Kentucky Fried Chicken

Original Recipe Chicken

Wing	118	12	67	387	92
Side Breast	276	17	96	654	55
Center Breast	257	14	93	532	49
Drum-stick	147	9	81	269	55
Thigh	278	19	122	517	62

* Chol = Cholesterol

N.A. = Not Available

	Calories	*Fat (gm)*	*Chol* (mg)*	*Sodium (mg)*	*% Fat*
Extra Crispy Chicken					
Wing	218	16	63	437	66
Side Breast	354	24	66	797	61
Center Breast	353	21	93	842	54
Drum-stick	173	11	65	346	57
Thigh	371	26	121	766	63
Kentucky Nuggets (6 pcs.)	276	17	71	840	55
Mashed Potatoes	59	.5	0	228	8
Mashed Potatoes w/gravy	62	1	0	297	15
Chicken Gravy	59	4	2	398	61
Corn-on-the-Cob	176	3	0	10	15
Cole Slaw	103	6	4	171	52
Potato Salad	141	9	11	396	57
Baked Beans	105	1	0	387	9
Buttermilk Biscuit	269	14	0	521	47

* Chol = Cholesterol

N.A. = Not Available

	Calories	Fat (gm)	Chol* (mg)	Sodium (mg)	% Fat
Long John Silver's					
Chicken Planks (4 pcs.)	440	24	60	1280	49
Fish w/batter (2 pcs.)	300	16	60	1020	48
Catfish Fillet (2 pcs.)	400	24	60	700	54
Breaded Shrimp (1 order)	190	10	40	470	47
Battered Shrimp (6 pcs.)	240	18	60	720	68
Breaded Clams	240	12	<5	410	45
Crispy Breaded Fish Sandwich	600	28	30	1220	42
Clam Chowder w/cod (7 oz.)	140	6	20	590	39
Gumbo (7 oz.)	120	8	25	740	60

* Chol = Cholesterol

N.A. = Not Available

	Calories	Fat (gm)	Chol* (mg)	Sodium (mg)	% Fat
(cont'd)					
Seafood Salad w/2 crackers	270	7	90	660	23
Ocean Chef Salad w/2 crackers	250	9	80	1340	32
Cole Slaw	140	6	15	260	39
Mixed Vege-tables	60	2	0	330	30
Corn-on the-Cob, buttered	270	14	<5	95	47
Hushpuppies (3 pcs.)	210	6	<5	75	26
Pecan Pie (1 slice)	530	25	70	470	42
Lemon Meringue Pie (1 slice)	260	7	<5	270	24

McDonald's

	Calories	Fat (gm)	Chol* (mg)	Sodium (mg)	% Fat
Hamburger	263	11	29	506	38
Cheeseburger	318	16	41	743	45

* Chol = Cholesterol

N.A. = Not Available

	Calories	Fat (gm)	Chol* (mg)	Sodium (mg)	% Fat
(cont'd)					
Quarter Pounder	427	24	81	718	51
w/cheese	525	32	107	1220	55
Big Mac	570	35	83	979	55
McD.L.T.	680	44	101	1030	58
Chicken McNuggets (6 pcs.)	323	21	73	512	59
Filet-O-Fish	435	26	45	799	54
Chef Salad	226	13	125	850	52
Shrimp Salad	99	3	187	570	27
Garden Salad	91	6	110	100	59
Chicken Salad Oriental	146	4	92	270	25
Side Salad	48	3	42	45	56
Egg McMuffin	340	16	259	885	42
Sausage McMuffin	427	26	59	942	55
w/egg	517	33	287	1044	57

* Chol = Cholesterol

N.A. = Not Available

	Calories	*Fat (gm)*	*Chol* (mg)*	*Sodium (mg)*	*% Fat*
(cont'd)					
Biscuit, Plain	330	18	9	786	49
w/sausage	467	31	48	1147	60
w/sausage & egg	585	40	285	1301	62
w/bacon, egg & cheese	483	32	263	1269	60
Scrambled Eggs	180	13	514	205	65
Hot Cakes w/butter & syrup	500	10	47	1070	18
Sausage	210	19	39	423	81
Hash Brown Potatoes	125	7	7	325	50
English Muffin w/butter	186	5	15	310	24
Soft Serve Cone	185	5	24	109	24
Sundae, all flavors	346	10	28	135	26
McDonaldland Cookies	308	11	10	358	32
Chocolaty Chip Cookies	342	16	18	313	42

* Chol = Cholesterol

N.A. = Not Available

	Calories	Fat (gm)	Chol* (mg)	Sodium (mg)	% Fat

Pizza Hut

(serving size—2 slices
of medium 13-inch pizza;
4 servings per pizza)

Thin' n Crispy

	Calories	Fat (gm)	Chol* (mg)	Sodium (mg)	% Fat
Standard Cheese	340	11	22	900	29
Superstyle Cheese	410	14	30	1100	31
Standard Pepperoni	370	15	27	1000	36
Superstyle Pepperoni	430	19	34	1200	40
Standard Pork w/mush- room	380	14	35	1200	33
Superstyle Pork w/mush- room	450	19	40	1400	38
Supreme	400	17	13	1200	38
Super Supreme	520	26	44	1500	45

* Chol = Cholesterol

N.A. = Not Available

	Calories	Fat (gm)	Chol* (mg)	Sodium (mg)	% Fat
Thick'n Chewy					
Standard Cheese	390	10	18	800	23
Superstyle Cheese	450	14	21	1000	28
Standard Pepperoni	450	16	21	900	32
Superstyle Pepperoni	490	20	24	1200	37
Standard Pork w/mushroom	430	14	21	1000	29
Superstyle Pork w/mushroom	500	18	21	1200	32
Supreme	480	18	24	1000	34
Super Supreme	590	26	38	1400	40
Taco Bell					
Bean Burrito	360	11	14	922	28
Beef Burrito	402	17	59	994	38

* Chol = Cholesterol

N.A. = Not Available

	Calories	Fat (gm)	Chol* (mg)	Sodium (mg)	% Fat
(cont'd)					
Burrito					
Supreme	422	19	35	952	41
Double Beef					
Burrito					
Supreme	465	23	59	1054	45
Tostada	243	11	18	670	41
Enchirito	382	20	56	1260	47
Mexican					
Pizza	714	48	81	1364	61
Pintos &					
Cheese	194	9	19	733	42
Nachos	356	19	9	423	48
Nachos					
Bellgrande	720	41	43	1312	51
Taco	184	11	32	273	54
Taco					
Bellgrande	351	22	55	470	56
Taco Light	412	29	57	575	63
Soft Taco	229	12	32	516	47
Taco Salad					
w/salsa	949	62	85	1763	59
Taco Salad					
w/o shell	525	32	82	1522	55
Fajita Steak					
Taco	236	11	14	507	42

* Chol = Cholesterol

  N.A. = Not Available

	Calories	Fat (gm)	Chol* (mg)	Sodium (mg)	% Fat
(cont'd)					
Chicken					
Fajita	225	N.A.	N.A.	N.A.	N.A.
Maxi Melt	264	N.A.	N.A.	N.A.	N.A.
Cinnamon					
Crispas	266	16	2	122	54
Cheesearito	312	13	29	451	38
Wendy's					
Hamburger	260	9	30	510	31
Cheeseburger	320	15	50	805	42
†Single					
Hamburger	430	22	70	805	46
w/cheese	490	28	85	1100	51
†Double					
Hamburger	640	36	145	910	51
w/cheese	700	42	160	1205	54
†Triple					
Hamburger	850	50	220	1015	50
w/cheese	970	62	250	1605	58
†Bacon					
Cheese-					
burger	535	31	78	993	52

* Chol = Cholesterol

N.A. = Not Available

† Includes mayonnaise

	Calories	Fat (gm)	Chol* (mg)	Sodium (mg)	% Fat
(cont'd)					
Philly Swiss Burger	510	24	65	975	42
†Bacon Swiss Burger	710	44	90	1390	56
†Wendy's Big Classic w/cheese	640	40	100	1310	56
Chicken Breast Fillet	200	10	60	310	45
†Chicken Sandwich	430	19	60	705	40
Crispy Chicken Nuggets (6 pcs.)	310	21	50	660	61
Chili	230	9	50	960	35
Hot Stuffed Baked Potatoes					
Plain (9 oz.)	250	2	0	60	7

* Chol = Cholesterol

N.A. = Not Available

† Includes mayonnaise

	Calories	*Fat (gm)*	*Chol* (mg)*	*Sodium (mg)*	*% Fat*
(cont'd)					
Sour Cream/ Chives	460	24	15	230	47
Cheese	590	34	22	450	52
Chili & Cheese	510	20	22	610	35
Bacon & Cheese	570	30	22	1180	47
Broccoli & Cheese	500	25	22	430	45
Garden Salad (take-out)	102	5	0	110	44
Chef Salad (take-out)	180	9	120	140	45
Taco Salad	660	37	35	1110	50
Delux Three Bean Salad (¼ cup)	60	0	N.A.	15	0
Red Bliss Potato Salad (¼ cup)	110	9	N.A.	265	74

* Chol = Cholesterol

N.A. = Not Available

	Calories	Fat (gm)	Chol* (mg)	Sodium (mg)	% Fat
Pasta Deli Salad (¼ cup)	35	0	N.A.	120	0
California Cole Slaw (¼ cup)	60	6	10	140	90
Turkey Ham (¼ cup)	50	2	N.A.	N.A.	36
Taco Shell (1)	50	2	N.A.	0	36
Flour Tortilla	110	3	N.A.	220	25
Taco Chips (2 oz.)	260	10	N.A.	20	35
Fettucini (1 cup)	296	7	0	7	21
Rotini (1 cup)	226	5	0	0	18
Pasta Medley (1 cup)	156	5	0	7	29
Alfredo Sauce (½ cup)	110	4	N.A.	44	33
Spaghetti Sauce (½ cup)	88	0	0	872	0

* Chol = Cholesterol

  N.A. = Not Available

	Calories	Fat (gm)	Chol* (mg)	Sodium (mg)	% Fat
Cheese Sauce (½ cup)	110	4	N.A.	916	33
Frosty (small)	400	14	50	220	32
Pudding, all flavors (½ cup)	180	8	0	156	80

Miscellaneous

Beverages (8 oz.)

Coffee	3	0	0	2	0
Tea	3	0	0	0	0
Orange Juice (6 oz.)	85	0	0	2	0
Chocolate Milk, Low-fat	180	5	5	150	25
Skim Milk	90	.4	5	125	0
2% Milk	140	5	5	145	32
Whole Milk	155	9	34	120	52
Soft Drink (12 oz.)	167	0	0	30	0

* Chol = Cholesterol

N.A. = Not Available

	Calories	Fat (gm)	Chol* (mg)	Sodium (mg)	% Fat
(cont'd)					
Diet Soft Drink (12 oz.)	1	0	0	58	0
Milkshake, vanilla	338	9	22	244	24
Milkshake, chocolate	398	11	36	276	25
Extras					
Catsup (2 Tbsp.)	30	0	0	310	0
Jelly (1 Tbsp.)	55	0	0	2	0
Table Syrup (2 Tbsp.)	100	0	0	4	0
Coffeemate (1 pkt.)	17	1	0	6	53
†Dressings (1 Tbsp.)					
Lemon Juice or Vinegar	0	0	0	0	0
Blue Cheese	75	8	4	165	96

* Chol = Cholesterol

N.A. = Not Available

† check packet to determine serving size

	Calories	*Fat (gm)*	*Chol* (mg)*	*Sodium (mg)*	*% Fat*
(cont'd)					
French	65	6	1	220	83
Italian	85	9	1	315	95
Thousand Island	80	8	8	110	90
Ranch	53	5.5	4	186	94
Oil & Vinegar	72	8	0	.1	100
Low-calorie Dress- ings (Avg.)	18	1	2	144	50
French Fries,					
regular order	221	11	10	120	41
large order	353	19	13	262	48
jumbo order	442	24	16	328	49
Onion Rings	328	20	27	536	55
Fried Pie	316	17	11	341	48
Tartar Sauce (1 pkt.)	80	3	5	80	34

* Chol = Cholesterol

N.A. = Not Available

† check packet to determine serving size

	Calories	Fat (gm)	Chol* (mg)	Sodium (mg)	% Fat
Sweet & Sour Sauce (1 pkt.)	40	0	0	160	0
BBQ Sauce (1 pkt.)	44	N.A.	N.A.	300	N.A.
Cocktail Sauce (1 pkt.)	32	0	0	206	0
Picante Sauce (1 Tbsp.)	7	0	0	74	0

* Chol = Cholesterol

N.A. = Not Available

† check packet to determine serving size

Calorie, Fat, Cholesterol, and Sodium Content of Commonly Used Foods

Food	Amount	Kcal	Fat (gm)	Chol (mg)	Sodium (mg)
Apple, fresh	1 medium	80	0	0	1
juice	½ cup	60	0	0	1
Applesauce, canned,					
sweetened	½ cup	105	0	0	3
unsweet-ened	½ cup	50	0	0	2
Apricots, fresh	3 small	50	0	0	1
canned, sweetened	½ cup (4 halves)	100	0	0	1
dried	¼ cup (4 halves)	80	0	0	9
nectar	½ cup	70	0	0	0
Asparagus, fresh	½ cup	20	0	0	1
canned	½ cup	20	0	0	235
Avocado, fresh	½ medium	190	18	0	5
dip (guacamole)	½ cup	140	13	0	165
Banana, fresh	1 6-inch long	100	0	0	1
Bacon, cooked	2 slices	109	10	16	303
bits	1 tablespoon	36	2	0	432
Canadian	1 slice	65	4	10	442
Baking powder	1 teaspoon	4	0	0	405
Baking soda	1 teaspoon	0	0	0	821
Bean dip	1 tablespoon	20	1	2	177
Bean sprouts	1 cup	35	0	0	5
Beans	½ cup	118	0	0	7
baked	½ cup	190	6	0	485
garbanzo, cooked	½ cup	134	2	0	6
green, cooked	½ cup	15	0	0	2

Food	Amount	Kcal	Fat (gm)	Chol (mg)	Sodium (mg)
(Beans-continued)					
kidney,					
canned	½ cup	112	0	0	4
navy, cooked	½ cup	88	0	0	0
pinto, cooked	½ cup	92	0	0	0
pork and					
beans,					
cooked	½ cup	160	4	1	59
refried beans	½ cup	230	12	0	340
Beef, barbecued					
sandwich					
with bun	1 sandwich	509	37	81	506
brisket, baked	3 ounces	367	33	80	46
barbecued	3 ounces	382	34	80	176
chicken fried					
steak	4 ounces	370	22	130	350
chop suey	1 cup	300	17	64	1052
chuck roast,					
baked	3 ounces	240	17	60	40
corned beef	3 ounces	372	30	83	1740
flank steak	3 ounces	158	5	50	47
hamburger					
patty,					
broiled	3 ounces	190	10	50	60
jerky	1 piece	38	2	10	418
liver, fried	3 ounces	200	9	255	155
meatloaf	3 ounces	171	11	50	555
paté	1 tablespoon	41	14	40	91
pot pie	1 piece	443	24	41	1008
prime rib,					
baked	3 ounces	380	33	80	40
round steak	3 ounces	220	13	60	60
short ribs	1 rib	290	24	24	39

Food	Amount	Kcal	Fat (gm)	Chol (mg)	Sodium (mg)
(Beef-continued)					
sirloin steak, broiled	3 ounces	330	27	80	50
stew	1 cup	220	11	63	90
stroganoff	1 cup	470	33	130	860
sweetbreads	3 ounces	143	3	466	0
tenderloin (fillet)	3 ounces	174	8	72	54
Beet greens, cooked	½ cup	15	0	0	55
Beets, canned	½ cup	30	0	0	200
Beverages, beer	12 ounces	150	0	0	25
beer, non-alcoholic	12 ounces	65	0	0	0
club soda	6 ounces	0	0	0	30
coffee	1 cup	3	0	0	2
Gatorade	1 cup	39	0	0	123
ginger ale	12 ounces	105	0	0	4
Kool-Aid	1 cup	100	0	0	1
lemonade	1 cup	110	0	0	1
mineral water	1 cup	0	0	0	5
quinine water	1 cup	74	0	0	16
soft drinks, all canned	12 ounces	150	0	0	10–30
Tang	1 cup	135	0	0	17
tea	1 cup	3	0	0	0
tonic water	12 ounces	132	0	0	0
V-8 juice	6 ounces	31	0	0	364
whiskey	1½ ounces	107	0	0	0
wine	4 ounces	85	0	0	5
Blackberries, fresh	1 cup	80	0	0	2

Food	Amount	Kcal	Fat (gm)	Chol (mg)	Sodium (mg)
Blackeyed peas, canned	¾ cup	81	0	0	602
dried, cooked	1 cup	72	1	0	2
Blueberries, fresh	1 cup	90	0	0	2
Bouillon cube	1 cube	18	1	0	960
low-sodium	1 cube	18	1	0	10
Bread, bagel	1 piece	180	2	0	260
biscuit	1 piece	90	3	2	270
diet	1 slice	40	0	0	115
breadstick	1 piece	23	0	0	100
cornbread	1 piece	180	6	3	265
cornbread muffin	1 2-inch muffin	130	4	2	190
croissant	1 piece	180	11	48	270
croutons	2 cups	359	1	0	1360
English muffin	1 muffin	138	1	0	203
French bread	1 slice	70	0	0	145
mixed grain bread	1 slice	64	1	0	103
pita pocket	1 pita	170	2	0	53
popover	1 medium	112	5	74	110
raisin bread	1 slice	65	0	1	90
roll, dinner	1 small	85	2	1	140
hard	1 small	160	2	0	315
whole wheat	1 small	90	1	0	197
rye bread	1 slice	65	0	1	140
sweet roll	1 medium	270	16	46	240
white bread	1 slice	70	0	1	130
whole wheat bread	1 slice	65	0	1	130

Food	Amount	Kcal	Fat (gm)	Chol (mg)	Sodium (mg)
Broccoli,					
cooked	½ cup	20	0	0	8
raw	1 cup	24	0	0	24
Brussels sprouts	½ cup	30	0	0	8
Butter, regular	1 teaspoon	35	4	13	40
unsalted	1 teaspoon	36	4	11	0
Cabbage,					
cooked	½ cup	15	0	0	10
Cake (1 piece),					
angel food	¹⁄₁₂ cake	135	0	0	60
brownie with- out icing	2-inch x 2-inch	146	10	25	75
cheese cake, plain	¹⁄₁₂ cake	255	13	60	170
chocolate cake with icing	¹⁄₁₂ cake	379	16	62	322
cupcake with icing	1 cupcake	190	6	54	160
fruitcake	¹⁄₃₀ cake	55	2	0	21
gingerbread	2-inch x 2-inch	170	5	0	190
pound cake	¹⁄₁₇ cake	140	9	48	35
Candy, caramels	3 pieces	120	3	2	65
chocolate chips	2 tablespoons	148	8	2	64
fudge	1 ounce	120	5	5	50
gum	1 piece	9	0	0	0
gum drop, small	2 tablespoons	100	0	25	10
hard candy	1 ounce	110	0	0	10
jelly beans	¼ cup	66	0	0	0

Food	Amount	Kcal	Fat (gm)	Chol (mg)	Sodium (mg)
(Candy-continued)					
milk					
chocolate	1.65 ounces	140	9	4	25
peanut brittle	1 ounce	120	3	2	10
peanut butter					
cup	1 piece	130	8	1	75
Cantaloupe	¼ melon	50	0	0	20
Carrots, cooked	½ cup	20	0	0	25
Cauliflower,					
cooked	½ cup	15	0	0	10
Celery, raw	1 stalk	15	0	0	100
Cereals,					
All Bran	1 cup	210	2	0	960
Alpha Bits	1 cup	119	0	0	227
bran	1 cup	120	2	0	60
Bran Buds	1 cup	210	2	0	516
bran flakes	1 cup	127	0	0	363
Cheerios	1 cup	89	1	0	297
corn flakes	1 cup	95	0	0	325
Cream of					
Wheat,					
cooked	½ cup	50	0	0	175
granola	1 cup	503	20	0	232
Grape Nuts	1 cup	402	0	0	299
Malt-O-Meal,					
cooked	½ cup	61	0	0	1
oat bran, dry	⅓ cup	110	2	0	0
oatmeal,					
cooked	½ cup	69	1	0	218
Product 19	1 cup	126	0	0	386
Puffed Rice	1 cup	54	0	0	1
Puffed Wheat	1 cup	50	0	0	1
Raisin Bran	1 cup	155	1	0	293

Food	Amount	Kcal	Fat (gm)	Chol (mg)	Sodium (mg)
(Cereals-continued)					
Ralston, cooked	½ cup	67	0	0	2
Rice Chex	1 cup	110	0	0	240
Rice Krispies	1 cup	112	0	0	340
Shredded Wheat	1 cup	180	1	0	2
Special K	1 cup	76	0	0	154
Sugar Crisp	1 cup	121	0	0	29
Sugar Pops	1 cup	109	0	0	103
Team flakes	1 cup	109	1	0	175
Total	1 cup	109	1	0	352
wheat flakes	1 cup	100	0	0	310
wheat germ	⅓ cup	120	4	0	0
Cheese,					
American	1 ounce	110	9	50	405
blue cheese	1 ounce	100	8	21	395
Brie	1 ounce	95	8	28	178
Camembert	1 ounce	85	7	20	239
cheddar	1 ounce	115	10	28	175
Colby	1 ounce	112	9	27	171
cottage cheese,					
regular	½ cup	120	5	24	455
low-fat	½ cup	81	1	12	459
cream cheese	2 tablespoons	100	10	32	85
Edam	1 ounce	101	7	25	274
feta	1 ounce	75	6	25	316
Gouda	1 ounce	101	8	32	232
gruyere	1 ounce	117	9	31	95
low-calorie cheese	1 ounce	52	2	5	606

Food	Amount	Kcal	Fat (gm)	Chol (mg)	Sodium (mg)
(Cheese-continued)					
low-cholesterol cheese	1 ounce	110	9	5	150
Monterey jack	1 ounce	106	9	26	152
mozzarella, part-skim	1 ounce	72	5	16	132
Muenster	1 ounce	104	9	27	178
Neufchâtel	1 ounce	74	6	22	113
Parmesan	⅓ cup	130	9	28	247
pimiento	¼ cup	106	9	27	405
provolone	1 ounce	100	8	20	248
ricotta cheese, regular	½ cup	216	16	63	104
part-skim	½ cup	170	10	38	153
Roquefort	1 ounce	100	8	45	395
Swiss	1 ounce	110	8	35	75
Cherries, fresh	½ cup	45	0	0	1
Chicken, breast, baked without skin	3 ounces	190	7	89	86
breast, fried	3 ounces	327	23	89	498
canned	½ cup	200	12	91	42
chow mein	1 cup	95	2	15	725
pot pie	1 piece	503	25	13	863
salad	½ cup	127	8	28	345
Chili, beef and bean	1 cup	340	15	34	1355
Chow mein noodles	½ cup	200	8	0	320
Cocoa powder	1 tablespoon	18	0	0	25

Food	Amount	Kcal	Fat (gm)	Chol (mg)	Sodium (mg)
Coconut	4 tablespoons	180	12	0	7
Coffee creamer, non-dairy					
liquid	1 tablespoon	20	2	0	12
powder	1 teaspoon	11	1	0	4
Cole slaw	1 cup	118	8	7	149
Cookies, animal					
crackers	5	43	1	4	30
chocolate					
chip	1	57	8	2	64
Fig Newton	1	50	1	17	35
ginger snaps	3	50	1	0	69
graham					
cracker	1	55	1	8	95
molasses					
cookie	1	71	3	7	58
oatmeal					
cookie	1	80	3	7	69
Oreo cookie	1	49	2	0	63
peanut butter					
cookie	1	232	10	0	85
Rice Krispie	2-inch x				
bar	2-inch	225	10	0	80
shortbread					
cookie	1	42	2	0	36
sugar cookie	1	98	3	0	109
vanilla wafers	3	51	2	9	28
Cool Whip	1 tablespoon	14	1	0	1

Food	Amount	Kcal	Fat (gm)	Chol (mg)	Sodium (mg)
Corn, on-the-cob	1 ear	169	1	0	0
canned	½ cup	70	1	0	195
creamed, canned	½ cup	110	1	0	300
frozen	½ cup	70	0	0	0
Crackers (see Snack foods)					
Cranberry, fresh	1 cup	46	0	0	0
juice	¾ cup	106	0	0	0
Cream,					
half and half	1 tablespoon	20	2	6	6
heavy	1 tablespoon	52	6	24	6
sour	1 tablespoon	26	3	5	6
whipped	½ cup	210	22	80	20
whipping cream,					
heavy	1 tablespoon	52	6	21	6
light	1 tablespoon	44	5	17	5
Cucumber	½ cup	10	0	0	4
Custard	½ cup	150	8	139	105
Dates	½ cup	220	0	0	1
Donuts, cake	1	160	8	33	210
glazed	1	180	11	16	100
Egg	1	80	6	252	60
Egg substitute	¼ cup	25	0	0	80
Egg noodles, cooked	1 cup	220	3	55	15
Figs, fresh	1 piece	80	0	0	2
dried	2 pieces	274	1	0	34
Fish,					
bass, baked	3 ounces	82	2	68	59
caviar	1 tablespoon	42	2	94	352

Food	Amount	Kcal	Fat (gm)	Chol (mg)	Sodium (mg)
(Fish-continued)					
cod, baked	3 ounces	180	6	56	115
crab	3 ounces	100	2	100	850
fish sticks	4	200	10	70	115
flounder, baked	3 ounces	200	8	51	235
haddock, baked	3 ounces	180	7	66	195
halibut, baked	3 ounces	175	4	51	86
herring, canned	½ cup	208	11	85	74
lobster	3 ounces	90	2	85	205
mackerel, baked	3 ounces	250	17	95	35
mussels	¼ cup	48	1	16	104
oysters, fresh	6	80	2	60	90
fried	6	138	8	131	116
perch	3 ounces	227	13	55	153
pike	3 ounces	116	2	55	64
red snapper	3 ounces	93	1	55	67
salmon, baked with butter	3 ounces	189	12	58	116
canned in water	½ cup	160	6	75	425
patty, fried	3 ounces	239	12	64	96
smoked	3 ounces	150	8	85	425
sardines	¼ cup	58	3	28	184
scallops	3 ounces	105	2	53	250
shrimp, boiled	1 cup	100	1	119	250
fried	1 cup	380	19	240	320
sole, baked	3 ounces	141	1	51	235

Food	Amount	Kcal	Fat (gm)	Chol (mg)	Sodium (mg)
(Fish-continued)					
sushi (raw fish)	3 ounces	93	1	50	67
swordfish, baked	3 ounces	174	6	43	98
trout	3 ounces	196	5	55	61
tuna, canned in oil	3 ounces	176	9	19	535
canned in water	3 ounces	109	2	30	399
canned in water, low-sodium	3 ounces	106	2	30	33
steak	3 ounces	145	4	60	0
Frankfurter	1	261	17	45	776
Fruit cocktail, canned, sweetened	½ cup	95	0	0	5
Grapefruit, fresh	½ medium	40	0	0	1
juice, unsweetened	1 cup	93	0	0	3
Grapes, fresh	1 cup	70	0	0	4
juice	¾ cup	120	0	0	4
Green chiles, canned	1 tablespoon	14	0	0	0
Green pepper, raw	½ cup	15	0	0	10
Greens, collard, cooked	⅓ cup	20	0	0	35
kale, cooked	1 cup	41	0	0	30

Food	Amount	Kcal	Fat (gm)	Chol (mg)	Sodium (mg)
(Greens-continued)					
spinach, cooked	½ cup	20	0	0	50
spinach, raw	½ cup	7	0	0	19
Swiss chard, cooked	½ cup	15	0	0	60
turnip, cooked	½ cup	15	0	0	19
Grits, cooked	½ cup	73	0	0	0
Ham, baked, lean	3 ounces	203	8	74	1684
Honey	1 tablespoon	65	0	0	1
Honeydew	¼ melon	55	0	0	20
Ice cream, regular (10 percent fat)	½ cup	135	7	36	60
rich (16 percent fat)	½ cup	266	14	72	120
soft serve	½ cup	163	10	0	51
Ice milk	½ cup	90	3	13	50
Instant breakfast	1 cup	280	8	28	242
Jalapeno pepper, canned	¼ cup	132	0	0	497
Jam or jelly	1 tablespoon	55	0	0	2
Jello	½ cup	70	0	0	0
Kiwi	1 piece	46	0	0	4
Knockwurst	3 ounces	278	23	65	483
Lamb chop, baked	3 ounces	340	28	85	50
roast, baked	3 ounces	160	6	59	60
Lasagna	1 cup	380	12	67	43

Food	Amount	Kcal	Fat (gm)	Chol (mg)	Sodium (mg)
Lemon, fresh	¼ lemon	22	0	0	3
juice	1 tablespoon	5	0	0	0
Lentils	⅔ cup	110	0	0	10
Lettuce	1 cup	6	0	0	6
Lima beans	½ cup	95	0	0	2
Lime, fresh	¼ lime	20	0	0	1
juice	1 tablespoon	3	0	0	2
Luncheon meats,					
bologna	1 ounce	85	8	28	370
pepperoni	1 ounce	139	13	70	492
pimiento loaf	1 ounce	74	6	10	394
salami	1 ounce	130	11	15	350
Macaroni and cheese	1 cup	430	22	42	1085
Macaroni, cooked	1 cup	210	1	0	0
Mandarin oranges, canned	½ cup	76	0	0	8
Mango	1 cup	110	0	0	10
Margarine, low-calorie	1 teaspoon	16	2	0	49
regular	1 teaspoon	35	4	0	50
unsalted	1 teaspoon	35	4	0	0
Marshmallows	½ cup	90	0	0	10
Milk, buttermilk, skim	1 cup	90	0	5	318
chocolate, low-fat	1 cup	180	5	5	150

Food	Amount	Kcal	Fat (gm)	Chol (mg)	Sodium (mg)
(Milk-continued)					
evaporated milk, regular	1 cup	340	20	77	265
evaporated milk, skimmed	1 cup	199	0	10	293
hot chocolate	1 cup	110	3	35	154
low-fat (1 percent fat)	1 cup	102	3	3	122
low-fat (2 percent fat)	1 cup	140	5	5	145
nonfat (dry)	¼ cup	109	0	6	161
skim	1 cup	90	0	5	125
whole (4 percent fat)	1 cup	155	9	34	120
Mixed vegetables, canned	½ cup	38	0	0	121
frozen	½ cup	54	0	0	45
stir-fried	½ cup	59	5	0	17
Mushrooms, canned	⅓ cup	17	0	0	400
fresh	½ cup	10	0	0	5
Nectarine, fresh	1	64	0	0	6
Nuts and seeds, almonds, unsalted	¼ cup	180	16	0	56
brazil nuts, unsalted	¼ cup	180	19	0	0
cashews, unsalted	¼ cup	320	26	0	120

Food	Amount	Kcal	Fat (gm)	Chol (mg)	Sodium (mg)
(Nuts-continued)					
macadamia nuts, unsalted	¼ cup	109	12	0	60
mixed nuts, unsalted	¼ cup	214	20	0	4
peanuts, salted	¼ cup	330	28	0	157
peanuts, unsalted	¼ cup	330	28	0	1
pecans, unsalted	¼ cup	200	20	0	0
pistachio nuts, salted	¼ cup	88	8	0	60
sunflower seeds, unsalted	¼ cup	200	17	0	10
walnuts, unsalted	¼ cup	200	20	0	0
Okra, cooked	½ cup	30	0	0	2
Olives, black	5	35	4	0	150
green	5	20	3	0	465
Onion, green	1 tablespoon	1	0	0	0
Orange, fresh	1 medium	80	0	0	1
juice	¾ cup	85	0	0	2
Pancakes (4-inch diameter)	3 medium	210	2	63	600
Papaya	½ medium	60	0	0	4
Parsnips	½ cup	66	0	0	8

Food	Amount	Kcal	Fat (gm)	Chol (mg)	Sodium (mg)
Peach, fresh	1 medium	40	0	0	1
canned, sweetened	⅔ cup	120	0	0	4
canned, unsweet-ened	⅔ cup	43	0	0	9
Peanut butter, regular	1 tablespoon	95	8	0	95
unsalted	1 tablespoon	95	9	0	5
Pear, fresh	1 medium	100	0	0	3
canned, sweetened	½ cup	65	0	0	2
canned, unsweet-ened	½ cup	35	0	0	3
Peas, canned	½ cup	75	0	0	200
frozen	½ cup	55	0	0	90
split	½ cup	115	0	0	15
Pickles, dill	1 large	15	0	0	1930
sweet	1 small	50	0	0	200
relish	1 tablespoon	20	0	0	105
Pie (1 slice), banana cream	⅛ pie	285	12	40	252
chocolate cream	⅛ pie	264	15	0	273
lemon meringue	⅛ pie	257	14	130	395
mincemeat	⅛ pie	365	16	0	604
pecan	⅛ pie	334	18	92	177
pumpkin	⅛ pie	320	17	150	325
rhubarb	⅛ pie	190	17	10	432
strawberry	⅛ pie	228	9	10	227

Food	Amount	Kcal	Fat (gm)	Chol (mg)	Sodium (mg)
Pimientos, canned	¼ cup	11	0	0	0
Pineapple, fresh	1 cup	80	0	0	2
canned, sweetened	1 cup	190	0	0	4
canned, unsweetened	1 cup	150	0	0	4
Pizza, cheese (13-inch diameter)	2 slices	340	11	2	900
combination (13-inch diameter)	2 slices	400	17	13	1200
pepperoni (13-inch diameter)	2 slices	370	15	27	1000
Plum, fresh	1 large	30	0	0	1
canned, sweetened	½ cup	110	0	0	1
canned, unsweetened	½ cup	51	0	0	1
Pork chop, broiled	3½ ounces	357	26	77	60
roast, baked	3 ounces	310	24	59	50
Potatoes, au gratin	½ cup	95	3	6	529
baked	1 medium	140	0	0	5
French fries	½ cup (10 pieces)	220	10	13	120
mashed	½ cup	100	5	15	350
tater tots	½ cup	200	12	20	545

Food	Amount	Kcal	Fat (gm)	Chol (mg)	Sodium (mg)
Prunes, canned	1 cup	245	0	0	6
dried					
(5 pieces)	¼ cup	130	0	0	4
Pudding, banana	½ cup	241	6	25	11
chocolate	½ cup	167	5	65	160
low-calorie	½ cup	76	0	0	146
tapioca	½ cup	110	4	9	130
vanilla	½ cup	140	5	16	85
Quiche (1 slice),					
cheese	⅛ pie	448	39	305	869
cheese and					
bacon	⅛ pie	520	42	310	970
Radishes	½ cup	7	0	0	10
Raisins	¼ cup	100	0	0	10
Raspberries,					
fresh	½ cup	40	0	0	1
frozen	½ cup	128	0	0	0
Rhubarb,					
cooked,					
sweetened	½ cup	190	0	0	2
Rice, brown	⅔ cup	160	1	0	370
white	⅔ cup	150	0	0	2
wild	1 tablespoon	33	0	0	1
Rice-a-Roni	⅔ cup	165	5	13	820
Rice cake	1 cake	31	0	0	8
Salad dressings					
blue cheese	1 tablespoon	75	8	4	165
blue cheese,					
low-calorie	1 tablespoon	10	1	4	177
French	1 tablespoon	65	6	1	220
French,					
low-calorie	1 tablespoon	22	0	1	128
green goddess	1 tablespoon	68	7	1	150

Food	Amount	Kcal	Fat (gm)	Chol (mg)	Sodium (mg)
(Salad dressings-continued)					
Italian	1 tablespoon	85	9	1	315
Italian, low-calorie	1 tablespoon	15	2	1	118
mayonnaise	1 tablespoon	100	11	8	85
mayonnaise, low-calorie	1 tablespoon	50	5	1	100
oil and vinegar	1 tablespoon	71	8	0	0
Ranch or buttermilk	1 tablespoon	53	5	4	185
Russian	1 tablespoon	76	8	0	133
Thousand Island	1 tablespoon	80	8	8	110
Thousand Island, low-calorie	1 tablespoon	24	2	2	153
Sauces and condiments					
barbecue	1 tablespoon	15	1	0	130
bearnaise	1 cup	701	68	189	1265
catsup	1 tablespoon	15	0	0	155
chili	1 tablespoon	17	0	0	228
chocolate	2 tablespoons	100	0	2	36
gravy	¼ cup	164	14	7	720
hollandaise	¼ cup	361	39	382	400
mustard	1 teaspoon	4	0	0	65
picante or salsa	1½ table-spoons	10	0	0	111
soy	2 tablespoons	25	0	0	2665
soy, low-sodium	2 tablespoons	25	0	0	1200
steak	1 tablespoon	18	0	0	149

Food	Amount	Kcal	Fat (gm)	Chol (mg)	Sodium (mg)
(Sauces and condiments-continued)					
tartar	2 tablespoons	75	8	10	100
teriyaki	1 tablespoon	15	0	0	690
white	½ cup	200	16	16	475
Worcester- shire	1 teaspoon	4	0	0	49
Sauerkraut	½ cup	20	0	0	880
Sausage, link	1	134	12	0	175
patty	1	112	8	34	418
Polish	3 ounces	276	24	60	744
Scallions	¼ cup	10	0	0	1
Shallots	⅓ cup	36	0	0	6
Sherbet	½ cup	134	1	0	10
Snack foods and crackers					
Cheetos	1 cup	153	10	9	329
corn chips	1 cup	155	10	0	183
peanut butter cracker sandwich	1 sandwich	61	4	3	103
popcorn, air-popped	2 cups	80	1	0	0
popcorn, caramel	2 cups	270	2	0	0
popcorn, cheese	2 cups	130	8	5	280
popcorn, cooked with oil	2 cups	106	5	13	466
potato chips	1 cup	115	8	0	200
pretzels, sticks	50 sticks	109	1	0	875

Food	Amount	Kcal	Fat (gm)	Chol (mg)	Sodium (mg)
(Snack foods and crackers-continued)					
pretzels, 3-ring	10 rings	120	2	0	500
rice cake	1 cake	31	0	0	8
Ritz crackers	5 crackers	76	3	8	180
Rykrisp crackers	2 crackers	40	0	0	110
saltines	4 squares	50	2	8	125
saltines, unsalted tops	4 squares	50	2	8	83
shoestring potato sticks	1 cup	152	10	3	280
tortilla chips	1 cup	135	6	0	99
trail mix	⅓ cup	189	10	0	236
Triscuit crackers	2 crackers	60	2	0	90
Wheat Thin crackers	4 crackers	70	3	0	120
Soups, bean	1 cup	170	6	10	1010
beef noodle	1 cup	84	3	5	952
black bean	1 cup	116	2	0	110
broth, beef	1 cup	16	0	0	782
broth, beef, low-sodium	1 cup	16	0	0	12
broth, chicken	1 cup	16	0	0	782
broth, chicken, low-sodium	1 cup	16	0	0	7
chicken noodle	1 cup	75	2	7	1107

Food	Amount	Kcal	Fat (gm)	Chol (mg)	Sodium (mg)
(Soup-continued)					
cream of mushroom	1 cup	203	14	20	1076
gazpacho	1 cup	57	2	0	1183
gumbo, chicken	1 cup	200	4	22	970
lentil	1 cup	108	0	0	1038
minestrone	1 cup	83	3	2	911
onion	1 cup	65	2	5	1051
onion, dehydrated	2 tablespoons	21	0	0	636
pea	1 cup	140	3	4	940
potato	1 cup	148	7	22	1060
tomato	1 cup	90	3	4	970
turkey	1 cup	136	4	9	923
vegetable	1 cup	78	4	0	1010
vegetable beef	1 cup	80	2	4	1050
vegetable, chunky	1 cup	122	4	0	1010
won ton	1 cup	92	2	1	2027
Spaghetti, cooked	1 cup	210	1	0	5
Spam	1 ounce	87	7	15	336
Squash (winter), baked	½ cup	65	0	0	1
Strawberries, fresh	⅔ cup	35	0	0	1
frozen, sweetened	⅔ cup	160	0	0	2
frozen, unsweetened	⅔ cup	119	0	0	2

Food	Amount	Kcal	Fat (gm)	Chol (mg)	Sodium (mg)
Succotash	1 cup	222	2	0	32
Sweet potato or					
yam, baked	¾ cup	160	0	0	15
canned	¾ cup	216	5	10	67
Syrup, corn	1 tablespoon	58	0	0	14
maple	1 tablespoon	50	0	0	2
Taco shell	1 piece	135	6	0	99
Tangerine, fresh	1 medium	46	0	0	2
Tofu	½ cup	85	5	0	10
Tofutti	½ cup	230	14	0	95
Tomato, fresh	½ cup	25	0	0	4
canned,					
regular	½ cup	25	0	0	155
canned,					
no salt					
added	½ cup	25	0	0	20
juice	¾ cup	35	0	0	365
juice, low-					
sodium	¾ cup	31	0	0	18
paste	½ cup	110	1	0	50
sauce, canned	½ cup	43	0	0	656
sauce, canned,					
no salt					
added	½ cup	43	0	0	25
Tortilla,					
corn					
(6-inch					
diameter)	1	65	1	0	1
flour					
(8-inch					
diameter)	1	105	3	0	134

Food	Amount	Kcal	Fat (gm)	Chol (mg)	Sodium (mg)
Turkey, dark meat, baked without skin	3 ounces	170	7	64	85
light meat, baked without skin	3 ounces	150	4	64	70
roll, light and dark meat	3 ounces	126	6	48	498
turkey ham	3 ounces	73	3	0	563
Turnips	½ cup	20	0	0	25
Veal cutlet	3 ounces	231	13	76	55
patty	3 ounces	298	19	90	51
Waffle	4-inch square	124	5	32	340
Water chestnuts, canned	¼ cup	20	0	0	5
Watercress	1 cup	5	0	0	20
Watermelon	2 ¾ cup	110	0	0	5
Yogurt, plain, nonfat	1 cup	127	68	4	174
frozen	½ cup	108	1	0	0
Zucchini, cooked	1 cup	22	0	0	2
raw	1 cup	38	0	0	3

Appendix V

Drugs and Dosages

Antihypertensive Drugs and Recommended Daily Doses

Trade Name	Chemical Components	Mode of Action	Usual Dosage		Manufacturer
			Min.	Max.	
Aldactazide	spironolactone hydrochlorothiazide	aldosterone antagonist; diuretic (spironolactone-minimizes K^+ loss)	25 mg	200 mg	G.D. Searle & Co.
Aldactone	spirondactone	aldosterone antagonist (distal tubule) K^+ sparing diuretic	25 mg	100 mg	G.D. Searle & Co.
Aldoclor	methyldopa chlorothiazide	increased central inhibitory alpha adrenergic drive and/or decreased renin diuretic (distal tubule)	1 tablet 2-3 x day (dosage may be increased or decreased)		Merck, Sharp & Dohme

Trade Name	Chemical Components	Mode of Action	Usual Dosage		Manufacturer
			Min.	Max.	
Aldomet	methyldopa	increased central inhibitory alpha adrenergic drive and or decreases renin	500 mg	3 grams	Merck, Sharp & Dohme
Apresoline	hydralazine	peripheral vasodilation (relaxation of smooth muscle)	40 mg	300 mg	CIBA
Apresoline-Esidrix	hydralazine hydrochlorothiazide	peripheral vasodilation diuretic	1 tablet 3 x/day	2 tablets 3 x/day	CIBA
Apresazide	hydralazine hydrochlorothiazide	peripheral vasodilation diuretic	1 capsule 2x day min. & max. (adjust to lowest effect level		CIBA

640

Trade Name	Chemical Components	Mode of Action	Usual Dosage		Manufacturer
			Min.	Max.	
Aquatensen	methyclothiazide	diuretic	2.5 mg	10 mg	Upsher-Smith
Arfonad (I.V.)	trimethaphan camsylate	autonomic ganglionic blocking agent and possibly peripheral vasodilation	3-4 ml/minute		Roche
Blocadren	timolol maleate	non-selective β-blocker ($\beta_1 + \beta_2$)	20 mg	60 mg	Merck, Sharp & Dohme
Calan	verapamil hydrochloride	calcium ion antagonist	$\frac{120 \text{ mg}}{\text{day}}$	$\frac{480 \text{ mg}}{\text{day}}$	C.D. Searle & Co
Capoten	captopril	ACE inhibitor	25 mg	50 mg	Squibb
Capozide	captopril hydrochlorothiazide	ACE inhibitor diuretic	25 mg	100 mg	Squibb
Catapres	clonidine hydrochloride	centrally acting alpha agonist	0.2 mg	2.4 mg	Boehringer Ingelheim

Trade Name	Chemical Components	Mode of Action	Usual Dosage Min.	Usual Dosage Max.	Manufacturer
Combipres	clonidine hydrochloride	central alpha adrenergic stimulation (decreases sympathetic flow)			Boehringer Ingelheim
	chlorthalidone	diuretic	0.2 mg	2.4 mg	
Corgard	nadolol	non-selective β blocker	40 mg	320 mg	Princeton Pharmaceuticals (Squibb)
Corzide	nadolol	non-selective β blocker	$\frac{1 \text{ tablet}}{\text{day}}$		Princeton Pharmaceuticals (Squibb)
	bendroflumethiazide	diuretic			
Demi-Regroton	chlorthalidone	diuretic	$\frac{1 \text{ tablet}}{\text{day}}$	$\frac{2 \text{ tablets}}{\text{day}}$	Rorer Pharmaceuticals
	reserpine	decrease CNS and peripheral tissue catecholamines			
Demser	metyrosine	inhibits catecholamine synthesis	1 gram	4 grams	Merck, Sharp & Dohme

Trade Name	Chemical Components	Mode of Action	Usual Dosage — Min.	Usual Dosage — Max.	Manufacturer
Diucardin	hydroflomethiazide	diuretic	50 mg	200 mg	Wyeth-Ayerst Laboratories
Diulo	metolazone	diuretic	2.5 mg	5 mg	G. D. Searle & Co.
Diupres	reserpine chlorothiazide	depletion of catecholamine stores diuretic	$\dfrac{1\ \text{tablet}}{\text{day}}$	$\dfrac{2\ \text{tablets}}{2\ \text{x day}}$	Merck, Sharp & Dohme
Diuril	chlorothiazide	diuretic	0.5 mg	2 grams	Merck, Sharp & Dohme
Diutensen-R	methyclothiazide	diuretic	$\dfrac{1\ \text{tablet}}{\text{day}}$	$\dfrac{4\ \text{tablets}}{\text{day}}$	Wallace Laboratories
Dyazide	hydrochlorothiazide triamterene	diuretic antikaliuretic agent	$\dfrac{1\ \text{capsule}}{\text{day}}$	$\dfrac{2\ \text{capsules}}{\text{day}}$	Smith, Kline & French
Enduron	methyclothiazide	diuretic	2.5 mg	10 mg	Abbott Laboratories

Trade Name	Chemical Components	Mode of Action	Usual Dosage		Manufacturer
			Min.	Max.	
Enduronyl	methyclothiazide deserpidine	diuretic depletion of catecholamine stores	1 tablet / day		Abbott Laboratories
Esidrix	hydrochlorothiazide	diuretic	25 mg	100 mg	CIBA
Esimil	guanethidine monosulfate hydrochlorothiazide	inhibition of sympathetic discharge (effects alpha and beta response) diuretic	1 tablet / day	2 tablets / day	CIBA
Eutonyl	pargyline	monoamine oxidase inhibitor	1 tablet / day		Abbott Laboratories
Exna	hydrochloride benzthiazide	action unknown diuretic	10 mg 50 mg	25 mg 200 mg	A.H. Robbins Co.
Harmonyl	deserpidine	depletion of tissue stores of catecholamines	0.25 mg	1 mg	Abbott Laboratories

Trade Name	Chemical Components	Mode of Action	Usual Dosage		Manufacturer
			Min.	Max.	
Hydro DIURIL	hydrochlorothiazide	diuretic	50 mg	200 mg	Merck, Sharp & Dohme
Hydromax	quinethazone	diuretic (saluresis)	50 mg	200 mg	Lederle Laboratories
Hydropres	reserpine hydrochlorothiazide	lowers tissue stores of catecholamines diuretic	$\frac{1\ tablet}{day}$	$\frac{2\ tablets}{2\ x\ day}$	Merck, Sharp & Dohme
Hygroton	chlorthalidone	diuretic	25 mg	100 mg	Rorer Consumer Pharmaceuticals
Hytrin	terzosin hydrochloride	alpha 1 adrenoreceptor blocker	1 mg	20 mg	Abbott Laboratories
Inderal	propranolol hydrochloride	beta-blocking agent	80 mg	640 mg	Wyeth-Ayerst Laboratories

Trade Name	Chemical Components	Mode of Action	Usual Dosage		Manufacturer
			Min.	Max.	
Inversine	mecamylamine	ganglion blocker	2.5 mg	25 mg	Merck, Sharp & Dohme
Ismelin	guanethidine-monosulfate	alpha and beta sympathetic release blockade. Inhibits neurotransmitter release.	10 mg	50 mg	CIBA
Isoptin	verapamil hydrochloride	calcium ion influx inhibitor (channel blocker)	120 mg	480 mg	Knoll Pharmaceuticals
Isoptin SR	verapamil hydrochloride (sustained release)	calcium ion influx inhibitor (channel blocker)	120 mg	480 mg	Knoll Pharmaceuticals
Loniten	minoxidil	peripheral vasodilator	5 mg	100 mg	Upjohn Company
Lopressor	metoprolol tartrate	selective beta 1 blocker	100 mg	450 mg	Geigy Pharmaceuticals

Trade Name	Chemical Components	Mode of Action	Usual Dosage		Manufacturer
			Min.	Max.	
Lopressor HCT	metoprolol tartrate hydrochlorothiazide	selective beta 1 blocker diuretic	25 mg	450 mg	Geigy Pharma- ceuticals
Lozol	indapamide	decreases peripheral resistance	2.5 mg	5.0 mg	Rorer Pharma- ceuticals
Metahydrin	trichlormethiazide	diuretic	2 mg	4 mg	Merrell Dow Pharma- ceuticals
Minizide	prazosin hydrochloride polythiazide	decreases peripheral resistance diuretic	2 mg	40 mg	Pfizer Labora- tories
Minipress	prazosin hydrochloride	decreases peripheral resistance	2 mg	40 mg	Pfizer Labora- tories
Moderil	rescinnamine	depletion of tissue stores of catecholamines	.25 mg	.5 mg	Pfizer Labora- tories

Trade Name	Chemical Components	Mode of Action	Usual Dosage Min.	Usual Dosage Max.	Manufacturer
Moduretic	amiloride-hydrochlorothiazide	potassium sparing diuretic	1 tablet / day	2 tablets / day	Merck, Sharp & Dohme
Mykrox	metolazone	diuretic	.5 mg	1 mg	Pennwalt Corporation
Naqua	trichlormethiazide	diuretic	2 mg	4 mg	Schering Corporation
Naquival	trichlormethiazide reserpine	diuretic lowers tissue stores of catecholamines	1 tablet / 2 x day		Schering Corporation
Naturetin	bendroflumethiazide	diuretic	2.5 mg	15 mg	Princeton Pharmaceuticals
Normodyne	labetalol hydrochloride	selective alpha 1 blocker and non-selective beta blocker	200 mg	2400 mg	Schering Corporation

Trade Name	Chemical Components	Mode of Action	Usual Dosage		Manufacturer
			Min.	Max.	
Normozide	labetalol hydrochloride	selective alpha 1 blocker and nonselective β blocker diuretic	$\frac{1\ \text{tablet}}{2 \times \text{day}}$		Schering Corporation
	hydrochlorothiazide hydrochlorothiazide	diuretic	50 mg	200 mg	Abbott Laboratories
Oretic					
Oreticyl	hydrochlorothiazide deserpidine	diuretic depletion of tissue catecholamines	$\frac{1\ \text{tablet}}{2 \times \text{day}}$		Abbott Laboratories
Prinivil	lisinopril	ACE inhibitor	10 mg	80 mg	Merck, Sharp & Dohme
Raudixin	rauwolfia serpentina	depletion of tissue catecholamines	50 mg	400 mg	Princeton Pharmaceuticals
Rauzide	rauwolfia serpentina bendro flumethiazide	depletion of tissue catecholamines diuretic	$\frac{1\ \text{tablet}}{\text{day}}$	$\frac{4\ \text{tablets}}{\text{day}}$	Princeton Pharmaceuticals

Trade Name	Chemical Components	Mode of Action	Usual Dosage		Manufacturer
			Min.	Max.	
Regroton	chlorthalidone reserpine	diuretic sedative; depletion of tissue catecholamines	$\frac{1 \text{ tablet}}{\text{day}}$	$\frac{2 \text{ tablets}}{\text{day}}$	Rorer Pharmaceuticals
Renese	polythiazide	diuretic	2 mg	4 mg	Pfizer Laboratories
Renese R	polythiazide reserpine	diuretic depletion of tissue catecholamines	$\frac{1}{2} \frac{\text{tablet}}{\text{day}}$	$\frac{2 \text{ tablets}}{\text{day}}$	Pfizer Laboratories
Saluron	hydroflumethiazide	diuretic	50 mg	100 mg	Bristol Laboratories
Salutensin	hydroflumethiazide reserpine	diuretic depletion of tissue catecholamines	$\frac{1 \text{ tablet}}{\text{day}}$	$\frac{2 \text{ tablets}}{\text{day}}$	Bristol Laboratories
Serpasil	reserpine	depletion of tissue catecholamines	0.1 mg	1.0 mg	CIBA

Trade Name	Chemical Components	Mode of Action	Usual Dosage Min.	Usual Dosage Max.	Manufacturer
Ser-AP-ES	reserpine hydralazine hydrochloride hydrochlorothiazide	depletion of tissue catecholamines peripheral vasodilation diuretic	$\frac{1 \text{ tablet}}{3 \text{ x day}}$	$\frac{2 \text{ tablets}}{3 \text{ x day}}$	CIBA
Serpasil Apresoline	reserpine hydralazine hydrochloride	depletion of tissue catecholamines peripheral vasodilation	$\frac{1 \text{ tablet}}{4 \text{ x day}}$		CIBA
Serpasil Esidrix	reserpine hydrochlorothiazide	depletion of tissue catecholamines diuretic	$\frac{1 \text{ tablet}}{\text{day}}$	$\frac{2 \text{ tablets}}{\text{day}}$	CIBA
Tenoretic	atenolol chlorthalidone	beta 1 selective blockade diuretic	$\frac{1 \text{ tablet}}{\text{day}}$		ICI Pharma
Tenormin	atenolol	beta 1 selective blockade	50 mg	100 mg	ICI Pharma
Tenex	guanfacine hydrochloride	alpha 2 adreno-receptor agonist	1 mg	3 mg	A.M. Robbins Company

Trade Name	Chemical Components	Mode of Action	Usual Dosage		Manufacturer
			Min.	Max.	
Timolide	timolol maleate hydrochlorothiazide	nonselective beta blocker diuretic	$\frac{1 \text{ tablet}}{2 \times \text{day}}$		Merck, Sharp & Dohme
Vaseretic	enalapril maleate hydrochlorothiazide	ACE inhibitor diuretic	$\frac{1 \text{ tablet}}{\text{day}}$	$\frac{2 \text{ tablets}}{\text{day}}$	Merck, Sharp & Dohme
Vasotec	enalapril maleate	ACE inhibitor	5 mg	40 mg	Merck, Sharp & Dohme
Visken	pindolol	beta blocker with ISA (intrinsic sympathomimetic activity)	5 mg	60 mg	Sandoz Pharmaceuticals Corp.
Wytensin	guanabenz acetate	alpha 2 adreno-recepter agonist	$\frac{4 \text{ mg}}{2 \times \text{day}}$	$\frac{32 \text{ mg}}{2 \times \text{day}}$	Wyeth-Ayerst Laboratories
Zaroxolyn	metolazone	diuretic	2.5 mg	5 mg	Pennwalt Corp.
Zestril	lisinopril	ACE inhibitor	10 mg	80 mg	Stuart Pharmaceuticals

Drugs for Hypertensive Emergencies

Clonidine (*Catapres;* and others) can control blood pressure in less seriously ill patients within six hours (RJ Anderson and WG Reed, Am Heart J, 111:211, 1986). If there is no response to a total dose of 0.8 mg, another drug should be used. Clonidine acts too slowly for true emergencies.

Captopril (*Capoten*) has also been used to lower blood pressure in hypertensive emergencies; the response to the drug is variable and severe hypotension can occur, especially in patients with renal artery stenosis or previously treated with diuretics.

Drugs for Hypertensive Emergencies

Drug	Class	Route and Dose	Onset	Duration	Comments
		PARENTERAL			
Nitroprusside[1] (*Nipride*; others)	Arteriolar and venous vasodilator	IV infusion pump 0.25 μg/kg/min to 8 μg/kg/min	seconds	3–5 min	Thiocyanate toxicity with prolonged (>48 hours) or too rapid infusion (>15 μg/kg/min) when thiocyanate concentrations exceed 10 mg/dl (particularly in renal insufficiency); cyanide toxicity with rapid infusion; not used in pregnancy
Nitroglycerin	Venous >> arteriolar vasodilator	IV infusion pump 5 to 100 μg/min	2–5 minutes	5–10 min	Headache, tachycardia can occur

654

Drug	Class	Route and Dose	Onset	Duration	Comments
PARENTERAL					
Diazoxide[2] (*Hyperstat*; others)	Arteriolar vasodilator	IV: 50–150 mg q5 min or as infusion of 7.5–30 mg/min	1–5 minutes	4–24 hrs	Not for patients with angina pectoris, myocardial infarction, dissecting aneurysm or pulmonary edema; can increase blood sugar; will arrest active labor
Trimethaphan (*Arfonad*)	Ganglionic blocker	IV infusion pump 0.5–5 mg/min	1–5 minutes	10 min	Preferred by many for emergency treatment of aortic dissection
Labetalol (*Trandate*; *Normodyne*)	Alpha- and beta-adrenergic blocker	IV: 2 mg/min or 20 mg initially, then 20–80 mg q10 min (300 mg max)	5 minutes or less	3–6 hrs	80% to 90% response rate; can be followed by same drug taken orally

Drug	Class	Route and Dose	Onset	Duration	Comments
PARENTERAL					
Hydralazine[2] (*Apresoline*; others)	Arteriolar vasodilator	IV: 10–20 mg	10–30 minutes	2–4 hrs	May precipitate angina, myocardial infarction; not used for aortic dissection; main use is in pregnancy
Propranolol (*Inderal*; others	Beta-adrenergic blocker	IV: 1–10 mg load then 3 mg/hr PO: 80–640 mg daily	immediate beta-adrenergic blockade	2 hrs 12 hrs	Useful as adjunct to potent vasodilators to prevent or treat excessive tachycardia; usually will not lower blood pressure acutely
Enalaprilat (*Vasotec I.V.*)	Angiotensin converting enzyme inhibitor	IV: 1.25–5 mg q6h	15 minutes	12–24 hrs	Variable, sometimes excessive response; not for use in pregnancy

Drug	Class	Route and Dose	Onset	Duration	Comments
		ORAL			
Nifedipine[3] (*Procardia; Adalat*)	Calcium entry blocker	PO, sublingual or buccal: 10–20 mg	5–15 minutes	3–5 hrs	Not yet standardized; somewhat variable, sometimes excessive response
Clonidine (*Catapres;* others)	Central sympatholytic	PO: 0.2 mg initial then 0.1 mg/hr (0.8 mg max)	0.5–2 hours	6–8 hrs	Sedation prominent; rebound hypertension can occur
Captopril (*Capoten*)	Angiotensin converting enzyme inhibitor	PO; 6.5–50 mg	15 minutes	4–6 hours	Excessive response with renal artery stenosis or after diuretics; not for use in pregnancy

1. Propranolol sometimes given concurrently; see text

2. Propranolol often given concurrently

3. Not approved for this indication by the US Food and Drug Administration

From *The Medical Letter on Drugs and Therapeutics*, Vol. 31, Issue 789, April 7, 1989, page 34.

Index

Acid, 169
Acta Medica Scandinavica, 258
Adolescents, 97
  accepted limits, 302
Adrenal
  gland disorders, 526–27
  steroids, 46
Adrenalin. *See* epinephrine
Adrenergic inhibitors. *See* Beta
  blockers
Aerobic exercise, 27, 83, 84,
  86, 126, 128, 132,
  249, 272, 274–75,
  304, 305, 306–08,
  313, 522
  aqua, 323–36
  effect, 285–86, 308–10
Aerobics, 3

Aerobics Institute, 98, 104
Aerobics Newsletter, 336
Alcohol, 6, 13, 22, 121–26,
  127, 249, 341
  abuse, 44–45, 103, 151,
  173, 189
  hypertension and, 122–23
  sensitive people, 20, 125–
  26
Aldosterone, 203–04
Aldosteronism, 203
Alpha-beta blockers, 24, 197,
  207–09, 213–14,236–
  37, 241, 255–56, 266,
  281, 527
  prazosin hydrochloride,
  197, 208, 229, 236,
  255, 256, 281, 312
  terazosin hydrochloride,

Recipe Index